Child Development and Teaching Pupils with Special Educational Needs

This thought-provoking book provides a framework for understanding the physical, sensory, emotional, social, linguistic and cognitive development of children with special educational needs. It gives practitioners and students a sound grasp of the theoretical ground needed to fully understand cognitive development, and will help them track children's developmental progress in order to optimise learning opportunities.

The authors handle complex topics in a highly accessible manner, explaining how to put theory into practice. In three lucidly argued sections they present:

- an overview of the work of key theorists and thinkers, including Vygotsky, Piaget, Freud, Erikson, Bruner and the Korning theorists;
- an evaluation of the educational implications of the work of each theorist, using illustrative case studies;
- a consideration of areas of development in learning and teaching children with special educational needs.

This book will be a beacon for teachers, headteachers, educational psychologists and all practitioners involved in special needs education who seek the opportunity to help empower their pupils, and enhance their own understanding.

Christina Tilstone is now retired, but was previously Senior Lecturer in Special Education at the University of Birmingham. **Lyn Layton** is Lecturer in Inclusive and Special Education at the University of Birmingham.

Child Development and Teaching Pupils with Special Educational Needs

Christina Tilstone and
Lyn Layton
with Anne Anderson,
Richard Gerrish, Jenny Morgan and
Anna Williams

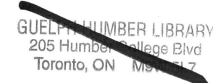

 RoutledgeFalmer
Taylor & Francis Group

LONDON AND NEW YORK

First published 2004
by RoutledgeFalmer
11 New Fetter Lane, London EC4P 4EE

Simultaneously published in the USA and Canada
by RoutledgeFalmer
29 West 35th Street, New York, NY 10001

RoutledgeFalmer is an imprint of the Taylor & Francis Group

© 2004 Christina Tilstone and Lyn Layton

Typeset in Baskerville by
HWA Text and Data Management, Tunbridge Wells
Printed and bound in Great Britain by
TJ International, Padstow, Cornwall

British Library Cataloguing in Publication Data
A catalogue record for this book is available from the British Library

Library of Congress Cataloging in Publication Data
Tilstone, Christina.
 Child development and teaching pupils with special educational needs /
Christina Tilstone and Lyn Layton ; with Anne Anderson ... [et. al].
    p.   cm.
Includes bibliographical references and indexes.
 1. Children with mental disabilities–Education–Great Britain. 2. Child
psychology. 3. Learning, Psychology of. I. Layton, Lyn. II. Title
  LC4636.G7T55 2004
   371.92´0973–dc22   2003025402

ISBN 0–415–27621–7 (hbk)
ISBN 0–415–27578–4 (pbk)

Contents

Notes on contributors

Christina Tilstone was, until she retired, Senior Lecturer in Special Education at the University of Birmingham where she was responsible for the co-ordination of the Distance Education Course in Learning Difficulties. Most of her teaching in schools has centred on pupils with severe difficulties in learning, but she has also taught pupils with a range of special educational needs in mainstream schools. Her doctoral research was on the design and development of the curriculum for pupils with learning difficulties and she has published widely on many aspects of the teaching and learning of pupils with special educational needs.

Lyn Layton is Lecturer in Inclusive and Special Education at the University of Birmingham. She has carried out research into the education of children and adults with a range of special needs and has a particular interest in literacy development. Her doctoral research focused on the phonological precursors to learning to read and to spell. Before joining the University of Birmingham she taught children and adults with dyslexic-type difficulties for a number of years, at the same time teaching GCSE and A-level psychology in a college of further education.

Anne Anderson is currently teaching Key Stage 3/4 and post-16 students in a school for pupils with physical disabilities; she also works for Hereford and Worcester Dyslexia Association where she tutors students with specific learning difficulties. Previously Anne taught in a unit for pupils with multi-sensory impairments within a school for students with profound and severe learning difficulties, and in a mainstream primary school where she was responsible for pupils with special educational needs. The focus of her doctoral research is on the provision for secondary-age pupils with specific learning difficulties.

Richard Gerrish teaches in an 11-to-18 mainstream comprehensive school where he is Head of Learning Support. His responsibilities include taking on the role of a SENCo (Special Educational Needs Co-ordinator), co-ordinating social inclusion and, in addition, acting as a professional mentor for students in initial teacher training and as an induction tutor for qualified teachers. He previously taught in residential schools for pupils with emotional and behavioural difficulties, an area that provided the main focus for his MEd degree.

Jenny Morgan is an Educational Consultant and a SENCo at a small, rural comprehensive school in Cumbria. The work she undertook for her Diploma in Speech and Language Difficulties and her Masters Degree in Learning Difficulties provided the impetus for her current research, which is on the teaching of spelling using a visual system.

Anna Williams is the Head of a Support Service for teachers of pupils with special educational needs and an advisory teacher for pupils with physical impairment and/or medical conditions in the London Borough of Havering. Her current post includes working with pupils and their teachers from pre-school to post-16. She has taught in mainstream primary schools and was a 'class-based' SENCo. Her work for her Masters Degree centred on pupils who had a range of difficulties in learning and she is now a distance education tutor for a number of special needs courses at the University of Birmingham. Anna also has strong links with the National Association for Special Educational Needs (NASEN), including a role on its Editorial Board.

Acknowledgements

We would like to thank all those pupils and teachers with whom we have worked over many years and who have been the inspiration for this book. Our thanks also to our co-writers, Anne Anderson, Richard Gerrish, Jenny Morgan and Anna Williams, for their willingness to share insights into the teaching and learning of their pupils and to respond to our heavy demands. We also wish to acknowledge the advice given to us by our 'critical friends' – Professors Harry Daniels and Ann Lewis; Drs Mike McLinden and Judith Watson; Heather Sullivan, Val Cooter, Claire Marvin and Stephen Mason – and for their penetrating comments on the early drafts of individual chapters. Any shortcomings are, however, our own.

We are indebted to the staff of RoutledgeFalmer, particularly to Alison Foyle, for their patience and support during some unavoidable delays. Finally, we wish to thank Philip Tilstone and Chris Layton for their encouragement and belief in our work.

Christina Tilstone and Lyn Layton

Abbreviations

AAC	alternative and augmentative communication
ACA	Affective Communication Assessment
ADHD	attention deficit and hyperactivity disorder
ASD	autistic spectrum disorders
dB	decibel
DfEE	Department for Education and Employment
EBD	emotional and behavioural difficulties
IQ	intelligence quotient
LAD	language acquisition device
LEA	local education authority
LSA	learning support assistant
LTM	long-term memory
MDVI	multiple disabilities and visual impairment
NASEN	National Association for Special Educational Needs
OT	occupational therapist
PE	physical education
PMLD	profound and multiple learning difficulties
PSHE	personal, social and health education
QCA	Qualifications and Curriculum Authority
SEN	special educational needs
SENCo	Special Educational Needs Co-ordinator
STM	short-term memory
TTA	Teacher Training Agency
ZPD	zone of proximal development

Introduction

In order to understand and promote development in typically developing children, practitioners in training are directed to study the views of a selected number of theorists. The collected works of these individuals, although analysed, evaluated and sometimes challenged, stand as authoritative and respected accounts of how humans develop from helpless newborn infants into mature, able and independent adults.

When teachers re-focus on pupils with special educational needs (SEN) they might be forgiven for thinking that these perspectives have little, if any, relevance for the teaching of pupils whose development is atypical. For our part, as practitioners, researchers and theorists, we agree that seminal texts on child development have much to offer but argue that they cannot claim to provide inclusive and comprehensive accounts of key aspects of development unless they have been interpreted in terms that can encompass atypical patterns.

To summarise our view, there is an ongoing need to interrogate theoretical frameworks for their contribution to our understanding of the potential, the progress and the attainment of any child with special educational needs. By examining the development of children, particularly those who require a high level of support in many different ways, we can evaluate and elaborate the frameworks. Our focus is their journey on a path of lifelong learning where pupils must acquire the skills of *learning how to learn*. These skills are explored throughout the book, particularly in Part 3, Chapter 9 (Cognition and learning).

In the first section of the book, we provide an overview of the work of an elite group of scientists and thinkers: Jerome Bruner, Erik Erikson, Sigmund Freud, Jean Piaget, Burrhus Frederick Skinner and Lev Vygotsky. At the same time, we recognise that there are many others on whom we might have focused but we believe these writers have much to offer the teaching and learning of children with special educational needs. Throughout the discussions original source material is referenced, and in the process the references reflect the cultural biases of the theorist in question. For example, writers in the past usually referred to the child as 'he' and, for contrast, the professional as 'she' and where this is the case we have adopted the same style. No sexist implications, however, are intended. As well as quoting from the theorist's own work we offer contemporary examples to illustrate major aspects or key concepts.

The educational implications of the work of each theorist are discussed in depth in the second part of the book and again, illustrative examples are provided. Our co-writers in their day-to-day contact have collected all the examples of pupils with special educational needs. Their backgrounds and areas of expertise in the special needs field are different and diverse and their collective experiences are extensive. Each offers distinctive perspectives on a wide range of pupils with difficulties and disabilities, including those from ethnic minorities.

We have attempted to draw out the 'educational implications' of the theories that we describe but it is important here to establish the range of applications of the term. Education can be narrowly or broadly interpreted: it might be regarded as a series of aims that are defined at national levels with specified outcomes in terms of knowledge, skills and understanding, to shape the learning experiences of groups of individuals. Alternatively, the educational implications may lie in identifying the content, the process and the timing of learning as well as the influence of other people and their contribution; a practice referred to as 'teaching' in the learning context. Current views on education, particularly in relation to pedagogy, tend to emphasise the active role of the learner and the ways in which 'teachers' and 'learners' interact, but this was not always the case, as accounts of different theoretical perspectives show.

In the final section we take the educational implications of each theorist further, and consider the learning and teaching of children and young people with special educational needs in four major areas of development:

*   communication and interaction
*   cognition and learning
*   behaviour and social development
*   sensory and physical development.

These cohesive themes relate to areas where professionals consider they need further insights. The areas have been identified by the Teacher Training Agency (TTA) in England as those where additional specialist skills and understanding are necessary if pupils with complex needs are to be taught effectively (TTA, 1999) and are referred to in the SEN Code of Practice (DfES, 2001). It is, however, inevitable that the areas overlap and development should be seen as a complex process of interaction between all of them. For example, sensory experiences feature importantly in communication, and language development is significant in the emergence of communication skills and for intellectual growth. It is necessary though to tease apart strands of development in an attempt to understand it. The narratives supplied by our co-writers are similarly intended to focus narrowly on aspects of pupil behaviour, student responses or teachers' approaches in order to illustrate the more theoretical dimensions of the strands. In diverting to real-life situations in this way, readers will be reminded of the richness of human experience and may see, in the examples, new links between the identified areas of development, or approaches and applications additional to those intended by the writers.

Finally, the potential scope of our endeavour remains enormous and in order to produce an accessible and thought-provoking text we have tried to identify a theme which is a crucial aspect of the education of *all* pupils and one which, we believe, unites us in a common purpose towards the education of pupils with special educational needs. Our collective aim, we propose, is their empowerment. In the chapters that follow we interpret theories about development in terms of a progression towards empowerment with a view to identifying why and where it might be compromised for individuals with disabilities or learning needs. We hope that the book will give readers the frameworks for supporting other people in their growth towards empowerment and that it will provide readers with the opportunity to reflect on their own development, both personal and professional.

References

DfES (2001) *Special Educational Needs: Code of Practice on the Identification and Assessment.* London: DfES.

TTA (1999) *National Special Educational Needs Specialist Standards.* London: TTA.

Chapter 1

Self-advocacy, autonomy and empowerment

What do we mean by empowerment?

At the dawn of the twenty-first century, views on the role of education include an emphasis on creating opportunities for all children to grow into self-determining citizens: people who will make, or contribute to, decisions about their lives and determine their interface with the wider community. Self-advocacy and autonomy are prerequisites to becoming a self-determining or 'empowered' citizen. We do not regard 'empowerment' as a fixed state, but as a lifelong *process* and therefore one aim of the current chapters is to provide a framework for conceptualising empowerment through learning that is inclusive of *all* learners; we will return to this theme later.

Meanwhile in England, the National Curriculum now sets out a framework for promoting personal autonomy through personal, social and health education (PSHE) and citizenship, thus acknowledging the importance of the development of 'empowerment' for *all* pupils (DfEE/QCA, 1999a; 1999b). Whereas the extension of PSHE to the National Curriculum is a relatively new subject area for the vast majority, it has, for some time, been advocated for pupils with significant learning needs by many teachers, academics and researchers (Byers, 1998; Mittler, 1996a, 1996b; Rose *et al.*, 1994; Sebba *et al.*, 1993) as the backbone of their wider learning and an essential element in the gaining of access to the same curriculum as their peers without such needs. However, the notion of including *all* learners within the same learning curriculum is, in itself, a relatively new phenomenon.

In the past, pupils whose learning needs are now described as complex or severe were considered to be ineducable, and under the 1913 Mental Deficiency Act of 1913 adults and children with difficulties in learning were categorised as 'idiots' and 'imbeciles'. People so labelled were thought to be unable to guard against common physical dangers and were, in their own interests and the interests of the society of the time, placed in institutions. They were 'cared for' in a medical regime where they were expected to accept a 'dependent' model of care. In addition to being segregated from society, 'patients', as they were known, were considered to be 'sick' and, consequently, experiences were minimised and expectations of them (by those who cared for them and by society in general) were reduced (Fraser, 1984). Their rights and powers to make decisions of any kind were removed and Stevens (1997) reminds us that 'doctors ran institutions, nurses controlled patients, and patients were "passive" victims of the staff' (p.52).

Later the labels of 'idiots' and 'imbeciles' were replaced under the 1959 Mental Health Act by definitions of 'subnormality' and 'severe subnormality'. Categorisations depended on the result of intelligence quotient (IQ) tests: subnormals were classified on the basis of an

IQ between 51 and 75, and severe subnormals, 50 and below. Both groups were regarded as mentally, socially and emotionally immature (Tilstone, 1991). They were denied access to education but were either 'cared for' in institutions or 'trained' in local health authority centres. It was not until 1971 (under the Education [Handicapped Children] Act, 1970) that their right to education was recognised, they entered the education system and so their potential to learn was given due consideration.

Thirty years have passed since formal education in the UK was extended to children and young people with significant learning difficulties, through schooling. While legislation creates the framework for opportunities, it cannot, of itself, immediately bring about new insights or changes of attitudes towards learners whose educational needs do not match typical profiles. Instead, the process of enhancing the learning experience of this group is ongoing but has been given an added impetus by the Salamanca Statement (UNESCO, 1994) that confirmed the right of all children to education and which, in turn, is reflected in the ideals and principles of the revised National Curriculum (England) (DfEE/QCA, 1999a; 1999b). A central theme of the revised curriculum focuses on how, through education, individuals might be empowered, in order to become effective citizens.

Empowerment through learning

The starting point for our deliberations must be a consideration of the early experiences that engage each of us in the acquisition of knowledge, the attainment of skills and the development of understanding. Such experiences are generic for all learning and depend to a great extent on the development of external opportunities such as the promotion of active learning and the identification of key experiences.

The work of the QCA/DfEE (2001) project team pulled together work from researchers engaged with infants and children at early levels of development (Uzgiris and Hunt, 1975; Brown, 1996; McInnes and Treffrey, 1982; Coupe O'Kane and Goldbart, 1998; Aitken and Buultjens, 1992) in an attempt to provide a framework for thinking about individual responses to new learning opportunities. Many of these researchers are concerned with learners who have complex special educational needs and they have therefore taken into account that, although these learners are at early developmental stages or are developmentally immature, they may be *chronologically* mature; a factor that applies to many pupils with special educational needs in all, or most, areas of their development. The broad bands of responses in the framework below apply to all new learning.

Framework for New Learning

Encounter

Here the learner is *introduced* to an experience or an activity. At this point it is unlikely that there will be a learning outcome. It is only by presenting the same activity or experience over a period of time that a reaction is established.

Awareness

The learner shows an *awareness* that something is happening when either engaged in an activity or taking part in an experience. Such an awareness may be fleeting.

Attention and response

The learner begins to respond, although not always consistently, to an object, event or a person.

Engagement

In this area the learner will attend for longer periods and make a greater response to stimuli.

Participation

Learners engage in turn taking and begin to anticipate familiar sequences of events.

Involvement

Learners actively join in some experience or activity. They may become involved in a range of different ways, which includes reaching out, or communicating in some way about what is going on.

Gaining skills and understanding

Learners use the activity or experience to demonstrate some knowledge, skills or understanding about it. They then strengthen and build upon their knowledge and skill base and generalise their learning to other areas.

(adapted from QCA/DfEE 2001, p.17)

The members of the project team who designed this framework were quick to point out that children will move through the early learning process in both hierarchical and linear ways. Children may, for example, move fairly rapidly hierarchically from encounter to awareness in the learning of a skill or the acquisition of new knowledge or understanding. They may, however, need to encounter experiences many times (in a linear way) when learning other skills or when acquiring new knowledge in order to establish a base for further development. We propose, however, that these processes are not restricted to children who are developmentally young, or who have special educational needs, but can be seen whenever *any learner* (at whatever age) is presented with something new. Consequently, all learners will move through this framework at different rates and in different ways and, therefore, we refer to it throughout this book as the Framework for New Learning. In the following example one of us describes her own learning in these terms.

Learning something new

'Working with computers? Yes, I must have *encountered* computers earlier but only became *aware* of them as something that impacted minimally on my own work during the late 1960s. My *attention* was drawn to computers during the 1970s when my undergraduate assignments were computer-marked, but I had no way of distinguishing between the different types or functions of computers, so it would not be true to say that I had much knowledge of them. At the same time, learning at the awareness level was extended because I was made more *aware* of the potential of computers as they further infiltrated everyday life and there was talk of a new Industrial Revolution. To some extent I *engaged* with the idea of the computer age as I read about computers and their potential and *encountered* more contexts where they were used. When I returned to paid work in the early 1980s I made limited use of word-processors, thus I *participated* in computer use. For example, I followed instructions about starting up the computer and saving documents but my participation was limited to applications with which I had become familiar and I was at a loss if, for example, the start-up programme did not follow its anticipated course. I did not become *involved* with them until the late 1980s when I had access to a computer for word-processing. From that time I have made regular use of increasingly sophisticated computers and gained more *skills*, for example a facility for e-mail usage. I have also generalised my word-processing skills to gain an *understanding* of, for example, how to edit texts for publication and even to cope with the erratic responses of some computer programmes.'

Empowering the learner

Contemporary perspectives on learning are increasingly likely to reflect the view that learning is essentially a 'shared social activity' (Watson, 2001, p.140). In pedagogic terms the perspectives are represented in *social constructivist* approaches which emphasise learners' active role in constructing and re-constructing their knowledge and understanding in a social context. This immediately places the learner in a position of power, at the centre of the teaching-learning experience. The teacher's role focuses on facilitating the construction of knowledge, by, for example:

* assessing the learner's baseline level of understanding;
* analysing the task or body of knowledge that is the learning objective;
* providing opportunities for exploring the area of knowledge in line with the learner's preferred learning style or personal learning resources.

Clive

Clive was 25 years old with specific learning difficulties. When he enlisted for help at his local Adult Education Centre he could not spell or write anything apart from his name, and his reading was restricted to a few social sight words such as 'Toilets', 'Exit' and 'Bus Stop'. His ambition was to become a long-distance lorry driver but he had not yet attained a driving licence for any vehicle because he was unable to read the Highway Code, although, mercifully, it was not necessary at that time for him to take a written test. His teacher developed resources based on the content and presentation of the Highway Code in order to make use of Clive's good visual memory for shapes and to help him to memorise sufficient content to pass the test. She decided that there was little point in adopting an approach that sought to establish spelling rules or other written language conventions. Instead, she tried to establish Clive's self-concept as an able learner through building on his road knowledge, acquired as a pedestrian and car passenger, in order for him to gain access to the necessary information about road-usage to become a competent driver.

This example contrasts with a didactic approach to teaching whereby knowledge and power reside with the teacher who dispenses or delivers a body of knowledge to passive learners. A substantial body of literature (see, for example, Brooks and Brookes, 1993;

Littledyke and Huxford, 1998) provides support for adopting a social constructivist approach with all learners, but the theoretical perspectives analysed in this book will build on Watson's work (Watson, 1999, 2000, 2001).

It is important to remember that the perspectives emphasising a dynamic relationship between learners and their environments will necessarily recognise the significance of a learner's membership of an ethnic minority group. If we conceptualise learning needs as those arising when a learner, with his or her own profile of skills, abilities and life history, encounters a specified curriculum of learning, it is clear that issues relating to ethnicity assume importance and we draw attention to such factors later in the book.

Social constructivism is a philosophical perspective on teaching and learning that can be used to analyse any encounter in which an individual extends his or her knowledge, skills or understanding. In relation to planned curricula of learning, the revised National Curriculum of England similarly stresses pupil participation, but as part of a wider emphasis on promoting personal development towards a position of autonomy from which true citizenship can be exercised. Lawson and Fergusson (2001) discuss how personal and social education has steadily assumed a higher priority in the curriculum. They note that dedicated curriculum subjects – PSHE and, for Key Stages 3 and 4, Citizenship – exist to foster explicitly the attitudes, competencies and understanding that are valued in modern society. In particular, the empowerment of all pupils to assume active roles as responsible citizens is a central theme, which necessarily entails the development of independence, of autonomy and of self-advocacy. Whereas such qualities may emerge naturally in pupils without special needs, Lawson and Fergusson point out that opportunities for reinforcement arise across the curriculum that will be seized by schools with an ethos of promoting personal and social skills.

In order to take account of the diversity of learning profiles and needs of the range of pupils with special educational needs, we regard the PSHE curriculum as a central element in the *process* of empowerment. There are, however, a number of principles that provide the basis for work on empowerment, both in the home and in schools. These can be summed up as the:

- recognition of a link between empowerment, choice and decision-making;
- understanding that relationships with others are significant to the process of empowerment;
- acknowledgement of the importance of being valued and of a belief in one's own value (the need to develop a feeling of self-worth);
- provision of opportunities to develop skills and competences from a basis of awareness and experience;
- encouragement of an element of risk taking.

It is important to place this list in context in this chapter, but all of these principles are implicit within the detailed discussions in the chapters that follow.

Recognising the link between empowerment, choice and decision-making

Choice is concerned with making a difference, and the hundreds of choices that we make in a day influence and change the environment around us. These changes may be subtle: for example, choosing to listen to a particular piece of music may drive other members of the family out of the room. On other occasions, the outcome of a choice might be dramatic: choosing to take a new job may mean relocating the family and leaving the country. Choice is also concerned with 'making *oneself* different' and acting as a unique person 'rather than acting as a piece of furniture in the lives of others' (Henderson and Pochin, 2001, p.67).

At a basic level the 'right' to choose may be an expression of preference, but at a more sophisticated level it will inevitably involve the active selection of a range of alternatives which take into account:

- one's own needs;
- the perceived needs of others;
- the recognition of constraints;
- the ability to comprehend the impact of actions on future goals.

(adapted from Swain, 1989)

Choice, at this level, has changed into decision-making, resulting in the recognition of autonomy and self-determination, which is a fundamental right. Consequently, to deny someone 'choice' is to exercise oppression. The theorists whose work we have chosen to discuss have much to teach us about the creation of environments, methods and approaches that foster the development of relationships, communication and social responsiveness, all of which serve the process of empowerment.

Understanding that relationships with others are significant to the process of empowerment

While we suggest that empowerment is a *process* which includes the development of a person's ability to direct his or her own actions and influence his or her environment, empowerment does not mean that we operate in isolation. We are all reliant on other people in many different ways and, as Henderson and Pochin (2001) point out, throughout the course of life it is our relationships with others that tend to be the most significant source of our personal development. The impact and significance of this observation is apparent throughout this book and is discussed at length in many of the chapters.

Although individual empowerment is also concerned with the development of self-advocacy skills, for some pupils and people with learning difficulties directing their actions or influencing their environment will need to be carried out *through* other people. Others become the advocates for that person, and advocacy takes many forms: for example, it can include professional case-work advocacy, citizen advocacy, peer advocacy, and volunteer advocacy. Although different in nature, all are primarily concerned with aiding a person to make choices and therefore to enhance his or her acceptance and independence within society. In recognising the importance of self-advocacy, we suggest that advocacy partnerships should be celebrated in the same way. The development of relationships are the cornerstone of what Atkinson (1999) regards as 'an advocacy culture'.

Acknowledging the importance of being valued and a belief in one's own value

A person feeling good about him- or herself and responding to others in positive and effective ways also fosters empowerment. In an approach to raise the 'feel-good factor' of children with special educational needs, Curry and Bromfield (1994) quote Illsley and Clarke (1978) who suggest that:

> People who have positive self-esteem know that they are lovable and capable and that they care about themselves and other people. They do not have to build themselves up by tearing others down or by patronising less competent people.
>
> (Curry and Bromfield, 1994, p.26)

This observation can be linked to Maslow's famous *hierarchy of needs* (Maslow, 1943) where he gives a prominent position to self-esteem and self-actualisation. Self-esteem, which in his view leads to self-actualisation, has two elements: first the desire to have confidence in oneself (know that you are lovable and capable) and the second a wish for respect and prestige *from* others (which is not achieved by trying to succeed *above* others) as the second part of the Illsley and Clark quotation suggests).

Thwarted opportunities for boosting self-esteem result in feelings of inferiority, weakness and helplessness. In Maslow's terms self-actualisation involves aspiring to achieve and is dependent on self-realisation. Put simply, we have to know what is possible before we know we are doing it. Often pupils, particularly those with difficulties in learning, are not encouraged to define their own tasks, specify the outcomes of those tasks or assess their own work (Tilstone *et al.*, 2000). Instead they may receive feedback from others which signals that they are inadequate or worthless, and consequently they see themselves as inferior. If they continue to see themselves as poor or as failures in areas that they perceive as being highly valued by others, their self-worth will be deeply affected. Many of the theorists, whose work we have considered, place an emphasis on the development of high self-esteem and provide helpful pointers for effective school and classroom practice.

Providing opportunities to develop skills and competences from a basis of awareness and experiences

We have considered the Framework for New Learning on which, we propose, all learning is based and in using the example of *learning something new* we have already placed this framework into context. It is worth reiterating, however, that many of us, particularly those who have complex learning needs, may need to encounter experiences many times in order to learn skills or acquire knowledge and understanding which will encourage the process of empowerment.

Encouraging risk-taking

As we have already discussed, choice forms a basis for empowerment and Wertheimer (2000, p.108), in the context of a research programme which looks at the choices offered (or not) to people with high dependency needs, reminds us that: '… choice for all of us involves trying things out, making mistakes, changing our minds and a process of trial and error.' There is an element of risk for each of us in making new relationships, in going to new places, in experimenting with new things and, as professionals concerned with the education of children and young people, in supporting them in their learning.

The issue of 'risk' for pupils with special educational needs is usually centred on considerations of vulnerability, physical protection and health and safety, and it is not our intention to undermine these important considerations. We do wish to emphasise, however, the impact on children and young people when choice and control are denied them. As research in the 1980s showed (Garber and Seligman, 1980; Sutherland, 1981; Swain, 1989), the psychological consequences of powerlessness are 'learned helplessness'. People can learn that events are independent of their actions and therefore the consequences of what happens to them are beyond their control. Over time, oppression is internalised and Swain (1989) reminds us that what seem to be the characteristics of some pupils with special educational needs (such as apathy, under-confidence, fatalism and depression) are actually the 'direct manifestations of the dynamics arising from the lack of power' (p.116). Powerlessness and learned helplessness are also characteristics of people *without* special educational needs: for example, those who are clinically depressed.

The foundations that we have built in this chapter are intended to make our own perspectives on the significance of empowerment and its relationship to learning clear to readers. In the next part of the book we describe and analyse the work of major theorists who, we believe, can contribute greatly to our understanding of the process involved in the empowerment of *all* children, *particularly* those who have difficulties in learning and whose needs are 'special'.

References

Aitken, S. and Buultjens, M. (1992) *Vision for Doing*. Edinburgh: Moray House.

Atkinson, D. (1999) *Advocacy: A Review*. Brighton: Pavillion Books.

Brookes, J. and Brookes, M. (1993) *In Search of Understanding: the Case for Constructivist Classrooms*. Alexandria, VA: Association for Supervision and Curriculum Development.

Brown, E. (1996) *Religious Education For All*. London: David Fulton Publishers.

Byers, R. (1998) 'Personal and social development', in C. Tilstone, L. Florian and R. Rose (eds) *Promoting Inclusive Practice*. London: Routledge.

Coupe O'Kane, J. and Goldbart, J. (1998) *Communication Before Speech: Development and Assessment* (2nd edition). London: David Fulton Publishers.

Curry, M. and Bromfield, C. (1994) *Personal and Social Education for Primary Schools through Circle Time*. Tamworth: NASEN.

DfEE/QCA (1999a) *The National Curriculum: Handbook for Primary Teachers in England*. London: DfEE.

DfEE/QCA (1999b) *The National Curriculum: Handbook for Secondary Teachers in England*. London: DfEE.

Fraser, B. (1984) *Society, Schools and Handicap*. Stratford: NCSE.

Garber, J. and Seligman, M.E.P. (1980) *Human Helplessness: Theory and Applications*. New York: Academic Press.

Henderson, R. and Pochin, M. (2001) *A Right Result? Advocacy, Justice and Empowerment*. Bristol: Policy Press.

Lawson, H. and Fergusson, A. (2001) 'PSHE and citizenship', in B. Carpenter, R. Ashdown and K. Bovair (eds) *Enabling Access* (2nd edition). London: David Fulton Publishers.

Littledyke, M. and Huford, L. (1998) (eds) *Teaching the Primary Curriculum for Constructivist Learning*. London: David Fulton Publishers.

Maslow, A.H. (1943) 'A theory of human motivation', *Psychology Review*. 50, 370–96.

McInnes, J.M. and Treffrey, J.A. (1982) *Deaf-Blind Infants and Children*. Toronto: University of Toronto Press.

Mental Deficiency Act (1913). London: HMSO.

Mittler, P. (1996a) 'Laying the foundations for self-advocacy', in J. Coupe O'Kane and J. Goldbart (eds) *Whose Choice?* London: David Fulton Publishers.

Mittler, P. (1996b) 'Preparing for self-advocacy', in B. Carpenter, R. Ashdown and K. Bovair (eds) *Enabling Access*. London: David Fulton Publishers.

QCA/DfEE (2001) *Planning, Teaching and Assessing the Curriculum for Pupils with Learning Difficulties*. London: QCA.

Rose, R., Fergusson, A., Coles, C., Byers, R. and Banes, D. (eds) (1994) *Implementing the Curriculum for Pupils with Learning Difficulties*. London: David Fulton Publishers.

Sebba, J., Byers, R. and Rose, R. (1993) *Redefining the Curriculum for Pupils with Learning Difficulties*. London: David Fulton Publishers.

Stevens, A. (1997) 'Recording the history of an institution: the Royal Eastern Counties Institution at Colchester', in D. Atkinson, M. Jackson and J. Walmsley (eds) *Forgotten Lives: Exploring the History of Learning Difficulties*. Kidderminster: BILD.

Sutherland, A. (1981) *Disabled We Stand*. London: Souvenir Press.

Swain, J. (1989) 'Learned helplessness theory and people with learning difficulties: the psychological price of powerlessness', in A. Brechin and J. Walmsley (eds) *Making Connections*. London: Hodder and Stoughton.

Tilstone, C. (ed.) (1991) *Teaching Pupils with Severe Learning Difficulties*. London: David Fulton Publishers.

Tilstone, C., Lacey, P., Porter, J. and Robertson, C. (2000) *Pupils with Learning Difficulties in Mainstream Schools*. London: David Fulton Publishers.

UNESCO (1994) *The Salamanca Statement and the Framework for Action on Special Needs Education*. Paris: UNESCO.

Uzgiris, I.C. and Hunt, J.M. (1975) *Assessment in Infancy: Ordinal Scales of Infant Development*. Urbana: University of Illinois Press.

Watson, J. (1999) 'Working in groups: social and cognitive effects in a special class', *British Journal of Special Education*. 26 (2), 87–95.

Watson, J. (2000) 'Constructive instruction and learning difficulties', *Support for Learning*. 15 (3), 135–41.

Watson, J. (2001) 'Social constructivism in the classroom', *Support for Learning*. 16 (3), 140–7.

Wertheimer, A. (ed.) (2000) *Everyday Lives; Everyday Choices*. London: The Foundation for People with Learning Disabilities.

Part 1

The theorists

Chapter 2

The cognitive developmental theorists

Cognitive development or intellectual development are terms used to indicate the processes whereby children gain an understanding of their physical, social and psychological worlds. Without subscribing to any specific theory about cognitive development, it can be said that an infant encounters the environment through the senses and through physical exploration to make sense of, or 'know', its features and how it works. In order to organise these experiences, to learn from them and, ultimately, to elaborate the experiences at a mental level, in short, to think, it is necessary to construct representations.

Discovering how children represent their experiences of the world (form concepts), in order to learn and eventually to think as adults, has long been a major concern of both philosophers and, more recently, psychologists. The outcomes of philosophical enquiry and research can be categorised and evaluated in numerous ways, but a major strand of investigation remains focused on the interplay between the developing child and the environment. For example, to what extent are children biologically prepared to process knowledge of the environment in specified ways, or how big a role does the environment play in what knowledge they acquire and how they acquire it? This is, of course, one formulation of the classic 'nature versus nurture debate', and its central tenets are evident in the summary of the theories of Jean Piaget, Jerome Bruner and Lev Vygotsky presented in this chapter.

Jean Piaget

A biographical background sometimes serves to bring a remote, but important, figure to life in order to capture a reader's interest before introducing his or her theories. Beyond that, there is rarely any significance between, say, where a man or woman was born, how they spent their early years and their contribution to the advancement of science. This is not true of Jean Piaget. To have some insight into the events and context of his early life is to understand his perspective on the development of the intellect. Knowing something about his background in science, we can evaluate his theories and assess their contribution to our understanding of cognitive development.

Piaget was born in Neuchâtel in Switzerland in 1896 and developed an early scientific interest in biology, publishing, at the age of only ten, a monograph about an albino sparrow that he had seen in the local park. His postgraduate research at the University of Geneva focused again on the natural sciences, but soon afterwards his career direction changed when he undertook a project to collect data from young schoolchildren to standardise a test of reasoning. The project awakened in Piaget a keen interest in the similarities between normally developing children of the same age, in terms of their problem-solving abilities. He was particularly drawn to explaining the consistency of wrong responses within age groups and this led him to propose a stage-related theory about intellectual, or cognitive, development. In the expression of the theory we see that Piaget conceptualises the dynamics of intellectual growth in terms of a progressive adaptation to the world of adult reasoning, reflecting the biological discipline within which his own thinking developed.

An outline of Piaget's theory of cognitive development

According to Piaget, the forces that drive intellectual growth are, in essence, the same as those underpinning any other aspect of development. In short, human beings, in common with all other living organisms, have to adapt in order to 'survive', either in a literal sense of 'life-sustaining' or, metaphorically, 'functioning as a member of a society'. The process of adaptation involves the simultaneous action of the organism on the environment and that of the environment on the organism. To translate this into the terms of the developing individual, the child acts on the external world, at first in terms of physical activity in order to 'survive', by which we mean to gain control over specified aspects of reality. To the extent that the child can act appropriately towards features of his or her environment, we say that he or she can *understand* them. In Piaget's terms, the store of knowledge that the child possesses can assimilate those features. However, the environment continually acts on the child's cognitive structures by presenting new features so that the cognitive structures are compelled to change in order to accommodate these novel features. Intellectual development strives towards adaptation whereby cognitive structures or, in Piagetian terminology, schemes (sometimes schemas), most closely represent to the individual an external reality within which he or she can function. A simple example can perhaps illustrate this whole process.

A baby grasps and manipulates a toy, say a rattle, in a rudimentary fashion. Progressively, she assimilates the properties of the rattle so that her knowledge of it, evidenced through her physical actions, is refined. From then on, her schema for the rattle leads her to have certain expectations of it and how she behaves towards it. If presented with a different rattle, the baby will attempt to apply the same 'rattle' schema but will quickly discover that the new object is different: in weight, colour, texture, sound, etc. Thus the existing schema is modified as the special properties of the second rattle are accommodated, and the knowledge base that underpins the baby's capacity to control this particular aspect of reality is extended.

As well as emphasising the role of action on the environment as the vehicle for intellectual development, Piaget also cited characteristic ways of responding that he believed to be associated with different stages of development. These stages are qualitatively different from each other. They proceed in a sequence that is, according to Piaget, invariable and universally observable because, to some extent, the characteristics that mark out each stage are determined by maturational factors. The four stages of development that Piaget identified are: sensori-motor; pre-operational; concrete-operational and formal operational.

The sensori-motor stage of development

An infant's earliest action schemes are reflex behaviours; that is, they are not under conscious control but are quite literally survival behaviours such as rooting, sucking and grasping. After the first four weeks the infant's behavioural repertoire is still limited to responding to sensory input with stereotypical motor activities. These are termed primary circular reactions, thus suggesting that they are repetitious and dependent on the infant's perception of their association with positive or pleasurable sensations. They are not therefore goal-directed but, even so, Piaget regarded this early part of the sensori-motor stage as the beginning of intelligent behaviour.

During the sensori-motor stage, reflex behaviour is steadily replaced by purposeful activity denoting the baby's increasing control over the environment during a series of sub-stages. In the third sub-stage, termed secondary circular reactions, there is evidence that babies are acquiring an understanding of the link between action and consequence. This is gradually consolidated so that, by the time of the first birthday, the baby has a well-established notion of cognitive intentionality: that is, her or his understanding of features of the world is conventional and she or he is able to set goals. Developments in understanding are matched by motor development: for example, independent mobility that brings with it an essential component of personhood – choice, about where to go, what to look at, and what to touch, grasp or reject. At the same time, and partly because of the opportunities presented through mobility to adopt new perspectives, there is a slow but definite decrease in egocentricity. In everyday usage, this is a pejorative term that implies selfishness: people are egocentric when they fail to consider another person's needs and desires. In relation to the developing child, it is initially identified in the inability to distinguish between oneself and the rest of reality. A gradual decentering allows the child to recognise this distinction, but the egocentric focus is evident in a failure to accept any reality other than that of which she or he is immediately aware. Therefore, before the age of six months a baby will watch a toy (as an object of interest) but, when it is covered with a cloth she or he will then act as if it has simply gone out of existence. Again, gradual understanding of *object permanence* or the acknowledgement that objects continue to exist even when we have no direct contact with them is characteristic of the sensori-motor stage.

Binda

Binda is a 15-year-old student with Angelman's syndrome (a chromosomal abnormality, the features of which often include slow psychomotor development and lax muscle tone, unco-ordinated arm movement, and unprovoked bouts of laughter). Children with this syndrome usually have severe difficulties in learning. Much of her development is at the sensory motor stage but Binda has benefited from effective physiotherapy, and she is ambulant and very mobile in familiar surroundings. She has developed an interest in, and obsession with, plastic wallet sheets and if she sees them anywhere in the room she makes strenuous efforts to obtain them. She vocalises and becomes distressed and agitated if they are out of reach or taken away from her. If, when she is watching, the plastic folders are put away in a drawer or a cupboard she will initially vocalize loudly, but then calms down and makes no attempt to retrieve them even though she is capable of opening both the cupboards and the drawers.

Full attainment of object permanence, according to Piaget, is not apparent until typically developing infants are between 15 and 18 months of age, when they will search for an object even though they did not see it being hidden. This implies some form of mental representation of the object and is therefore the beginnings of intelligent thought, in contrast to earlier logical processes that were demonstrated solely through intelligent action. The internalisation of events or cognitive representation of actions after the age of 18 months is paralleled by a rudimentary awareness of causality. This means that the infant is able to reflect on possible associations between events in which she or he is a player. For example, babies come to realise that they can make things happen; they link specific actions (causes) with specific outcomes (effects) and they experiment by varying their behaviours in order to achieve different effects. It is important to remember that this development, which enables the child to exert significant control over her or his environment, is borne out of the experiences gained through her or his sensory and motor exploration of that environment.

As we explore the significance of Piaget's observations for children with special educational needs, the sensori-motor stage will assume particular relevance because it could be thought that the development of many children who are considered at present to have profound and multiple learning difficulties may not progress beyond this stage. However, Piaget's emphasis on the importance of motoric and sensory development for intellectual development has been questioned, and in Chapter 9 (Cognition and learning) we examine contemporary views and the evidence that intellectual competence can exceed that predicted by severe sensory disability.

It is therefore necessary to digress briefly from the developmental pathway set out by Piaget in order to make some broad observations about his view on the child as a learner. In particular, we should note that, for Piaget, the developing child is a lone scientist striving to make sense of a complex world, initially endowed only with a set of instincts for responding to stereotypical events. Variations on these events mean that this learner has to adapt but it seems that, at all stages, the process of adaptation is negotiated by the learner with little or no intervention from any other person. Motivation to learn stems from the imbalance created when incoming information cannot be assimilated within existing schemes, but motivation can be dissipated if too much accommodation is demanded.

Lucy

Lucy is a Key Stage 4 pupil with complex learning needs. In order to obtain a greater under-standing of her level of development her teacher observed her working with another more able pupil in an art lesson. It quickly became obvious that Lucy loved to feel, crinkle, scrunch, pull and tear different types of paper. Her classmates were using her efforts to create a large group collage. It was apparent from her level of attention and co-operation, and her smiles and vocalizing, that she enjoyed her task. At one point, however, the pupil working with her began to sort the tissue and cellophane papers into red and yellow heaps, and she tried to encourage Lucy to follow her lead. Lucy, however, quickly became unco-operative and distracted and reverted to rocking backwards and forwards in her wheelchair and to sucking her fist.

Operational thinking

To return to the course of development as proposed by Piaget, mature cognitive reasoning is characterised by operational thinking. In his terminology, operations are organised systems of mental actions that interrelate. Operational thinking enables complex and systematic problem-solving, firstly within the realm of concrete and actual events. Therefore a ten-year-old would probably respond correctly to questions such as the following: 'If Tom is taller than Kate and Kate is taller than Sam who is the shortest?' However, the concrete operational thinker would need to build up a mental representation of 'Tom', 'Kate' and 'Sam' and arrange them (mentally) in a line before she or he could give the correct answer.

By the age of 12 or 13 problem-solvers should be able to make use of the form of logical systems to generate and test hypotheses about events, both real and imagined (hypothetico-deductive reasoning); thus the final stage of development is referred to as the stage of formal operational reasoning. This stage appears to be mainly concerned with scientific and mathematical thought although, as Bee (2000) points out, its application to strategic planning is also evident. In the example below, Steven uses the form of such thinking to make life-plans:

Steven

If I take this course of study when I leave school, these career opportunities will be opened up although that wouldn't allow me to travel as that course of study would. At the same time I need to plan a range of options against the possibility of varying degrees of success in A-level exams.

It is, however, most likely that Steven, a typically developing 15-year-old, *learned* to apply this type of logic along with other school-based learning because these ways of thinking are favoured in most Western societies and are, therefore, routinely encouraged as part of education. This, then, casts doubt on Piaget's view that formal operational thinking is the invariable endpoint of intellectual development.

Pre-operational thinking

While development is seen as growth in the direction of operational thinking, important changes occur before then and after the sensori-motor stage. Piaget referred to this stage as pre-operational, which lasts approximately from the age of two years to six years in normally developing children, because he saw it as preparatory for operational thought. Obviously, this is also a period of rapid physical growth and major changes in children, when they become fully mobile and increasingly competent as users of spoken language. However, the restrictions on children's thinking during this time are largely the outcome of continuing egocentricity. The child's judgements are based on the evidence of her or his senses, on a form of logic that lacks reversibility and on a steadfast focus on one aspect of a problem to the exclusion of its other features. These characteristics are classically demonstrated in Piaget's conservation experiments: for example, the conservation of number experiment.

The child watches as the adult sets out two lines of equal numbers of sweets, with sweets matching one-to-one, in each line. The adult then spreads out one line to make it longer. The child is then asked whether there are the same numbers of sweets in each line. The pre-operational thinker is persuaded by the longer length of one line and fails to recognise that, if no sweets were added or subtracted, the two lines have to contain the same number of sweets as before.

As indicated earlier, a key development during the pre-operational stage is in the child's ability to produce and understand language. Elsewhere in this book, we examine the relationship between language and thought but it is worth noting here that Piaget regarded language only as the external manifestation of thought. That is, he regarded intelligent thought as evolving from intelligent behaviour and conceded the value of symbolic thought whereby thought could be dissociated from action, but he did not regard language as having a facilitative effect on the growth of intelligence.

Evaluations of Piaget's theories

Since its publication, Piaget's theory of cognitive development has been re-examined and, although the central tenets remain intact, details have been challenged. In particular, theorists have shown that he was inclined to take a conservative view about the ages at which major developments were likely to take place (see Wood, 1998 for details). Subsequent repetitions of classic experiments have been modified to take account of how the child might perceive an event or situation, or to employ language that a child might use. These have confirmed that young children are often able to reason at a more mature level than Piaget had been able to demonstrate (for example, Donaldson, 1978). More significantly for the population of children with whom we are concerned, Piaget, who died in 1980, did not have the advantage of present-day insights into the capacities of the newborn infant for imitation and remembering (Goswami, 1998). It now seems likely that the neonate is able to make use of mental representations and is therefore far better equipped for learning than Piaget could have known. With this knowledge, and the conviction that appropriate learning experiences can develop it, skilled teachers can advance the learning potential of all children.

Conclusion

For Piaget, the child is innately prepared for empowerment over a constantly changing environment. The cognitive structures that underpin intellectual activity adjust in response to challenges when incoming information cannot be accommodated within existing schemes, and modes of thinking develop with biological growth. However, as we have seen, most interpretations of Piaget's perspective, with its emphasis on child-directed learning, point to a view of individual progression that *could* be restricted by *within-child* factors so that the child may never exercise a degree of autonomy in line with his or her potential. An alternative view, particularly that of Vygotsky, emphasises the greater potential for intellectual and personal growth of individual learners when they interact with more advanced thinkers.

In his stage-related view of development, Piaget offers a framework within which to consider individual progress towards mastery over the environment, both physical and social. Critical analyses of the framework have questioned his view of the environment as passive and have stressed a more interactive relationship whereby the environment, suitably adapted by other people, can facilitate the growth of personal autonomy. Nevertheless, his contribution to the science of cognitive psychology is immense. While attempting to extract from his vast collection of data, he had a tendency to make generalisations about the development of human intellectual functioning, but he always retained an openness towards, and an interest in, individual variations. It is therefore entirely appropriate that his theories and approaches should inform an exploration of complex and variable learning needs.

Jerome S. Bruner

Jerome S. Bruner was born in New York in 1915. On leaving school he studied at Duke and Harvard Universities where he became interested in human development and its relationship to learning. His work has involved studying children in nurseries, schools, playgroups, African villages, hospitals and highly technical laboratories, and he has made a considerable contribution to research into learning readiness and its practical implications. During his career he has been Professor of Psychology at Harvard University where he became Founder and Director of the Center for Cognitive Studies. He left Harvard to become Professor of Experimental Psychology at the University of Oxford and was Director of the Oxford Pre-school Research Project, a landmark in practical research, which analysed the pre-school scene in Britain in the 1980s. He then became, concurrently, a professor at the New School for Social Research, New York City, and a fellow at the New York Institute for the Humanities, New York University. In addition, he has served as a member of various academic and government advisory boards and holds many honorary offices and degrees, including the American Psychological Association's Distinguished Scientific Award.

His work has been greatly influenced by Jean Piaget, to whom he dedicated his famous book written in 1966, *Studies in Cognitive Growth* (Bruner *et al.*, 1966a). His previous book *The Process of Education* (1960) was also an influential study of curriculum reform. In addition, Vygotsky also had a significant effect on his work, and between them they have concentrated on the functional aspect of the formation of concepts in young children.

An outline of his theories

As stated, Bruner's work has been greatly influenced by Piaget but as their individual work developed, Piaget became more interested in the *structure* of mature thinking, whereas Bruner sought to describe the different *processes* embedded in creative problem-solving. The similarities between the two theorists can be seen in the importance that both place on *action* and *problem-solving*; children will, for example, only arrive at abstract problem-solving and the generalisation of ideas if they have first been engaged in practical problem-solving which establishes the deep connections between activities and solutions (Wood, 1998). Similarly, both Piaget and Bruner stress the use of modes of representation to indicate ways in which children acquire knowledge, and Smith (1999) provides a useful overview of Bruner's modes of representation that can be summed up as:

- *enactive*, in which the child comes to understand the world by acting upon it;
- *iconic*, when sensory images or iconic representations are increasingly used for the storage and the transformation of knowledge;

- *symbolic*, which is characterised by the ability to use abstract symbol systems, like language and mathematics, and permits flexibility and complexity of thinking.

Smith (1999, p.20) shows the correspondence between Bruner's modes of representation and Piaget's stages of development below.

Piaget	Bruner
Sensori-motor (birth to 2 years)	Enactive
Pre-operational (2 years to 6 years)	Iconic
Concrete (6 to 11 years)	Symbolic
Formal (11 years +)	Symbolic

Bruner's three ways of representing the world resulted in what he defined as 'understanding reality' (Bruner, 1996). Children represent the world in 'action routines', in pictures, or in symbols, and as they become more mature they then move towards symbolism.

Bruner's three modes

Enactive mode

The enactive mode is crucial in guiding activity and results in directed activity, or what Bruner later termed 'work'. This is a stage when action and external experience are fused, when the senses are brought into play and the spatial world of vision corresponds with the serial world of action. Motor activity, visual development, kinaesthetic activity and perception provide a basic framework for growth. At this early stage, the identification of objects 'seems to depend not so much on the objects encountered but on the actions evoked by them' (Bruner, 1966a, p.12).

The examples below show pupils who are developmentally within the stage that Bruner refers to, but are chronologically much older. The first example illustrates the sensory experiences encountered by Tom using volleyball in physical education (PE). In a later session he attempted to generalise his new knowledge to what he regarded as a similar situation and became frustrated when he realised that his new 'volleyball' did not respond to his actions as before.

Tom

Tom is 16 and has profound and multiple learning difficulties and significant visual impairment. He is participating in a game of volleyball in a PE lesson with his peers (whose difficulties in learning are not so complex). His intervener supports him and, in order to facilitate his inclusion in the activity, the students are using a very large yellow balloon, which contains some dried pasta. This sensory object is chosen to help Tom to locate it, using his limited vision and hearing.

Tom is able to use his developing visual and motor skills in the game as he 'tracks' the balloon and reaches out towards it when it enters his field of vision. If it lands in his lap he feels the balloon, becomes 'still' and appears to listen to the sound when it moves. His intervener helps him to lift it towards his face and he is able to explore its surfaces with his mouth and tongue before pushing it away. The experiences appear pleasurable and he laughs and smiles.

Later, in a massage session, a teaching assistant blows a stream of bubbles in front of his face. Tom 'stills', smiles, starts to track the bubbles and reaches out for them, but when they burst he frowns and withdraws his hand. When a few bubbles touch his head he pushes his hand angrily over it, makes the noise he uses when he is unhappy, and bites his wrist.

Iconic mode

As the enactive mode of representation progresses, movement becomes independent and the child begins to represent the world without the necessity of action. Iconic representation is concerned initially with capturing the particularity of events and objects by manipulation (Rosch and Lloyd, 1978). The child uses actions to match something that he sees in his mind to something that he is encountering, but gradually there is a sharp separation between the child and the world around him and the early manipulation of the concrete becomes unnecessary. Bruner (1966a) explains that although there will often be some confusion, even in a three-year-old, between what is internal to his own experience and what is external (in the sense of it being shared by others), the separation becomes clearer as he matures.

Marie

Marie is a year younger than Tom. Her difficulties in learning are not so complex and she uses icons to help her to understand her world. In order for her to take responsibility for her daily routines and to help her to increase her independence, her weekly timetable is available in pictures and symbolic representation. In recognising the shapes, she is able to understand what lessons she will receive, and also to go further and calculate the equipment she needs for each one, the room to be used and who her teacher will be. She is using iconic representation for basic understanding, but the icons also help her to summarise actions.

Symbolic mode

It was Bruner's initial belief that before the child could use symbolic representation as an instrument of thought, he or she must first bring the world of experience under control through the other modes of representation. Although Bruner recognises the development of *communication* as being important within the symbolic mode, his research in the 1970s and 1980s focused mainly on the emergence of words as a vehicle for the growth of knowledge, and in 1977 he wrote:

> Once language becomes a medium for translation of experience, there is a progressive release from immediacy. Language has the new and powerful features of remoteness and arbitrariness; it permits productive, combinatorial operations in the absence of what is represented.
>
> (Bruner, 1977, p.217)

Not only does language provide a means of representing experience, but also of transforming it. Bruner is quick to recognise that without the help of others, namely adult intervention, in the symbolic representation of experience, the child would grow to adulthood still depending in large measure on the enactive and iconic modes of representing and organising the world, no matter what language or method of communication she or he uses (Bruner, 1966a). Bruner's theories are based on the premise that human mental activity does not happen in isolation, nor is it conducted 'unassisted', even when it goes on 'inside the head', but is shaped by others' responses, and the codes and conditions of the culture in which the human lives (Bruner, 1996). Wood (1998) takes this view further when he emphasises that the development of certain ways of reasoning and learning is a direct product of both spontaneous and organised social interactions between the developing child and the more mature members of his or her community (p.16). Bruner, however, felt that some adults never achieve the symbolic mode and consequently it is not easy to select an example of a child with difficulties in learning who is using the mode as 'an instrument of thought'. An alternative way of looking at it is to compare the development of a young person who does not have identified learning difficulties with a young person whose difficulties have been pinpointed through a Statement of Special Educational Need (the Statement is a legal document that outlines the resources necessary for a pupil to learn and to be taught effectively).

Royston's learning needs were diagnosed in his primary school (he is now 17), and he has been successfully included in mainstream secondary education with appropriate human and physical resources.

Royston

In Key Stage 4, Royston (who is slightly older than the other pupils in his class) and his peers are experiencing an increasing pastoral emphasis on the preparation for leaving school. The majority of the pupils (with support from parents and the career services) are able to choose areas of interest for their future careers including subject options for A-level study or vocational courses. They discuss possible career choices with staff and the effect such decisions will have on their lives.

In comparison, Royston is finding it hard to participate in this discussion without 'strong' direction from the pastoral team including his learning support assistant. Although he is able to think about the immediate future, it is 'an adult driven future' where he will continue to be directed by other people. His peers are beginning to work with ideas that are abstract and symbolic ('where would I like to be in three years' time'), but Royston is still working within Bruner's earlier stages and is relying on others to make the choices for him.

In the 1960s Bruner considered the course from enactive through to iconic and on to symbolic representation as a progression, but later questioned such a progression on developmental grounds (Bruner, 1996). Maturity is, in Bruner's terms, more to do with the interplay between biology and culture. Mental activity is, on the one hand, at the mercy of biological constraints and, on the other, the cultural setting and its resources. According to his theories, 'learning, remembering, talking, imagining: all of them are made possible by participating in a culture' (Bruner, 1996, p. xi).

The importance of the culture

We see that throughout Bruner's work there is a tacit belief that the culture in which a child is reared has a great bearing on the nurturing and shaping of growth. His theory that cognitive growth is influenced by outside actions and resources which are culturally determined is in line with the notion that learning difficulties are often created by the lack of experiences or the lack of responsive environments rather than by 'within child' factors (Tilstone *et al.*, 2000).

Bruner identifies three factors (or amplifiers), which are given different emphases in different cultures, and at different times as the child develops. These amplifiers are: motoric, sensory and reflective; all provide extensions to human powers. The examples he gives, particularly in his early work, are somewhat crude and simplistic, but it is easy to add new examples that apply to contemporary culture.

Amplifiers of human motor capacities

These are initially extensions of the limbs that in all societies can range from eating and cutting tools, and in primitive ones, to digging sticks and weapons to kill animals for food. In a more sophisticated society one can add writing tools, switches and computer keyboards. Later amplifiers of motor capacities go beyond extensions of the limbs and may involve devices that transport the body from one place to another. Bruner's devices include wheels and levers, but bicycles, wheelchairs and cars can be added to his list.

As far back as 1978, Bland described the practical aspects of amplifying the motor capacities of children who have profound and multiple learning difficulties. The approach to teaching was largely physical and the teacher must become part of the child. Sitting, turning, rolling and crawling may be partly, or wholly, the result of the teacher's physical identification with the taught. The teacher may use his or her body as a vehicle to allow the child to experience movement, or to provide the necessary structure and support for movement to take place. The approach was experimental, with the emphasis on gross motor activity in which the teacher is the main motivating force and is closely identified with the child. The later work of Veronica Sherborne (1990), which is based on Laban's analysis of human movement, also feeds into Bland's ideas. Sherborne emphasised the importance of developing relationships in movement. In order to help some children to experience movement, particularly those with profound and multiple learning difficulties, it is necessary for the adult (or in her experimental work, an older mainstream pupil under supervision) to provide basic physical support for children with complex needs. As in Bland's work, the bodies of the 'teachers' become the means of experiencing movement and of transportation.

Amplifiers of the senses

These are aids that enhance ways of looking and noticing things and other people, and Bruner's examples include primitive devices such as smoke signals and hailers. His more sophisticated ones encompass magnifying glasses and radar systems. In a culture which includes children and people with learning difficulties, it is possible to identify environments that provide particular sensory stimulus and teaching approaches that build on early sensory experiences (Longhorn, 1995; Davis, 2001).

Amplifiers of human rationactive capacities

It is here that Bruner's preoccupation with the formation of language comes to the fore. Language is used as the development of logical thought and involves the acquisition of symbol systems which are governed by rules and must be shared for effective use. Such 'sharing' starts with the way in which a caregiver 'talks' to his or her baby, and the approach is labelled by Bruner and other psychologists as 'motherese' (Bullowa, 1979). The caregiver watches the reactions of his or her charge, which are often non-verbal, leaves spaces or pauses for the response, and uses repetition to help the child anticipate and respond. Nind and Hewett (1994) have taken a similar approach in their work on intensive interaction in order to help pupils with extreme difficulties in learning to form relationships. A range of interactive games is used in an attempt to attract and hold the attention of the learner and the adult builds on the responses of the child. In this work the adult provides a 'scaffold' for the development of the child's own actions, initiative and thought (see also Wood *et al.*, 1976; Wood *et al.*, 1978). Bruner's notion of 'scaffolding' is neatly summarised in his own words: 'As a teacher you do not wait for readiness to happen; you foster or "scaffold" it by deepening the child's powers at the stage where you find him or her now' (Bruner, 1996, p.120).

Bruner originally intended 'scaffolding' to apply to the strategies that parents and caregivers employ to facilitate their children's acquisition of language by deliberately using language pitched at a level very slightly above that which the child can comprehend at a given point in time. In the example below, the teacher is using scaffolding in a number of different ways, to develop communication and language within the class and also to provide support for a wide range of pupils in the *content* of the lesson, in this case literacy.

Literacy work

The pupils are aged seven and eight years and include those with a wide range of special educational needs. Their mainstream teacher is asked how he 'scaffolds' his work for the pupils and his 'list' includes:

- PLAN–DO–REVIEW (where pupils plan their activities together, carry out individual tasks and then review them collaboratively at the end of the lesson, see Hohmann et al., 1979);
- asking a pupil to think aloud and providing support in recording his or her ideas, often through pictures or symbols;
- providing sentence support for older pupils to enable them to begin to be 'writers';
- carefully structured group work;
- using a 'jigsaw approach' to a group completion of a task (see Rose, 1991); such an approach can mean that each pupil is given a specific task to achieve which leads to the completion of a piece of work – in this case, a piece of writing by the class;
- recapping and identifying specific successful aspects of the work at the end of the session, again, often using pictures or symbols.

Conclusion

It is perhaps Bruner's overwhelming concern about the part played by the instructor or teacher in the child's development that offers important messages for the staff of schools. Social interaction is the bedrock from which progression through his modes is made, particularly in the development of language and communication. He provides a rich account of the development of language in the child in his chapters 'Teaching a native language' (Bruner, 1966b) and 'On cognitive growth' (Bruner, 1966a), all of which hinge on the importance of social interaction. Critics of his theory argue that social interactions vary between different cultures and yet children still learn to communicate at roughly the same rates in cultures where such interactions are not regarded as important (Hoff-Ginsburg, 1977). Nevertheless, as we argue in the second part of this section, Bruner's theories have much to offer in the development of empowerment and self-advocacy.

Lev S. Vygotsky

Vygotsky is recognised as a leading figure among Soviet psychologists and other intellectuals from the mid-1920s until his death in 1934 from tuberculosis at the early age of 38. The group was forced to leave Moscow to settle in the Ukraine during the political and social changes wrought by the Stalinists. After his death, Vygotsky's writings were officially suppressed, and did not re-emerge for over 20 years when supporting accounts of his views came, as oral contributions, from his former collaborators. Until recently, comparatively few of his publications were translated into English and those that were, according to Bakhurst (1996), may not be true to the original texts. Consequently, our interpretations of Vygotsky's perspective on the development of thinking are drawn from a range of secondary sources and, in all probability, have undergone subtle variations and modifications in the process. Nonetheless, it is possible to represent a general consensus among scholars on Vygotsky's views on intellectual development and its relationship to language and other cultural artefacts.

An outline of Vygotsky's theory of intellectual development

Like Piaget, Vygotsky believed that the basis of intelligence lies in the individual's activity in and on the world. He too wrote about the active construction of knowledge by the child and emphasised learning through discovery and curiosity, particularly during the first two years. Vygotsky believed that, during this period, the child is driven by biological needs to mature and termed it 'the natural line of development'. However, unlike Piaget, he gave the major role in development to the culture surrounding the child and termed the process, 'the cultural line of development'. Vygotsky argued that knowledge is culture-specific, the collective outcome of human thinking over time that is transmitted from one generation to another. Culture determines what we think about and how we think, and the process of transmission necessarily involves 'tools'. These, for Vygotsky, include psychological tools such as the spoken and written language, which are powerful sign systems that simultaneously liberate thinking beyond the 'here-and-now', but also structure and interpret experiences in specific ways. According to this view, as the child engages in social and cultural practices he or she internalises those experiences in order to become capable of intelligent thought. Thus, socio-cultural participation and the development of individual consciousness go hand-in-hand. An example, adapted from Lock (1980), illustrates how this process might start.

The very young baby cries as a response to some inner state, perhaps hunger or discomfort, but certainly not with the intention of communicating. At this developmental point, the baby's 'knowledge' is restricted to an awareness of sensation and is largely undifferentiated. However, the baby's mother interprets the child's crying as a sign of discomfort and takes appropriate action. Thus there is communication between the baby who unintentionally initiated it, and the mother, in Vygotsky's terms, at the intermental level. Such interactions provide the opportunity for the baby to develop an awareness of her or his ability to communicate and so she or he transfers this knowledge to the intramental level.

In this example the baby's experience of her or his inner state is interpreted by her or his mother who names it, 'You've got tummy ache.' That is, she constructs a meaning. Her interpretation, communicated verbally and through the response that she makes, perhaps by holding the baby and easing the discomfort, is internalised by her or him to become her or his understanding of the experience of crying with tummy ache. Thus, what was intermental or shared between two minds, those of mother and baby, is now also intramental or located in the consciousness of the infant.

Vygotsky himself described the same process of knowledge or thinking passing from the culture, via a more mature partner, to the developing infant. Daniels (1996) has termed this process the 'social formation of mind' and quotes Vygotsky:

> Any function in the child's cultural development appears twice, or on two planes. First it appears on the social plane, and then on the psychological plane. First it appears between people as an interpsychological category, and then within the child as an intrapsychological category. This is equally true with regard to voluntary attention, logical memory, and formation of concepts, and the development of volition ... Social relations or relations among people genetically underlie all higher functions and their relationships.
>
> (Vygotsky, 1981, p.163, cited by Daniels, 1996, p.6)

Thought and language

The sub-title here is also the translated title of Vygotsky's own account of the nature of language and its relationship with thought. In this publication Vygotsky set out his views on language as a psychological tool for mediating socio-cultural influences and concept formation. (This view stands in sharp contrast to that of Piaget, who maintained that language is the outer manifestation of thought and, in relation to the developing child, a reflection of that child's stage of development.) As we have seen in the example above, focusing on a very young baby, the child spontaneously communicates with others in the course of everyday activity and this communication is interpreted and fed back, principally through speech. In this way the child acquires an understanding of the functions of speech: for example, as a means of exerting some control over the environment via the agency of other people.

Polly

Polly is a teenager, she has profound difficulties in learning and is a wheelchair user. She has good receptive language and is able to follow short sets of instructions. She also understands positional concepts. Her expressive vocabulary is, at present, limited and consists of about 50 words. She is able to string two or three of these together ('Wendy gone now', for example).

The speech and language therapist and a clinical psychologist have recently joined the multidisciplinary team involved with Polly as her parents have become very concerned about her inappropriate behaviours. She often gets very excited and will then blow loud 'raspberries'. These professionals noticed that Polly's 'raspberry blowing' only happened during interactions with specific people including two of her peers who were disruptive and made a lot of noise.

The psychologist suggested that when in close contact with Polly these two children were annoying her and that her raspberry blowing was a way of expressing her frustration with the situation. Staff working with Polly had not interpreted her behaviour in this way and, consequently, had responded in ways which served to magnify the behaviour and to interpret it as a 'problem' rather than as an act of communication.

At the same time, the child's knowledge of the world is organised and structured by the language with which it is described. Vygotsky considered a further role for speech in the development of thought and this is best represented by the distinction between 'external' speech and 'inner' speech. Developmentally, inner speech follows external speech and is used by the child to regulate her or his activities and behaviour. Initially, inner speech is spoken aloud and it is egocentric in that it is not addressed to another listener, but it eventually exists at a sub-vocal level where it constitutes verbal thought.

Carol

Carol is a 16-year-old student with severe learning difficulties. She has good receptive language, uses a vocabulary of around 40 words appropriately and is beginning to string two or three words together. One of her favourite activities is to listen to stories and to look at books. Sometimes if she is sitting, alone, in the 'comfy corner' she will pick up a book or a photograph album and turn the pages. She occasionally starts to smile, laugh and talk quietly to herself and appears to be telling her own 'story' as she looks at the pictures and turns the pages. This activity is very much for Carol alone; if she becomes aware that she is being observed or if another student approaches she immediately ceases to talk and simply continues to look at the pictures or photos.

The zone of proximal development

As we have already emphasised, the essence of Vygotsky's view on the development of the intellect is socio-cultural. That is, the defining aspects of human mental activity are endowed through the operations of a range of psychological tools, including spoken language, written language and number systems to transmit the collective conceptual understanding of the wider culture of which the individual is a member. The PSHE/Citizen curriculum in England (DfEE/QCA, 1999a; 1999b) is culturally appropriate, for example, in that it emphasises democratic values through free-thinking and participatory practices. It also places value on the importance of the development of responsibility and self-regard, but such an emphasis would not be appropriate in either non-democratic countries, or societies where humility and servility are highly valued.

Through the socio-cultural customs of the society, the child develops towards membership of a specified culture. While the process of development is constrained by biologically endowed factors – in particular, maturational constraints – it was firmly held by Vygotsky that the human intellect is considerably extended by learning through instruction. The specifically pedagogic aspect is captured in Vygotsky's amplification of the zone of proximal development (ZPD). The ZPD suggests a distance between what a child can do when left to learn alone and what the same child can achieve through negotiation with a more able individual. In educational terms, the zone of proximal development underpins the proposal that the child's capacity to learn should not be assessed on the basis of unassisted learning but according to that child's aptitude for learning with appropriate guidance.

Conclusion

Vygotsky's theory about cognitive growth was founded on the notion that it is external cultural forces that create human intellectual functioning. Accordingly, 'reality' is socially constructed and exists initially on an external plane, to be internalised by members of each successive generation. Internalising socially constructed knowledge is, of course, a lifelong process: consider how our 'knowledge' of *disability* and *learning difficulties* has been reconstructed over the last few years. We return to the concept of social constructivism elsewhere in this book, when we examine these issues in more detail. Meanwhile, it is important to note that Bruner was greatly influenced by Vygotsky's theories of the development of thinking and, as we have described in that section, has elaborated those theories to provide practical applications, as in his descriptions of scaffolding.

References

Bakhurst, D. (1996) 'Social memory in Soviet thought', in H. Daniels (ed.) *An Introduction to Vygotsky*. London: Routledge.

Bee, H. (2000) *The Developing Child* (9th edition). Needham Heights, MA: Allyn and Bacon.

Bland, G.A. (1978) *Ten Years On*. Stratford: NCSE.

Bruner, J. (1960) *The Process of Education*. Cambridge, MA: Harvard University Press.

Bruner, J. (1966a) 'On cognitive growth', in J. Bruner, R.R. Oliver, and P.M. Greenfield (eds) *Studies in Cognitive Growth*. London: John Wiley.

Bruner, J. (1966b) *Toward a Theory of Instruction*. Cambridge, MA: Harvard University Press.

Bruner, J. (1977) 'The course of cognitive growth', in D. Child (ed.) *Readings in Psychology for the Teacher*. London: Holt, Rinehart and Winston.

Bruner, J. (1996) *The Culture of Education*. Cambridge, MA: Harvard University Press.

Bruner, J., Oliver, R.R. and Greenfield, P.M. (1966) *Studies in Cognitive Growth*. London: John Wiley.

Bullowa, M. (ed.) (1979) *Before Speech: The Beginning of Interpersonal Communication*. Cambridge: Cambridge University Press.

Daniels, H. (ed.) (1996) *An Introduction to Vygotsky*. London: Routledge.

Davis, J. (2001) *A Sensory Approach to the Curriculum for Pupils with Profound and Multiple Learning Difficulties*. London: David Fulton Publishers.

DfEE/QCA (1999a) *The National Curriculum: A Handbook for Primary Teachers in England*. London: DfEE.

DfEE/QCA (1999b) *The National Curriculum: A Handbook for Secondary Teachers in England*. London: DfEE.

Donaldson, M. (1978) *Children's Minds*. London: Fontana/Collins.

Goswami, U. (1998) *Cognition in Children*. Hove: Psychology Press.

Hoff-Ginsburg, E. (1997) *Language Development*. Pacific Grove, CA: Brooks-Cole.

Hohmann, M., Banner, B. and Weikart, D.P. (1979) *Young Children in Action*. Ypsilanti, MI: High/Scope Press.

Lock, A. (1980) 'Language development – past, present and future', *Bulletin of the British Psychological Society*. 33, 5–8.

Longhorn, F. (1995) *A Sensory Curriculum for Very Special People*. London: Souvenir Press.

Nind, M. and Hewett, D. (1994) *Access to Communication*. London: David Fulton Publishers.

Rosch, E. and Lloyd, B.B. (1978) (eds) *Cognition and Categorisation*. Hillsdale, NJ: Erlbaum.

Rose, R. (1991) 'A jigsaw approach to group work', *British Journal of Special Education*. 18 (20), 54–8.

Sherborne, V. (1990) *Developmental Movement for Children.* Cambridge: Cambridge University Press.

Smith, B. (1999) 'Child development', in C. Tilstone (ed.) *Learning Difficulties: Introduction to the Course. Distance Education Material for Teachers of Children with Learning Difficulties (Severe and Moderate).* Birmingham: University of Birmingham.

Tilstone, C., Lacey, P., Porter, J. and Robertson, C. (2000) *Pupils with Learning Difficulties in Mainstream Schools.* London: David Fulton Publishers.

Wood, D. (1998) *How Children Think and Learn.* Oxford: Blackwell.

Wood, D.J., Bruner, J. and Ross, G. (1976) 'The role of tutoring in problem solving', *Journal of Child Psychology and Psychiatry.* 17 (2), 89–100.

Wood, D.J., Wood, H.A. and Middleton, D.J. (1978) 'An experimental evaluation of four face-to-face teaching strategies', *International Journal of Behavioural Development.* 1, 131–47.

Chapter 3

The psychoanalytical theorists

Sigmund Freud

Freud's theories about the origins of the personality have had a major influence on the way in which individual differences in behaviour, as well as group behaviour and cultural traits, are explained in Western capitalist societies. This influence has extended beyond the boundaries of scientific disciplines – it has become embedded in everyday thinking and is illustrated in our frequent use of many Freudian terms. For example, we talk about 'unconscious motives', 'repression' and 'fixations': all notions that derive directly from his work. But in order to gain real insights into the development of behaviour through Freud's conceptual framework, we need to examine it in greater detail, consider how it emerged and understand the terminology that it engendered.

Freud was born in 1856 in Freiberg, then in Austria-Hungary, but his family moved to Vienna, the city with which he is most usually associated, when he was four. After completing his formal education, he trained and practised, first as a physician, later as a neurologist. He rigorously sought explanations for the symptoms of what we call 'mental illness' and developed a keen interest in the work of Jean Martin Charcot, a French psychopathologist who used hypnosis as a means of discovering the basis of 'hidden' causes of neurotic disturbances. Having studied under Charcot in Paris for a while during 1895/6, Freud based his own techniques for gaining access to the source of patients' neuroses on the notion that mental activity of which the thinker is totally unaware is the very activity that drives human behaviour. Collectively, the techniques are known as psychoanalysis and Freud used them extensively to diagnose and treat his patients in Vienna. As well as developing the therapeutic aspects of psychoanalysis, he used the techniques to research the origins of the 'normal' personality (Freud, 1960). He was curious to discover what lay behind specific traits and dispositions and what determined behaviour and marked out individual characteristics. It is important, however, to note that Freud was less interested in the significance of ability differences between people; as a result, variations in skills and aptitudes (intelligence, for example) do not feature in his explanation of personality development. Freud moved to London in 1938 to escape the Nazi Party who had earlier publicly burned his books in Berlin. His published output was immense and when he died in London in 1939, he was working on an exposition of the discipline that he founded, *An Outline of Psychoanalysis* (Freud, 1940), that remains unfinished.

An outline of Freud's psychoanalytic theory

As we have already stressed, the notion of unconscious mental activity (often called 'the unconscious') is an important part of Freud's psychoanalytic theory. Unlike its counterpart in contemporary general usage, the *unconscious* cannot be accessed (other than under the guidance of a psychoanalyst) and it is meaningless to say 'I forgot that arrangement because, *unconsciously*, I did not want to go'. Instead, unconscious mental activity is primary and does not, for example, respond to reason or to the constraints of moral directives. At birth, all mental activity is unconscious, driven by instinctual forces. At this point, the personality comprises one element only, *the id*. The id is the origin of the libido which, in turn, is the unconscious drive that provides the energy and motivation for all development. The id obeys the pleasure principle with no regard for the consequences of behaviour. Therefore, unchecked id impulses would produce behaviour that would destroy human society. As children mature they are forced to accept constraints on the behaviour that is aimed at satisfying the demands of the id. For example, in Freud's theory, which is also termed a 'psychosexual theory', the libido is primarily a sexual drive and its activity is evident from birth. Sexual pleasure is derived from stimulation of erotogenic zones: initially, the mouth, later the anus and, before going into the latency period that precedes mature sexual activity associated with reproduction, the genitals. Stimulation of erotogenic zones is discouraged (as with thumb-sucking which is often regarded as anti-social) or, in the case of anal-expulsive behaviour, closely regulated through toilet training.

Richard

Richard, a normally developing two-year-old, had apparently accepted the absence of his mother who left him, for the first time, in the care of his father while she was away on a week-long study. Richard had, for some time, been able to control his bowel functions but was wearing a nappy at night because bladder control was not fully established. On three occasions during the week-long absence of his mother, Richard defecated after he had been put to bed, removed the excrement and smeared it over the blankets and the bedroom wall.

Although the principles of psychoanalysis do not allow lay people to interpret the deeper meaning of behaviour, it is reasonable to conclude that Richard's behaviour was a response to his mother's absence that he perceived as threatening his view of the world. So perhaps he regressed to an earlier level, in which id impulses are not under the control of social conditioning, as a way of communicating that he did not feel ready to exercise such control in the absence of his mother.

When the child is aged between two and five years, the second component of the mind – that is, the seat of mental activities – begins to develop. This is the *ego*, which 'obeys the reality principle', meaning that the ego has to take account of the reality of living in society. Thus, one of its functions is to provide socially acceptable outlets, otherwise known as 'defence mechanisms', for id impulses in psychologically healthy individuals. Such mechanisms allow for the expression of id impulses and the release of libido in ways that will not attract social disapproval. For example, most people will admit to a pleasurable sensation when moulding wet clay. This, says Freud, fulfils the anal drive to handle faeces. Although defence mechanisms are unconscious, other ego mechanisms are conscious. All ego mechanisms seek to maintain a balance between the id and the *super-ego*, the latter being an internalised version of the child's parents or, more significantly, the same-sex parent. In the absence of parents, this process would emerge out of an analogous relationship with the dominant adult in the child's life, probably a permanent caregiver.

Internalisation is achieved through a resolution of the Oedipus conflict. During the phallic stage of psychosexual development, when the genital organs are the erotogenic zone, the boy is said to experience intense desire for his mother. Just as Oedipus in Greek legend killed his father and, without knowing her true identity, married Jocasta, his mother, the boy wants to replace his father in his mother's affections. However, he accepts the futility of his case and, fearing his father's revenge, identifies with him so that he can enjoy the same relationship with his mother (but vicariously). The counterpart theory for the female stresses an ongoing hostility or jealousy towards her mother, suggesting that the Oedipal conflict is never fully resolved in females, with the implication that they do not develop as strong a super-ego (often represented as the conscience) as males!

During the process of internalisation the boy comes to identify with his father – in other words, to act, feel and respond as if he were his father (conversely, a girl identifies with her mother). As part of that process, the boy monitors and restricts his own behaviour just as his father restrained him when he was younger. Therefore, the imperative, 'Don't do that!' becomes 'I mustn't do that' without the need for parental restraint; and so the conscience emerges.

Through the same process the child adopts the gender-appropriate behaviours that she or he has observed in mother or father. The super-ego develops before the ego has the opportunity to regulate its operation and, consequently, the super-ego, unchecked, is punitive and harsh, forcing the individual to feel guilty, almost without reason. For example, if parents place a heavy emphasis on the merits of hard work and self-denial, or they deplore any form of self-indulgence, their children will feel guilty about enjoying themselves through non-productive leisure activities or relaxation. Such children would not feel comfortable about idly hammering nails into wood or putting pieces of Lego together without purpose: they would be happier working to a plan, with a clear and useful outcome.

In Freud's view the behaviour that characterises the personality can be understood by reference to a dynamic balance between the ego, the id and the super-ego. If the super-ego dominates, guilt-ridden, anxious behaviour, and possibly mental illness, emerge. Where the id governs, the individual appears to be devoid of conscience and, in extreme cases, a psychopathic personality is the outcome. However, when the ego maintains the balance the individual is said to be mentally sound.

Conclusion

It is evident, even from a brief overview of Freud's theories, that the principal aim of developing individuals is to be *self-directing*: that is, independent of parental control and free from parental censure, either actual or through the operation of the super-ego. To achieve this freedom, children internalise the identities of their parents, to form their own personalities, as described above. Then, as mature, well-adjusted individuals, they make moral judgements, control destructive and other primitive urges, and choose their paths through life, apparently on the basis of rational decisions.Clearly, the child–parent relationship is crucial in the emergence of personal autonomy, but the mechanisms through which this is achieved are complex. It is, though, appropriate to draw out a few of the implications of Freud's theory (albeit in simplified form) in order to provide a basis for our explorations. For example, we should pay particular attention to the Freudian view that the handling of challenging behaviour, initially by the parent, later by members of the school community acting *in loco parentis*, is instrumental in determining the adult personality, which carries with it an expectation of self-advocacy and self-direction. Therefore, it is important to remember that some challenging behaviour may be the acting out of id impulses for which a socially acceptable outlet could be substituted, and it becomes the responsibility of parents and caregivers to identify how this can be achieved. The view that challenging behaviour can be understood as a response that has meaning for the person who engages in it is considered in more detail later on. At the same time, the management of challenging behaviour is viewed through several lenses, including one that owes its origins to Freud's psychoanalytic theories.Other aspects of the Freudian framework suggest the importance of parents' high expectations. Through the process of identification, parental attitudes towards the developing child and his or her abilities, skills and attributes, are adopted by the child to form the self-concept. In this way, low expectations of children's abilities, by their parents, will lead to a reduced capacity for self-advocacy as well as poor self-esteem. The operation of the self-fulfilling prophecy was first described by Rosenthal and Jacobson in 1968 to show how pupils respond to teachers' assessments of their learning potential but, in Freudian terms, the effects are more powerful when it is the parental prophecy that is internalised.

Gary

Gary is a Year 2 pupil in his local mainstream school. Although he appeared to be developing normally until the age of about two, it became apparent that his sight and hearing were starting to fail. It was subsequently discovered that he had an inherited, but rare, degenerative condition. After their initial shock and dismay, Gary's parents made a conscious decision that they would not treat him as multisensorily impaired and stated: 'We didn't treat him differently before we had the diagnosis, and he coped; why should we treat him differently now that we have the explanation for the various difficulties that we have *noticed* and that he has *handled*?'

Gary's current level of educational attainment is within age-predicted norms; the local education authority service for pupils with sensory impairments supports him and his school is generous in its response to his needs. He participates fully in a range of out-of-school activities with the blessing and support of his parents.

By internalising his parents' positive view of his abilities and potential, Gary presents to the world as an unusually empowered and lively seven-year-old who happens to have a medical condition that, in other circumstances, could debilitate and handicap him.

Freud's impact on modern thinking about personality, together with the individual's and society's development, has been incalculable. We return to evaluating his contribution to pedagogy in Part 2.

Erik H. Erikson

Erikson was born in Frankfurt, Germany in 1902. His parents, who were Danish, separated before he was born. His mother's family were Jewish and she later married a paediatrician, Dr Homburger, whose name Erikson took, and in 1939 he became known as Erik Homburger Erikson.

After his schooling, Erikson spent a year travelling through Europe. He decided to study art and was invited to teach in a small private school in Vienna for children whose parents were undergoing psychoanalysis, where he became interested in clinical psychoanalysis. At the same time he was curious about the effects on the children of the progressive educational methods practised at the school. As a result he trained as a teacher in the Montessori approach and was, according to his biographer and friend Robert Coles, one of only two men to graduate from the Montessori teachers' association, the Lehrerinnenverein (Coles, 1970).

The approach to education developed by Maria Montessori encouraged young children to learn through their senses by exploring the objects in their world, and then by making decisions about their explorations; she designed educational materials that encouraged cognitive understanding through exploration and manipulation. Possibly because of his interest in art, Erikson became fascinated in what children did with these materials and how, for example, they used or arranged them in a given space. His open-minded curiosity in teaching methods and in art had a profound influence on the way he approached psychoanalyis, a subject that he went on to study at the Vienna Institute.

After graduating in 1933, he lived in Denmark for a short time and then in the United States of America, and it was from an appointment at Yale University that he accepted an invitation to observe Indian children in South Dakota. In 1939 he went to California to take part in a large-scale study of child development and, later, wrote his first book *Childhood and Society*. It brought together his work with American Indians, his clinical research, his studies of anxiety in children, and his teaching and artistic background. He remarked in the foreword to the second edition:

> I came to psychology from art, which may explain, if not justify, the fact that at times the reader will find me painting contexts and backgrounds where he would have me point to facts and concepts. I have had to make a virtue out of a constitutional necessity by basing what I have to say on representative description rather than theoretical argument.
>
> (Erikson, 1965, p.15)

The book was regarded as revolutionary. His interpretation of human life through the search of 'identity' is one in which the child consciously develops an understanding of the world of adults through conflict, and gradually joins that world.

An outline of Erikson's psychosocial theory

Although Erikson's work is firmly embedded in the psychoanalytical tradition, he has focused his attention on the *conscious self* rather than on the unconscious drives and instincts which were Freud's interests. Erikson's concern for child development and his experience in South Dakota led him to consider the cultural and social influences on the child and not to delve deeply into instinctual drives. He regarded emotional functioning as the outcome of the resolution of key developmental tasks related to carefully selected psychosocial stages. Although these stages are well defined, the tasks which children and adults need to accomplish in order to pass through them are not, and Erikson has often been criticised for this omission (Miller, 1993; Keenan, 2002). Throughout his work, Erikson mostly refers to the child as 'he', and as we have emphasised at the beginning of the book, when we make use of original source material we have adopted the theorists' approaches.

Although they came from very different *positions* we can identify similarities between the focus of Erikson's work and that of Bruner. Both were concerned with the effects of the *culture* upon the child, but Erikson's work went beyond a consideration of the child (or adult) making sense of the environment, and was more concerned with the development of each person's sense of *identity* within it. This search for a sense of identity is a lifelong process and stretches beyond childhood as the child (and later the adult) passes through Erikson's defined stages of development.

Bee (1989) breaks down his theoretical concepts into a series of basic propositions which, together with Erikson's original source material, are used to frame our discussions in Part 2 of this book. Bee's statements can be summarised as:

1   During a lifetime each person goes through a series of developmental stages, with specific developmental pointers at each stage. Central to all stages is the development of a particular 'ego quality' such as trust, autonomy, or intimacy.
2   The developmental stages are defined partly by maturation and partly by the society in which the person grows. Erikson differs from Freud in this respect who stressed maturation as the important element in development.
3   The person's success in completing the task at each stage relies on the interactions between the child and his or her caregivers/educators (parent, teachers), and their responses shape the development.
4   Any developmental task that is not successfully completed leaves a residue that interferes with later tasks. Put simply, a child who has not formed a trusting relationship will have greater difficulty in completing subsequent tasks.

(adapted from Bee, 1989, pp.340–1)

As we can see from Bee's last two points, the role of school staff is vital as the child moves through each stage, and embarks on developmental tasks which help to establish an 'identity'. An understanding of the stages can enable professionals to assist their pupils through the transitions between each, and to build in the necessary experiences for healthy growth through approaches to teaching and an examination of the curriculum offered.

We can understand Erikson's work, and Bee's interpretations, through a consideration of each of the stages, and the first four examples of each stage below illustrate how the social and/or cultural environment can have an impact on supporting primary and secondary pupils with special educational needs towards a position of autonomy. The last example (Identity versus role confusion) is rather different, as it clearly illustrates the conflict John is experiencing as he attempts to balance the ego quality of 'industry' with its opposite challenge of 'inferiority'.

The first example of an older pupil (older than the babies that Erikson identifies with his first stage of development) illustrates the careful way in which the teacher manipulates the situation in order to encourage the pupil with difficulties in learning to build up experiences that help to develop trust with both her and his normally developing peers.

The psychosocial stages

STAGE ONE: TRUST VERSUS MISTRUST

This initial stage centres on the oral-sensory first year of life. Erikson (1965) explains that a lasting ego-identity cannot develop without the trust acquired in this stage. The baby develops trust through physical comfort and social contact with a loving caregiver who provides continuity and consistency in pleasurable experiences. The behaviour of the major caregiver is crucial in the development of trust and love, and predictability and reliability are major elements in its formation. The development of basic trust helps the baby to become more active and to accept new experiences, but if his needs are poorly met (subjecting him to frustration and pain), a sense of basic mistrust becomes dominant and has a detrimental effect. At this stage, Erikson also places an emphasis on the development of a *healthy* sense of mistrust and stresses that an ability to discriminate is important. The baby, for example, is quite likely to mistrust strangers with whom he has had little contact because not only does the stranger act differently to his mother, but a pattern of pleasurable experiences has not been established. In the process of maturation, Erikson (1965) stresses, the general state of trust not only relies on trusting others through encounters of sameness and continuity, but babies begin to trust *themselves* through the gradual recognition of their own capacity to cope with their experiences, including those of their own bodies. Pupils with special educational needs will, of course, move through Erikson's stages at a much slower rate, and will often encounter more difficulties in establishing trusting relationships, as attitudes towards them may be hostile, unfriendly or suspicious (Tilstone, 2001).

Joel

The pupils in a mainstream school are engaged in a religious education lesson which involves a consideration of 'Muhammad's difficult decision'. They work in pairs and are being encouraged to tell the class about a difficult decision they once had to make. One of them is working with Joel, a pupil with severe difficulties in learning, and asks him a series of simple questions, some of which Joel finds difficult. They record the given answers together. The teacher then assists by asking Joel a question about a topic (sport) which she knows he is interested in and has little difficulty in answering. 'Joel, would you like to go to a football match or a rugby match?' Joel then chooses a piece of coloured paper to record his 'difficult' decision and he and his partner work on the language he will use to tell the class about his choice.

In this case, the 'rules' for decision-making (group work) are explicit and Joel is building up trust with other pupils as well as with staff.

STAGE TWO: AUTONOMY VERSUS SHAME AND DOUBT

Between the approximate ages of 15 and 30 months in the normal developing child (Freud's anal stage), the infant is naturally exploring his or her environment. Greater mobility enables greater independence, and the encouragement he or she receives to exercise autonomy from trusted caregivers is a crucial factor in the development of the child's feeling of self-control and sense of self-worth. Erikson writes about the child physically and metaphorically 'standing on his own feet' and that some control on the part of the caregiver is necessary to stop the child from 'falling over'. Nevertheless, excessive control will produce doubts in the child, about his or her ability, and then shame and doubt dominate and may force the child into a position of secretiveness and sneakiness. Gross (1987) explains that Erikson uses the words 'shame' and 'doubt' in a precise manner. 'Shaming' means the exposure of a deed or part of one's self which you do not want others to know about. Gross gives the example of getting caught with your hand in the 'cookie jar' or being found with wet pants (Gross 1987, p.28). 'Doubt', on the other hand, is concerned with *not* being able to accept what you cannot see, or being wary about hidden or unknown dimensions. The tussles between these dimensions last throughout life and, in order to be a rounded person, the child and emerging adult need more opportunities to be autonomous and proud of their achievements.

Hall and Lindzey (1978) comment that, as this is the stage that promotes freedom of self-expression and lovingness, the child should be encouraged to experience situations that require the use of free choice. Such a position is vital to teachers of children with special educational needs, particularly those who teach children with complex learning difficulties, as there may be a tendency for them unwittingly to make choices on behalf of their pupils. The following example illustrates how members of the staff of a school are helping Wendy to set out on a path of autonomy.

Wendy

Six-year-old Wendy, a pupil in a special school, has very complex needs, including visual impairment and a physical disability. She is beginning to make choices between two objects and is supported in this learning by all the staff that come into contact with her. It is their responsibility to ensure that she is placed in the best possible physical position in order to use her limited vision effectively (usually in a standing frame with a bright light coming from her right-hand side). As her choice-making involves reaching out with her right hand towards her chosen object, it is important that she has the necessary freedom of movement. As she is at an early stage of choice-making, it is also important that the two different, but highly coloured, objects (an orange beaker containing orange juice and a blue beaker containing milk), are presented in similar ways and that the language used to encourage her to make a choice is similar ('Wendy, what would you like to drink, orange or milk?') Her reward for the choice must be immediate: that is, the chosen drink.

Not only is Wendy learning to become autonomous but she is also becoming confident in her decision-making, and the staff are offering her consistent experiences in a 'safe' environment.

STAGE THREE: INITIATIVE VERSUS GUILT

This third stage corresponds to Freud's phallic stage of development and at this point the child uses his greater mobility, cognitive skills and energy to initiate actions that ultimately become part of his own behaviour. Erikson (1965) remarks that at this stage initiative adds to autonomy, and the endless role-play and rehearsal that children go through provide a vehicle for both practice and ways of adjusting to this newfound autonomy. On occasions this *trusting* autonomy is frustrated by feelings of guilt, and Gross (1989) draws a useful distinction between the meaning Erikson attributes to shame (stage 2) and emerging guilt. Shame is about being *caught*; guilt arises from the *fear* of being caught. The anticipation of being caught breaking rules which are laid down by parents, teachers or society, for example, results in feelings of guilt.

In the second part of this stage the child, through his or her purposeful play, enters into imaginative play, acting out and assuming the roles of parents and other adults in a make-believe world. Maier (1978) suggests that children become their own parents as they try to organise themselves and avoid parental disapproval. At this stage the child becomes forceful and aggressive which may be difficult for the caregiver to deal with. Consequently, the caregiver may react by employing over-strict discipline and punishment. Such actions on the part of others can also arouse feelings of guilt in the child and, as in the example given below, children shape their own behaviour by drawing up the rules (acceptable to their society) and by formulating the criteria by which responses to those rules can be judged.

School rules on bullying

These were devised by pupils aged 11 (including those with a wide range of special educational needs). Mainstream pupils in a secondary school have come to decisions about bullying, through a series of 'circle time' activities, which now constitute school rules.

One of the many decisions they have agreed upon is that if a pupil complains of unfair treatment/bullying from other pupils, he or she should be involved in the investigations and should listen to what others have to say in order to gain a wider perspective. In this way, if the pupil understands the situation, he or she is in a better position to appreciate how the so-called bullying started in the first place. Similarly, if found guilty of bullying by his or her peers, gaining this wider perspective will enable the pupil to recognise that responsibility for his or her actions is an essential part of fair play. He or she should then be helped, by the others, to face the consequences.

STAGE FOUR: INDUSTRY VERSUS INFERIORITY

During this fourth stage (which in Freud's schemes is the 'latency period') the child is beginning to settle down to a more formal education. He or she develops a sense of work or industry and learns that he or she is rewarded if he or she works well. At this time he or she becomes a member of a large peer group, and wants to be liked and accepted. Bee (1989) points out that 'the task at this time is to develop the repertoire of abilities that society demands of the child' (p.343). The hazard at this stage is a feeling of inferiority brought about by:

*   unacceptance by peers;
*   an inability to master tasks set by teachers or parents.

Teachers and parents of children with special educational needs may unwittingly force children into a situation of rejection by their normal peers, insisting on inclusion without adequate preparation, or imposing tasks which are too difficult for children to complete. The following is an example of the challenges facing the teacher as she attempts to structure relevant learning experiences and to encourage the acceptance of peers.

Raj

Raj is a seven-year-old pupil who has recently transferred to a mainstream school. He has moderate learning difficulties and is having difficulties in accessing all the core, and many of the foundation, subjects of the National Curriculum. He only 'works' when he has support from a learning support assistant (which he is entitled to for two hours per day). The teacher became extremely worried about his lack of progress for many reasons which included:

*   her inability to differentiate the curriculum to meet his needs;
*   his growing isolation from his peers;
*   his lack of self-confidence and self-esteem.

She wishes to build on his strengths and interests and after much thought she uses his abilities and interests in computers to overcome some of the challenges. She introduces a particular computer program (Wordshark) which he is enthusiastic about. His peers become interested in the program and this gives him an opportunity to demonstrate aspects of his work to them. Through these interactions, he is in control of the situation and his self-confidence and self-esteem are improving, and the teacher is able to use computer-assisted learning as a way into other subjects.

STAGE FIVE: IDENTITY VERSUS ROLE DIFFUSION

Erikson (1965) emphasises that at this stage, which corresponds with the onset of puberty, young people undergo a crisis of identity, best summed up in his own words quoted by Gross (1989, p.19):

> I have called the major crisis of adolescence the Identity Crisis: it occurs in that period of the life cycle when each youth must forge for himself some central perspective and direction, some working unity out of the remnants of his childhood and the hopes of his anticipated adulthood; he must detect some meaningful resemblance between what he has come to see in himself and what his sharpened awareness tells him others judge and expect him to do.

Because of this crisis, adolescents are likely to suffer more deeply than before from a confusion of roles as two identities come strongly into conflict: a sexual identity and an occupation identity. As he or she struggles with these identities, the adolescent's behaviour becomes inconsistent and unpredictable and the young person is apt to display self-consciousness and embarrassment. Although sexually mature, the adolescent is not yet adequately prepared emotionally to become a partner.

It is during this difficult time that the young person attempts to formulate a set of values which Erikson calls 'fidelity'. He defines fidelity as 'the ability to sustain loyalties freely pledged in spite of the inevitable contradictions of value systems' (Erikson, 1976, p.25). He sees this stage as one of searching for something worth being faithful to: for example, a message or a way of life. Here there is a tendency for the adolescent to find out what they are *against* (which is a stage in knowing what they are *for*). Time and space are essential prerequisites at this stage for the emergence of an awareness of who he or she is (Stevens, 1983).

John

John is a Year 8 pupil who has been diagnosed as having dyspraxia. He has been one of the school's librarians since he started secondary school, and has always been keen to do things to the best of his ability, albeit in a certain way. He is regarded by staff as a gentle, biddable student who, although he struggles to achieve academic success, is generally well motivated and eager to learn.

Recently he has had a growth spurt and is now about six feet tall. Strangely, he has been very weepy without any traceable reason and staff have become concerned about his swings of mood. Tears do not 'sit well' with Year 8 students, particularly when there seems to be no real cause, and John has experienced some teasing. His confidence has become low, and consequently, in an effort to rebuild it, support staff have found an excuse for John to be 'needed' and to carry out particular tasks; they in turn usually offer hot chocolate and 'tender loving care' as a reward.

John has, rather unexpectedly, started to 'rebel' by refusing to do simple tasks in the library when requested. He declared, 'I just do not want to do that', and stormed off, to the surprise of the member of staff. When assisting at the school's Book Fair, John decided to take off all the elastic bands holding the books together and to give one to each boy he met in the corridor. When asked why he had abandoned his post and why he had taken such an action he ran off.

At present, John has switched from being a happy well-adjusted student for most of the time, to becoming an angry young man for all of the time. Members of staff are now planning other strategies to support him through his crisis.

The last three stages of Erikson's psychosocial stages are concerned with adulthood and are therefore outside the remit of this book. They are:

STAGE SIX: INTIMACY VERSUS ISOLATION

The main activities at this stage are the formation of intimate relationships which may, or may not, involve marriage and the formation of family groups.

STAGE SEVEN: GENERATIVITY VERSUS STAGNATION

Here the emphasis is on bearing and rearing children and on occupational achievement, with an overarching concern for training the next generation.

STAGE EIGHT: INTEGRITY VERSUS DESPAIR

It is finally at this stage that the integration of previous stages is fully realised and that each individual comes to terms with his or her basic identity. This is the true acceptance of *self*.

Conclusion

Erikson's theory is not a coherent theory of development and for this reason, as we have already pointed out, he has been criticised, particularly as his stages do not lend themselves to empirical testing (Miller, 1993; Keenan, 2002). His theory is better thought of as a loosely connected set of ideas which describes 'roles' (trust and autonomy, for example) and aspects of those roles (mistrust, shame and doubt). Taking on each 'role' and striking a balance between its centrality and its conflicting aspects is difficult for all pupils, particularly those with special educational needs who are inevitably the 'victims' of their society and of their environment. Despite its limitations it is the importance that Erikson places on the integration of social and cultural factors (Keenan, 2002; Waterman, 1985) which is the strength of his work for school staff, and provides useful pointers for their role in the development of self-advocacy and empowerment.

References

Bee, H. (1989) *The Developing Child* (5th edition). New York: Harper Collins.
Coles, R. (1970) *Erik H. Erikson: The Growth of His Work*. New York: Da Capo Press.

Erikson, E.H. (1965) *Childhood and Society* (2nd edition). Harmondsworth: Penguin Books.

Erikson, E.H. (1976) 'Reflections on Dr Borg's life cycle', *Daedalus*. 105, 25.

Freud, S. (1940) *The Standard Edition of the Complete Psychological Works of Sigmund Freud, Vol 23: An Outline of Psycho-analysis* (J. Strachey, ed., 1964). London: Hogarth Press and Institute of Psycho-analysis, pp.144–71.

Freud, S. (1960) *A General Introduction to Psychoanalysis*. New York: Norton.

Gross, F.L., Jr. (1987) *Introducing Erik Erikson: An Invitation to his Thinking*. Lanham, MD: University Press of America.

Hall, C.S. and Lindzey, G. (1978) *Theories of Personality*. London: Wiley.

Keenan, T. (2002) *An Introduction to Child Development*. London: Sage Publications.

Maier, H. (1978) *Three Theories of Child Development* (3rd edition). New York: Harper and Row.

Miller, P.H. (1993) *Theories of Developmental Psychology* (3rd edition). New York: W.H. Freeman.

Rosenthal, R. and Jacobson, L. (1968) *Pygmalion in the Classroom*. London: Holt, Rinehart and Wilson.

Stevens, R. (1983) *Erik Erikson*. Milton Keynes: Open University Press.

Tilstone, C. (2001) 'Changing public attitudes', in B. Carpenter, R. Ashdown and K. Bovair (eds) *Enabling Access*. London: David Fulton Publishers.

Waterman, A.S. (1985) 'Identity in the context of adolescent psychology', in A.S. Waterman (ed.) *Identity in Adolescence: Processes and Contents*. San Francisco: Jossey-Bass.

Chapter 4

Skinner and the learning theorists

The whole of this section is concerned with outlining key influences on how we understand human development. In this final chapter of Part 1 we consider the theories of one psychologist within the school of thought that had its origins in nineteenth-century scientific thinking.

In the West in the nineteenth century, scientific methods were a major factor in rapid industrial and commercial progress. Developments in science and its potential to explain all phenomena gave rise to 'positivism' in which only observable, physical aspects of reality could be regarded as capable of yielding valid measurable data. Positivism can clearly be applied to the physical sciences but, given our tendency to impute intentions, wishes and other subjective motivations to our own and to other people's behaviour, it may appear an unlikely source of explanation for human activity. During the late nineteenth and early twentieth century, however, concepts and labels adopted by scientists to describe learning in lower animals replaced those of the introspectionists (the early psychologists whose data stemmed from reflections on their own thinking). The 'new' scientists were concerned with a more objective study of human behaviour and concentrated their efforts on what was observable; in other words 'how' people behaved. In this way human psychology began to align itself with the physical sciences.

Thorndike, Pavlov and Watson

Some of the earliest demonstrations of learning were conducted by physiologists using animals. E.L. Thorndike (1911) demonstrated trial-and-error learning, while, in Russia, Pavlov formulated the principles of *classical conditioning*. In laboratory experiments, Pavlov noted how hungry dogs salivate when they take food. This is a reflex response in mammals that initiates the process of digestion. After presenting food on several occasions, accompanied by the sound of a tuning fork or bell, Pavlov discovered that the sound alone could produce salivation in the dogs. The extent of the association was measured by the amount of saliva produced after conditioning in comparison with unconditioned or natural productions of saliva in response to food alone. This led to the general principle that a new, neutral stimulus can produce a reflex behaviour once it has been paired with the stimulus that naturally produces the response.

In the 1920s J.B. Watson considered the findings from animal experiments in relation to human subjects (Watson and Rayner, 1920). He was able to demonstrate *classical* or *Pavlovian* conditioning in a series of experiments with a nine-month-old boy, Albert. Prior to the experiments, Albert had played happily with a white rat but demonstrated fear in response to a loud noise. Watson created this noise each time Albert touched the rat so that eventually he showed the same fearful response to the animal in the absence of the noise. Mercifully, Watson and his co-workers were later able to condition a positive response in Albert, by pairing the presentation of the rat with sweets and toys.

The following is an example of naturally occurring classical conditioning.

Timothy

Timothy, aged three, was admitted to hospital with a severe fracture of the skull. This was the first time in his short life that he had been away from his mother and he was clearly alarmed by the attentions of doctors and nurses as they investigated his injury. The admissions ward was close to a heli-pad where helicopters landed frequently to bring patients to this busy city hospital. On his discharge from hospital Timothy showed terror bordering on hysteria if he saw or heard a helicopter, either in the sky or on television. A natural response, fear, had become tied to a new stimulus, helicopters, by association.

Central to Watson's work was the belief that the environment was crucial in shaping the development of the child. In fact, as Keenan (2002, p.24) emphasises, Watson believed that children could be moulded in any direction determined by an adult, provided that the stimulus-response associations were carefully controlled. To many of us it seems intuitively unacceptable, and highly unethical, that the strategies used by Watson to induce and then inhibit fear in Albert could be applied to shape an individual's entire life experience. However, classical conditioning has therapeutic applications: for example, careful control of stimulus-response associations is often used in helping people to overcome phobias or irrational fears.

The learning situations that were grounded in the prototypes from animal experimentation were relatively uncomplicated, but they could not explain new and complex behaviour patterns of human beings. Nonetheless, these demonstrations provided the basis of a conceptual framework that hinged on the collection of measurable data, and the early psychologists and physiologists showed that new responses can be elicited by old stimuli (trial-and-error learning) and that existing responses can be tied to new stimuli (classical conditioning). The links were referred to as stimulus-response bonds, and *behaviourists*, as these scientists were called, were able to demonstrate that bonds were consolidated by the reduction of some inner physiological drive: for example, hunger. Their demonstrations led to the consideration that rewards or reinforcements could arise from the satisfaction of inner needs and could provide a motivation for learning.

Burrhus Frederick Skinner

Skinner, who started his work at Harvard University in the USA in the 1930s, differed in one important respect from other behaviourists. He believed that it should not be necessary for animals or humans to experience some need before they are impelled to learn. Skinner is credited, instead, with establishing learning through the reinforcement of progressively closer approximations to a desired learning outcome, a process termed *operant conditioning*. In early demonstrations of operant conditioning, a target behaviour was identified and broken into smaller elements (operants). For example, when an animal first spontaneously or accidentally produced this behavioural element it was rewarded. Once the rewarded behaviour was consolidated, the animal had to produce behaviour that more closely matched the target behaviour in subsequent trials in order to gain the reward. The process of reinforcing different responses towards a desired outcome is termed shaping, and its advantage, particularly in comparison with trial-and-error learning, is the speed with which the animal arrives at the target behaviour.

Skinner devised apparatus with which to conduct simple operant conditioning. For example, rats were trained in the Skinner box.

The Skinner box

The Skinner box comprised a cage fitted with a lever and a food trough. On the first trial the rat was rewarded for approaching the lever by food being delivered into the trough. The next reward followed only when the rat sniffed or touched the lever. Once this was established, the food was only delivered when the rat depressed the lever. Using shaping, a rat could be taught to press a lever in less than 30 minutes.

Skinner's experiments in operant conditioning yielded further insights into the conditions of learning and how these affect learning outcomes. He was able to show, for example, that shaping is more efficiently achieved if a reward does not follow every correct response and this led to formulae or schedules of reinforcement, setting out the timing and presentations of rewards associated with the most effective learning. Skinner's work can be seen in the principles adopted by makers of one-armed bandits or fruit machines where players are encouraged to 'work' (respond) by putting more money into the machine in the hope of getting a reward.

Skinner further demonstrated the differences between positive reinforcements, negative reinforcements and punishment. The examples that follow show these differences.

Positive reinforcement

Positive reinforcement occurs when rewards follow correct responses.

Jasmin

Jasmin, whose learning difficulties are profound, has acquired the necessary hand–eye co-ordination to operate the switch on her wheelchair, and is being encouraged to travel independently from classroom to classroom, as part of a programme to develop more autonomy. She is not particularly keen to learn this new skill, preferring instead to be wheeled around the school by members of staff. She is, however, passionately fond of yoghurt and it has been decided that this provides an ideal reinforcer (reward) for any efforts she makes. Small pots of yoghurt are placed at strategic points within her reach around the classroom and Jasmin is encouraged to travel to them – a skill she quickly acquires. The reinforcer is then used to encourage her to move around the school and, consequently, she is quickly learning the basic skills of independent travel. She is becoming so proficient that members of staff are now considering strategies to keep her in her classroom!

Negative reinforcement

Negative reinforcement is said to have occurred when behaviour changes because of its association with the cessation of something unpleasant, as in the following example.

David

David has severe language and behavioural problems. He is now 15 and although these difficulties have been evident throughout primary school, it was not until he was 11 that the extent of the difficulties was recognised. At that time a speech and language assessment revealed that his receptive language was equivalent to that of a four-year-old. Nonetheless he was placed in a mainstream school but through a statement of special educational needs, extra support is now provided. David has a learning support assistant (LSA) to help him with half his lessons. She is able to interpret what the teacher is saying, in words that he understands, and explains concepts carefully to ensure that instructions or ideas are presented one at a time. During these lessons, David copes reasonably well, although he is prone to outbursts of temper when he finds the work hard.

In the lessons where such support is *not* available his teachers are unable to give him the time he needs, or to simplify their language. Consequently, David struggles to understand what is expected of him, which has a detrimental effect on his self-esteem. In some lessons, when the rest of the pupils are working, he will flick paper at his neighbours, call their names under his breath or sing loudly. On other occasions, he will lose his temper and throw books or equipment on to the floor.

His teachers respond by telling him off which allows him to stop work, albeit for a few moments. Frequently, however, he is sent out of the room to 'cool down'. In either case, the *escape*, however temporary, from the situation that he finds challenging brings a sense of relief that, in turn, reinforces the behaviour that preceded the *escape*. He has now learned that if he disrupts the lesson, he will escape from the work that he finds hard, and he now starts to behave badly as soon as he enters the classroom.

Through negative reinforcement, David has been conditioned to adopt bad behaviour, thus avoiding the pressure of work before it begins.

Punishment

Classically, punishment is a technique that involves the presentation of an adverse physical stimulus. Naturally this has no place in the education of children and is ethically unacceptable. For some attention-seeking behaviours, however, where it is known that the pupil finds the reward of the *attention of adults* reinforcing when he or she behaves inappropriately, it is possible to use a technique to remove the attention. This *ignoring* technique is not punishment in the traditional Skinnerian sense but is the non-presentation of the reward termed 'time out from reward'. Such an approach should not be confused with 'time out rooms', where, in the 1960s, children with learning difficulties who behaved inappropriately were removed to an isolation room. This punitive approach proved to be of little success (Foxen and McBrien, 1981), and is now considered unethical.

In certain circumstances, however, 'time out from reward' can eliminate attention-seeking behaviour. There can be 'challenges' when adopting this technique which are clearly shown in the example of Adam below. You will find that there are similarities between Adam's and David's behaviour. Their reasons for their behaviour are, however, different.

Adam

Adam also has speech and language difficulties. He is seven and his statement shows that his difficulties in learning in most subjects are similar to those of his peers in the class of the special school he attends. Like David, he constantly makes excessive demands upon his teacher, usually by calling out in class and butting into her conversations with other children. Unlike David, he does not have the support of an LSA in lessons and he is in a class with a smaller number of pupils.

His teacher decides to record this behaviour over a period of weeks and her records show that his behaviour is not a figment of her imagination: he certainly does repeatedly interrupt, but there is no substantial evidence to suggest that he needs specific help with his work when he is acting in this way. She considers that he may be attention seeking and surmises that by providing attention, which she always does when he behaves badly, even if it is to reprimand him, she is effectively giving him consistent rewards. She makes a conscious decision to ignore this inappropriate behaviour but is aware that it will increase as he works harder to attract her attention. In order to positively reinforce good behaviour she decides to give him very regular attention (and praise) at times when he is not disruptive. She expects that the experience will not be pleasant for her or the class at first (and she is right as Adam's adverse behaviour becomes worse) but anticipates that it will become extinct over time.

Some of her challenges are:

- establishing a true record on which to base judgements (is attention-seeking really Adam's reward?);
- dealing with the situation in a calm and objective way;
- not reinforcing him as his attention-seeking behaviour increases;
- providing a highly rewarding environment where he is able to earn rewards (her attention) for *positive* behaviour;
- ensuring that his initial reinforcement (her attention) is linked to praise, which she hopes he will work for in the future.

Social learning theory

While radical learning theorists such as John Watson believed that an individual's total life history could be explained by reference to the way he or she had been 'conditioned', other researchers, notably Albert Bandura, pointed out the limitations of a behaviourist explanation (1986). First, it was noted that we acquire complex behaviours far more quickly than we could if they were being progressively shaped out of spontaneous occurrences. Second, as any parent can testify, babies, from their earliest days, imitate. Bandura therefore added to the key concepts of learning theorists, the propositions that social behaviours (in particular, those that we regard as personality characteristics) are acquired through observation and imitation. It is evident, however, that whereas we all observe a great number of people, we imitate very little of their behaviour and therefore the social learning theorists were required to explain how selective imitation occurs within the framework of learning theory.

Certainly the concept of reinforcement may explain why children imitate some behaviours and not others. For example, extrinsic reinforcement, when a child is rewarded directly, usually with praise, for copying behaviour or a pattern of behaviours, probably accounts for some learning. Other powerful mechanisms that determine which social behaviours a child will adopt include vicarious reinforcement. In the latter case, the child perceives that someone else is rewarded for behaving in a particular way and by imitating that behaviour the child experiences the sense of reward, even without any expectation of actually receiving it. Social learning theory has been invoked to explain why children may adopt aggressive behaviour simply by viewing it on videos and television: for example, where it is possible that the aggressor attracts some special status or attention that the child would like to experience. A more familiar illustration of social learning theory in action is the adoption of gender appropriate behaviours. Learning theorists maintain that children are subtly rewarded for adopting behaviour and mannerisms typical of the gender to which they have been assigned. However, social learning theorists argue for the wholesale adoption of male or female characteristics through identification with an individual of the same gender, usually in the course of a close emotional relationship such as that between parent and child.

It is evident, then, that learning through observation, identification and imitation gives a role to cognitive or intellectual deliberation on the part of the learner. This aspect, of course, was rejected as unimportant by traditional learning theorists. Bandura (1986), however, acknowledged the influence of such inner factors, suggesting that the potency of learning through identification-imitation will vary according to the cognitive maturity and competence of the learner. Moreover, as summarised by Bee (2000), Bandura's reconceptualisation of the processes underpinning imitation and modelling puts him into a theoretical position which resonates, to some extent, with that of Piaget. Bee explains this similarity in the following way: a child has, among his or her schemes, a self-scheme (Bee, 2000, p.273). This is a view of one's own abilities, standards, modes of behaviour – in short, what we more usually term the 'self-concept'. Once children have formed a self-concept, they will choose to interpret other people's behaviour (when deciding which to adopt for their own) so that comparatively little adjustment to their self-concept is required. In this way, the self-concept serves to mediate potential influences on their behaviour and developing personality, a point discussed in greater detail in Chapter 10.

The development of self-concept is complex and begins with an awareness of both the child's own actions and the presence of others. Details are considered in Chapter 10, but it is important to note here that it begins with self-awareness, which manifests itself in statements like: '*I am Luke, I am six, I like to play with Fred, our dog.*'

Later there is an acknowledgement by the child of the differences between himself and others: '*I am a boy; I am bigger than my friend Pete; my skin is darker than Pete's.*'

As they become more aware of others, children begin to describe their own personalities in terms of others' perceptions of them. Damon and Hart (1992) suggest they begin to construct a theory of their own personalities, which becomes more complex as their cognitive and social abilities develop. For children with special educational needs, often such theories illustrate the labels assigned to them: '*I am not clever; I can't do maths; I am a spastic.*'

Conclusion

Skinner and the learning theorists have undoubtedly had a great impact on the teaching and learning of all children. It is through their work that the behavioural methods of teaching described later in the book have emerged and have entered the everyday repertoire of those who care for children. The radical learning theorists placed strong emphasis on environmental changes and considered that learning is the same for *all*, irrespective of the age of the learner. As Bee (1989) reminded us, 'what we call development in this view, is really just a long series of individual learning experiences' (p.14). Other theorists, such as Bandura, who have introduced a cognitive element into the debate, have thus softened the emphasis on observable behaviour. Nevertheless, learning theorists have encouraged us to think about the fundamental ways in which pupils carry out tasks and how they have (or have not) acquired skills. By concentrating on the *observable* these psychologists have encouraged us to be systematic in our approach, to undertake meticulous record keeping and analysis, and to attempt a more structured evaluation of our work.

References

Bandura, A. (1986) *Social Foundations of Thought and Action: A Social Cognitive Theory*. Englewood Cliffs, NJ: Prentice-Hall.

Bee, H. (1989) *The Developing Child* (5th edition). New York: HarperCollins.

Bee, H. (2000) *The Developing Child* (9th edition). Needham Heights, MA: Allyn and Bacon.

Damon, W. and Hart, D. (1992) 'Self understanding and its role in social and moral development', in M.H. Bornstein and M.F. Lamb (eds) *Developmental Psychology: An Advanced Textbook* (3rd edition). Mahwah, NJ: Erlbaum.

Foxen, T. and McBrien, J. (1981) *Training Staff in Behavioural Methods: Trainee Workbook*. Manchester: Manchester University Press.

Keenan, T. (2002) *An Introduction to Child Development*. London: Sage Publications.

Thorndike, E.L. (1911) *Animal Intelligence*. New York: Macmillan.

Watson, J.B. and Rayner, R. (1920) 'Conditioned emotional reactions', *Journal of Experimental Psychology*. 3, 1–14.

Part 2

The educational implications

Chapter 5

The cognitive developmental theorists

In this section we consider the educational implications of the work of the theorists and the relationship of their ideas to the process of empowerment. As we emphasised in the Introduction, we have interpreted the term 'educational implications' broadly, and therefore we will be reviewing the theories in order to extend and explain our interpretation. In particular, we will examine the theories for their contribution to the process of teaching and learning and for their identification of the role of others in an individual's emerging knowledge, understanding and empowerment.

As in the first part of the book, we have examples of a range of pupils with special educational needs to illustrate our ideas. We hope that these will provide a starting point for your reflections on the contributions that the theorists can make to your practice and to the special features of your working environment.

Jean Piaget

The educational implications of his work

As accounts of his early professional life reveal, Jean Piaget did not set out to provide a comprehensive account of all aspects of development and their interrelationships, neither did he have any commitment to exploring the pedagogic implications of his theories. Consequently, scholars have pointed to the 'gaps' in his theory: for example, he did not examine the influence of language on the development of thinking. In fact, although his work was first translated into English during the 1940s, it was 20 years before its impact on educational practice was felt, particularly in the widespread adoption of *discovery learning*, both for normally developing children and for those with learning difficulties, as in the High/Scope programme (Hohmann and Weikhart, 1995; Mitchell, 1994).

High/Scope was developed initially as an approach for disadvantaged children of nursery age, but its principles can be seen reflected in approaches for older children with learning difficulties, specifically those whose cognitive abilities could be regarded as within the sensori-motor stage. In particular, it relies on the principles of PLAN–DO–REVIEW and stresses that children must be self-directed, active learners. Consequently tasks must be set at the appropriate developmental level in order that children may drive their own learning, and the approach provides *all* learners with opportunities to make choices. Children PLAN together, DO (carry out their agreed plan, which may mean working independently or co-operatively) and REVIEW together. In applying this approach to children with special educational needs, Mitchell (1994) stresses the importance of the element of active learning mentioned above in the PLAN–DO–REVIEW sequence. She identifies five active ingredients that should be present for active learning to take place:

- the availability of, and easy access to, a variety of interesting materials;
- the freedom of pupils to work and experiment with the materials and, where appropriate, explore their properties;
- an element of choice for pupils in approaching a task;
- the sharing of experiences (through a range of methods of communication appropriate for each pupil);
- the provision of adult support in three ways; help with:

  - building on skills
  - problem-solving
  - entering into their 'play'.

(adapted from Mitchell, 1994, p.69)

The following example charts Hugo's experiences of the approach during a lesson on design and technology.

Hugo's active learning

Hugo and his peers are being educated in a unit for children with difficulties in learning within a mainstream school and much of their learning takes place in the mainstream classrooms. The lesson is part of a scheme of work that focuses on musical instruments, based on a Qualifications and Curriculum Authority (QCA) scheme of work for Key Stages 1 and 2 (QCA/DfEE, 1998). In previous lessons the children had made sounds, compared different instruments and felt and talked about the different materials used to make some basic instruments. In this lesson, carried out in the unit, the teacher wants them to carry out a practical task as independently as possible.

Planning together

At the beginning of the lesson, the teacher discusses with the pupils what they are going to do in the session, and together they consider how each one is going to set about the task. Some pupils want to experiment with making sounds by making musical instruments; others want to explore ways of making different sounds. Two pupils want to find out how a keyboard produces sounds, but Hugo has rather different ideas. He tells the group that he wants to make a video camera. Instead of dissuading him, the teacher suggests that his work could be used to 'record' the work of the other children. In discussing how Hugo might go about his task in this lesson the teacher and the children suggest he should:

- draw a plan or picture of the camera;
- find a magazine cutting of a camera;
- compare his plan with the picture.

Doing

Hugo finds his own materials to make a plan and, with adult support, makes a basic model. Throughout the activity he talks about what he is doing and is encouraged to question his decisions. He cannot find a picture of a camera in the classroom and so is accompanied by a member of staff to the school library.

Reviewing

The children are brought together at the end of the session to talk about what they have done and what they are going to do in the next lesson. Hugo is at a loss to consider what he was going to do next but, with gentle prompting, it is decided that he should find out what the components of the camera are and then make a model. He is very clear on the materials he is going to use for this (Duplo) and goes to the drawer where it is kept.

Over the following weeks Hugo made his camera and 'filmed' other pupils. He also talked over the process of filming which he must have observed at home. Through the process of PLAN–DO–REVIEW he was encouraged to return to his original plan and the picture, and to compare them with his model. He then modified his work. In the final session he was allowed to use (with help) the school's camera to video the results of his classmates' contribution to this scheme of work. The video recording was later shown in a whole school assembly.

The teacher, far from discouraging Hugo's unusual choice of activity, used Mitchell's five components of the High/Scope approach to extend and develop Hugo's learning within a specific lesson.

At the very heart of Piaget's theories lies the notion of logical thought proceeding towards formal operational thinking, in universal, invariant stages. According to this view there is an optimal point in the child's development when particular types of learning can take place; conversely, it would be unhelpful, possibly counter-productive, to introduce ideas that depend on an understanding of, for example, the concept of object permanence before it was established. This interpretation of Piaget led to a pedagogical approach based on 'readiness', which assumed that the child would, through behavioural responses, indicate when she or he was intellectually prepared to progress to new ways of learning. The readiness approach should not, however, suggest that teaching and learning are entirely 'child centred', in the sense that the child makes arbitrary choices over how, when and what to learn or (indeed) *whether* to learn.

Although Piaget's ideas about development had only limited influence on mainstream educational approaches before the 1960s, Piaget, with his colleague, Barbel Inhelder, extended his theories to learners with special needs, and these views were more widely adopted by practitioners while his research was ongoing (see Hodapp, 1998, for details). In summarising the evidence from research and practice, Hodapp reports that children with learning difficulties show the same *sequences* of development as those without difficulties but development for the former is characterised by more regressions and oscillations. Thus, children might indicate one level of reasoning in relation to a task yet, when completing the task at a later date, perform at a lower level.

This is particularly true when pupils are receiving medication. Naturally, the effect of medication on a pupil's learning is a contentious issue and has been brought to the fore in recent years with the use of Ritalin, or similar amphetamine-based Class A drugs, for pupils with attention deficit and hyperactivity disorder (ADHD). In some cases, the effects of medication can be that pupils show a 'bumpy' profile of performance from one day to the next or from lesson to lesson. In the case of Ben, however, the regressions and fluctuations occurred *before* medication was introduced. It is not our intention to make a case for or against a drug regime to alleviate certain characteristics, but simply to highlight the variations in the day-to-day patterns of learning of a child with special educational needs.

Ben

Ben, a pupil in Year 3, was constantly fidgeting and was unable to sit still. His concentration varied, was often fleeting, and accessing information or completing tasks was challenging. The impact of Ben's behaviour on the class gave the teacher and support assistants concern, as he would constantly attempt to disturb others and it was impossible to tell whether he had acquired the knowledge and understanding to progress or if he needed more support and experiences of the same aspects of learning. His ability to work was often very limited and, although he showed that, on a day when he was 'on task', he could reach his target, on another day he was unable to achieve the same standard or to cover the same amount of work. On a 'bad' day his usual work pattern was to begin a task with support, usually from an adult, but he was unable to sustain concentration for more than two minutes.

The gap between Ben and his peers was widening, and he appeared to be aware of this, which in turn exacerbated the situation. In addition to his ADHD behaviours, Ben's self-esteem was decreasing and he began to view all school experiences negatively. Despite his difficulties Ben could respond positively in one-to-one situations when he was engaged in a topic of his choice and he had a sense of humour and liked to tell jokes.

In addition to his irregular learning profile, Ben often found himself in conflict situations in the playground as a result of inappropriate behaviour. On some days he had a 'very short fuse' and reacted aggressively towards his peers. Although he frequently said that he wanted to play with his friends, he would want his own way on one day, but be willing to co-operate on another. Ben's peers were confused, and became reluctant to include him in playground games.

Ben's poor relationships were mirrored in his home life and his parents described similar incidents when his siblings were equally bewildered. In addition Ben needed very little sleep and his parents were finding it increasingly difficult to cope as he would be awake at frequent intervals during the night. This pattern of challenging behaviour in and out of school suggested that it was not caused by the situation, but had an organic origin, and therefore the family sought a medical opinion.

Ritalin was prescribed and the effect of the medication was dramatic. Ben became quieter and calmer, and he was able to concentrate for the same length of time consistently. Gradually, his concentration span increased and his work patterns became constant.

The example above shows how a child with evidence of cognitive reasoning on one day could, when undertaking the same task, regress on the next. In this case, medication helped to stabilise Ben's 'bumpy' profile, but for other children it can contribute to the cause of regression and oscillations, and professionals need to be aware of the effects of drugs like Ritalin.

In addition, research has shown that some children with severe learning difficulties who are working broadly within the sensori-motor stage will provide evidence of different levels in response to different tasks or materials, whether on medication or not (Hodapp, 1998). This suggests that it would be a mistake to make judgements about overall capacity on the basis of a single task or a set of tasks completed on one occasion; a view that has come to be reflected in relation to the wider population of learners. On the contrary, Piaget's approach to establishing children's developmental levels has special advantages over psychometric techniques when planning intervention for pupils with any learning difficulties. As previously noted, Piaget placed great emphasis on the value of 'wrong' or unconventional responses, believing that they hold the key to a child's intellectual processes; as a result, practitioners and researchers have used Piagetian tasks diagnostically, in order to discover why and how a child arrives at the 'wrong' response.

By this 'diagnostic' method, it is possible to make inferences about the child's knowledge, understanding and reasoning abilities, which yield information with a greater value than a score on an intelligence (IQ) test or a developmental rating, on which to base further teaching.

Piaget's theory and empowerment

At first sight, Piaget's view of the developing child as drawing principally on his or her own resources in order to gain mastery over the environment might seem to imply severe limitations for some children with special educational needs. The frameworks and concepts that emerge from his theories have, however, been adopted by subsequent theorists and practitioners to enable them to devise effective approaches to promoting understanding and skills that are fundamental to all learning. To cite just one example, Piaget recorded 'contingency learning' in his own son; he described how and when notions of causality emerge in typically developing children whose growing competence is evidenced, firstly in their physical, and secondly in their mental, action on their environment. His hypothesis about an area of understanding that is crucial to empowerment is a reminder that physical or intellectual disabilities can limit children's experiences of associations between actions and results, thereby depriving them of valuable learning. Intervention to promote contingency awareness in children with special educational needs has been framed around the recognition that it is the lack of experiential learning that is more significant for them than the fundamental 'handicapping' condition. Compensatory approaches are outlined in later chapters in this book.

Empowerment through learning may not have been a central concern of Piaget as he attempted to account for the development of thinking. Nonetheless, his theories continue to inspire and direct other researchers with a more specific focus on promoting the cognitive abilities of all learners; in particular, his influence is evident in Jerome Bruner's views on school-based learning.

Jerome S. Bruner

The educational implications of his work

Much of Bruner's work is concerned with the development of the curriculum and the social structures that support it and, therefore, it is fitting that we should consider the educational implications of his theory in terms of the curriculum offered in schools in England and in other countries at present. Schools in England have a responsibility to provide a broad and balanced curriculum that, since 1988, includes the National Curriculum. It is recognised that the whole curriculum for all pupils aims to:

- 'provide opportunities for all pupils to learn and achieve;
- promote pupils' spiritual, moral, social and cultural development, and prepare all pupils for the opportunities, responsibilities and experiences of life' (DfEE/QCA 1999a, p.11; 1999b, p.11).

All the theorists discussed in this book could be said to subscribe to these aims, although it is the key skills embedded in all the subjects of the whole curriculum which we feel are of particular relevance to Bruner's theory. They are particularly important in the process of empowerment as they have been identified as those that 'will improve learning and performance in education, work, and life' (QCA/DfEE, 2001, p.6).

The key skills which span the whole curriculum and are identified in the revised National Curriculum Handbooks (for England) of 1999 are:

- language and communication;
- application of numbers;
- information technology;
- working with others;
- improving own learning and performance;
- problem-solving.

All are worthy of scrutiny in relation to Bruner's theory, but in order to provide a flavour of their relevance to his work we have chosen to highlight two in this chapter: communication and problem-solving. These will also be discussed in more detail, along with the other skills listed above, in later chapters.

Key skills: Language and communication

The emphasis in this area is on teaching pupils to express themselves appropriately and to read accurately and with understanding. Elements of the key skill are speaking and listening, and reading and writing, all of which contribute importantly to empowerment. Bruner (1966) suggests that language and communication are '... not only a powerful way of saying something, but an instrument that can now be seen as a tool for organising thoughts about things' (p.105).

The following example, adapted from the QCA booklet, *Developing Skills* (2001), illustrates this point and indicates the role that staff must play in structuring experiences in order to enhance their pupils' ability to organise their thoughts.

Maria

Maria is a Year 8 pupil in a unit in a mainstream school. Her communication needs are similar to many of the pupils in her class, all of whom need some support. One of her targets in her individual education plan (IEP) is to organise her speaking and writing to produce clear descriptions and evaluations.

In science some pupils are focusing on freezing and thawing various foods, and they have to identify and describe changes, and record their findings. Maria is learning to describe the process in the correct order, to identify changes and to work with others to decide which foods are likely to freeze successfully. She needs extra help to order her thoughts in a logical way and staff help her by the use of questions, prompts, examples, symbols and pictures, and by clustering ideas together.

(adapted from QCA/DfEE, 2001b, p.5)

Key skills: Problem-solving

Problem-solving involves a process which we loosely call 'thinking'. Early problem-solving involves an understanding of cause and effect and is promoted by the play and social routines that Bruner regards as so important in early childhood. The booklet issued by QCA (2001), *Developing Skills*, lists the attributes of problem-solving as:

PERCEPTION: in which the pupil recognises and identifies problems (a favourite toy out of reach, a missing bus pass before a journey, or being in an uncomfortable position);

THINKING: which involves: breaking a problem down into elements (for example, preparing, cooking, serving a meal and clearing away afterwards); thinking through the relevant features of a problem (what to do when there is no water in the kettle for a cup of tea); planning ways of solving the problem;

ACTION: remembering how to solve a problem (for example, using strategies such as rehearsal, or using symbols, signs or objects of reference as clues);

EVALUATION: evaluating how the plan of action worked and what needs changing in order to make the situation better.

All these attributes contribute to Bruner's notion of 'thinking' and he is clear about the central role that adults, including the staff of schools, play in the development of cognitive abilities and in fostering their pupils' powers of perception, thinking, action and evaluation. He categorically states that teachers must be trained to encourage problem-solving, and to provide their children with the materials and lessons that permit legitimate problem-solving. The task for the curriculum maker is to provide exercises and opportunities that nurture problem-solving and thinking skills – a task which has now been made simpler by the identification of the key skills across the curriculum.

Bruner's theories and empowerment

Two aspects of the human condition, identified earlier as 'empowering', are embedded in our discussion at the beginning of the book and can be defined as:

* choice and decision-making;
* the opportunity to access and make effective use of communication.

Although acts of choice and decision-making can be undertaken by individuals on their own (choosing to watch a favourite TV programme, for example), they often involve other people. Exposure to a range of relationships is a fundamental requirement for the growth of empowerment. Firth and Radley (1990) consider that the opportunities for empowerment come firstly from learning about ourselves, and then by learning about others; often from learning *from* others, but, most importantly, learning *through* others. At one level, 'learning through others' can be interpreted as the 'scaffolding' necessary for the development of mental activity, but at another level it involves, in Bruner's words: '… a deep human need to respond to others and to operate jointly with them towards an objective' (Bruner, 1966, p.125).

By examining these prerequisites, and using them as a starting point for discussion, it is possible to give an indication of how Bruner's theories and principles contribute to our understanding of the development of empowerment in everyday life.

Choice and decision-making

In order to make choices, children need to become active learners, as the decision-making process involves grasping opportunities to investigate, predict, anticipate and make judgements, all of which are embedded in Bruner's theories. Choosing can, on the one hand, be a very simple opportunity to indicate a yes/no preference in response to stimuli provided by one person. On the other hand, it can become a complicated process that involves collecting information from a range of sources and, subsequently, making complicated decisions. Cooper and Hersov (1986), for example, list the choices available to us when making up our minds on what to eat or drink. At a basic level, such choices can involve whether or not to have a cup of tea or coffee, but, at the other extreme, choices become more complicated and involve:

*   the selection of the restaurant (and the type of food) required;
*   how to get there;
*   the time to eat;
*   the decision whether to eat alone or with others;
*   the choice of the number of courses in line with the budget;
*   the choice of the food and drink from a complicated menu.

The latter extreme involves a complex level of reasoning and Bruner states categorically that:

> ... intellectual development is marked by the increasing capacity to deal with several alternatives simultaneously, to tend to several sequences during the same period of time, and to allocate time and attention in a manner appropriate to these multiple demands.
> (Bruner, 1966, p.6)

The need to access and to make effective use of communication

The strong emphasis on communication in Bruner's theory naturally supports the notion of empowerment, and the structure that he provides, ranging from the enactive to the symbolic mode, enables children to progress from a state of total dependence to one of control. It is his view that language (and for pupils with special educational needs it is important to add *communication*) does not come about by chance. Children require specific experiences to make it happen, and they require external support. Trust, a loving and caring environment, and the reciprocal nature of early relationships that include social routines, all contribute to the development of language and communication. Some of the ideas put forward on the development of language and communication by other theorists are difficult to interpret for children at very early stages of development, for example those with profound and multiple difficulties. Bruner's theories, however, are as applicable to children with profound and multiple learning difficulties as they are to more intellectually able children.

The importance he attaches to play and to the social interactions that take place between child and adult provide a firm basis for work with *all* children. In the early stages, his emphasis on the importance of the adult and child experiencing events and playing with objects together ensures that they are provided with *topics* for further exchanges (Harris, 1990). Through such social play, not only is the child learning some of the fundamental principles of the *give and take* of communication, but both child and adult have something to communicate about, with a joint understanding of the focus of their 'communication'. The child, however severe the difficulties in learning, is seen as an intentional communicator (Goldbart, 1994) and learns that he or she is a conversational partner.

The pre-verbal responses that stem from the social routines of early childhood enable the adult to continually check the child's intent. Even if the methods of communication are idiosyncratic and involve a particular movement of a muscle or of the eyes, the adult is likely to make a good guess as to the meaning, and to put the necessary *scaffold* in place to help to extend the child's communicative efforts. Research shows that for some children with special educational needs, patterns of non-verbal communication can aid the development of spoken language (Harris, 1990; Goldbart, 1994; Nind, 1996). For other children, these early patterns can pave the way for non-verbal communication that is understood by a wider range of people, thus ultimately promoting empowerment and self-advocacy.

Finally, Bruner's overarching principle is perhaps the most powerful in terms of fostering self-advocacy and empowerment: 'Growth is characterized by increasing independence from the immediate nature of the stimulus' (Bruner, 1966, p.5).

Lev S. Vygotsky: the educational implications of his work

The influence of Vygotsky on contemporary pedagogy is widely recognised, particularly his theory concerning the mechanisms by which optimal learning takes place when the developing child (the learner) interacts with a more mature individual (the teacher). Having acknowledged that, beyond pedagogy, the learning situation does not have to be formal, nor does 'the teacher' have to be a professional – or, indeed, an adult – his notion of the zone of proximal development has particularly important implications for how teachers utilise pupils' responses in planning further intervention and support: 'Instruction is only useful when it moves ahead of development. When it does, it impels or awakens a series of functions that are in a stage of maturation lying in the zone of proximal development' (Vygotsky, 1987, p.212 cited by Daniels and Lunt, 1993, p.82).

According to Vygotsky, as interpreted in this quotation, instruction must be based on clear assessments of individual differences in rates and directions of development. In short, the teacher must be aware of the child's capability in any area of problem-solving so that teaching can be structured appropriately. Therefore, assessment, in its broadest sense of gaining an holistic view of a learner's profile of strengths and needs in different learning contexts, must be sensitive to both the task-demands and individual pupils' responses to them. Such assessment approaches are termed, collectively, dynamic assessment (see, for example, Elliott, 2000). Contrasting with static assessment, in which a judgement about a child's capacity to learn in any given sphere is based on a 'snapshot' of the child's performance on assessment tasks, dynamic assessment is interwoven with the teaching–learning process. Thus, during the process of instruction the teacher learns progressively more about the learner's maturational level and mode of thinking and learning.

Mandy

Mandy is in Year 5 and has Down syndrome. Faced with the task of writing the word 'yet' on a blank sheet of paper, she becomes tearful and refuses to write anything. The teacher assumes that Mandy does not know how to write 'yet' but he does not have any idea about the reason for her difficulty with this word. Can't she hear the word clearly? Does she only know some of the constituent letters? Does she know all the letters but not the order? Is she unsure about how to form some or all of the letters? Perhaps her pencil is broken and she's afraid to say so?

Using an alternative approach the teacher produces a white magnetic board and plastic letters. He constructs the words *met, set, let* and *yes* and invites Mandy to read them after him. He demonstrates where the rime of the word stays the same, '-et' and emphasises how different words are created with fresh onsets. If Mandy can spontaneously create *yet* using this technique the teacher may assume that certain alphabetic skills are secure, thus providing the basis for focused literacy teaching. Otherwise, the teacher will be better placed to judge precisely what input is needed to establish the host of skills that are needed to spell the family of words that includes 'yet'.

Dynamic assessment informs the way that the teacher guides the learner and advances the learner's problem-solving ability. Campione (1996) reviewed dynamic assessment approaches, under the heading of 'assisted assessment', as well as its implications for teaching, contrasting it with the product-oriented view of traditional unaided, static assessment and didactic instruction. He pointed out the dangers of relying on the techniques of the latter to identify pupils' learning difficulties. For example, in the past there have been significant and long-term implications for the placement of learners who have failed to perform satisfactorily in assessment tasks at or above the baseline for 'normality'. It is hypothesised that a different picture of their abilities might emerge through the process of dynamic assessment when adults structure learning to activate cognitive competence, which lies within an individual learner's zone of proximal development.

Robyn

Robyn attends a school for children with moderate learning difficulties and is nine years old. She and her peers enjoy their daily literacy hour, which is based on the structure used in the Reception Year. The school has developed its own literacy policy, firstly by analysing the developmental progression implicit in the *Framework for Teaching the Literacy Hour* (the guidance document for supporting the implementation of a national initiative in England), which has the aim of promoting literacy achievements in all primary-aged children (DfEE, 1998). The school approach is then based on *rolling back* the process of development to examine the prerequisite skills that are not addressed in the document. The resulting policy reflects a more highly differentiated schedule of skills than that represented in the Literacy Hour Framework.

Working with Robyn, her teacher found out that she appeared to have no concept of 'same' and 'different', which is obviously crucial to making the sort of judgements that underpin early reading skills, and establishing this concept became a target. Robyn can now categorise concrete objects in this way and her teacher is hopeful that they will soon start working with plastic letters, making the same judgements. Her teacher commented that the Literacy Hour has provided the staff with the opportunity to look at what individual children *can* do in a constructive way, as an alternative to dismissing complex activities, such as reading, as 'beyond these children'. As a result, the teacher says, 'We have been amazed at what our children have achieved.'

The notion of 'co-operatively achieved success' (Wood, 1998, p.27) also underpins Bruner's view of scaffolding; a similarity that is demonstrated in the quotations from Vygotsky (above) and Bruner (in Chapter 2). However, in Vygotsky's view, the teacher or other adult does more than help a child to acquire a skill or a concept: she or he mediates the child's cultural context, which will go on to create a framework for wider learning and the 'acculturation' of the child.

In the narrative involving Robyn and the Literacy Hour activities, it is evident that learning about the 'sameness' of letters will be tackled shortly. The teacher will show Robyn a variety of presentations of the letter 'a' and help her to see that they are all called 'a'. They will then progress to looking at the letter 'a' written in a variety of media: in pencilled script, in coloured script, in printed text, in sand. Eventually, Robyn will need to learn that the letter represents a variety of sounds (as in 'hat', 'father', 'all'); afterwards, that a number of sounds blend together to make the words that we hear when people speak. Through this approach the learner moves towards establishing 'decoding': that is, the skill of working out a pronunciation for previously unseen words from visual stimuli (letters), which is the hallmark of an independent reader. We widely regard readers as empowered by their participation in a literate society or, conversely, we recognise the disempowerment of people who cannot read at a functional level made possible through decoding.

In another culture, supporting a child's access to literacy might not follow the same route. For example, in what is now the USA and prior to the War of Independence, literacy was encouraged in the masses only for reading the Bible and designated patriotic texts that could be taught using sight-reading and learning by rote (Adams, 1994). In this case, it is clear that neither empowerment of the individual, nor the independent reading skills that support empowerment, were socio-cultural ideals.

Vygotsky and empowerment

Vygotsky emphasised that learning is essentially a social process: the outcome of an interaction between individuals sharing a cultural environment, which gives rise to an enhanced state of knowledge, skills and understanding. In this respect, the 'cultural environment' may refer to what Evans (1993) describes as 'educational micro-cultures' (p.41) and he goes on to review research conducted within a Vygotskyan paradigm that indicates the impact that different schools, with their own organisations and methods, have on pupils' understanding of the world. As shown, for example, by Daniels (1988, cited by Evans, 1993), members of staff at schools for pupils with moderate learning difficulties may mediate a different world view for their pupils from that of mainstream schools. Evans suggests that, as a result, pupils' knowledge and understanding of the world may, at the end of formal schooling, be incompatible with that of the wider society, therefore creating obstacles to full participation. He proposes that Vygotsky's theories about the socio-cultural basis of cognition offer a framework for illuminating these potentially negative effects, and addressing them by focusing on the structures of knowledge that schools implicitly or explicitly impart. To illustrate these complex notions, Evans cites the example of deaf people who, historically, received a segregated education with their own sign language that effectively excluded users from the hearing community, and thus denied them access to the culture of the wider society.

In confronting the issue of integration, which as an area of concern has more recently been replaced by considerations of inclusion, Evans identifies the importance of the philosophies underpinning education systems or 'micro-cultures' for individual empowerment.

For our part, we would argue that the current educational climate, with its emphasis on the inclusion of all learners within the same curriculum, offers opportunities for mainstream and special provision to examine the world views that they separately or jointly promote. In England, *The Index for Inclusion* (Booth *et al.*, 2000) provides a framework within which schools can assess their policies and practices in order to respond to the diversity of all learners. The *Index* identifies schools as communities or cultures but emphasises that the inclusion process will involve merging the school culture with that of the wider community, for example:

*   'Inclusion is concerned with fostering mutually sustaining relationships between schools and communities.
*   Inclusion in education is one aspect of inclusion in society' (Booth *et al.*, 2000, p.12).

Evans' argument, which reflects on how individual empowerment can be enhanced by looking at institutional organisation and policy, is based on a key concept in Vygotsky's theory, that of mediation. Mediation also has a major role in the formation of self-concept. Recalling that human consciousness derives from experience of the world that is somehow mediated by other, more mature individuals using cultural artefacts such as language or signs, it follows that the self-concept is formed from other people's views of the *self* and its capabilities. Hodapp (1998) interprets Vygotsky as adopting a social definition of disability: that is, an understanding of disability as defined by non-disabled people who focus on the difficulties resulting from some physical, emotional or mental difference. This view is subsequently transmitted to become internalised as the self-concept in affected learners, who consequently regard themselves as 'disempowered'.

Jordan

Jordan is a 17-year-old student with spina bifida. He has only mild learning difficulties, is a wheelchair user and has a high level of physical care needs. Jordan is a lively and likeable student, but he is very disorganised; he is reluctant to take any responsibility and does not attempt to be independent if he can find someone else to help him. For example, if his wheelchair tyres need air he will wait for someone else to notice and take action rather than pushing himself to the physio department to ask for the tyres to be inflated.

Jordan's mother is very caring, but is anxious and overprotective. She does everything for Jordan, saying that he is not able to do anything for himself 'because of his condition'. This attitude, which may be typical of many well-meaning people, has helped to create many problems for Jordan; in particular, it has limited his potential for independence. He has a place at a residential college, but his failure to see himself as capable of independent living, means that he has not actively sought or practised independent living skills that, in turn, suggests that he will find it difficult to cope with life away from home.

Alternatively, by reference to the zone of proximal development, educators and service providers can assess and establish what all children *can* do with appropriate support. This will involve investigating how individual children may be encouraged or taught to communicate. For example, Vygotsky took special note of intervention for deaf children. He was strongly critical of mechanistic training programmes to teach individual language sounds, arguing that, if this group of learners was going to regard itself as part of wider society, members needed to acquire language interactively as hearing children do (Hodapp, 1998).

Vygotsky's theory has been adopted in Russia, specifically to develop approaches and materials for pupils with special educational needs. Indeed, Vygotsky founded the Russian Institute of Defectology in 1934, where research into learning difficulties, as well the development of teaching approaches, takes place. However, as Daniels and Lunt (1993) explain, the interpretation of his theory, its application to special education and the identification of learning difficulties are fraught with contradictions and complexities. For example, children who, in the UK, would be described as having severe learning difficulties or profound and multiple learning difficulties would be regarded in Russia as ineducable and therefore outside the remit of education policy and practice. In short, an unknown proportion of children in Russia are permanently excluded from schooling. Interested readers are invited to study the paper by Daniels and Lunt (1993) for further insights into the work of the Russian Institute and to assess the differences between British and Russian views on the nature and purpose of education, of special education and educability. In viewing these differences through a Vygotskyan lens, it is evident that their effect is not solely to deny an education to children with severe and complex learning difficulties: in wider, sociocultural terms, the children are effectively disempowered.

References

Adams, M.J. (1994) *Beginning to Read: Thinking and Learning about Print*. Boston, MA: MIT Press.

Bakhurst, D. (1996) 'Social memory in Soviet thought', in H. Daniels (ed.) *An Introduction to Vygotsky*. London: Routledge.

Booth, T., Ainscow, M., Black-Hawkins, K., Vaughan, M. and Shaw, L. (2000) *The Index for Inclusion: Developing Learning and Participation in School*. Bristol: CSIE and London: DfEE.

Bruner, J. (1966) *Toward a Theory of Instruction*. Cambridge, MA: Harvard University Press.

Campione, J.C. (1996) 'Assisted assessment: a taxonomy of approaches and an outline of strengths and weaknesses', in H. Daniels (ed.) *An Introduction to Vygotsky*. London: Routledge.

Cooper, D. and Hersov, J. (1986) *We Can Change the Future* (A staff training resource for people with learning difficulties). London: SKILL.

Daniels, H. and Lunt, I. (1993) 'Vygotskian theory and special education in Russia', *Educational Studies*. 19 (1), 79–89.

DfEE (1998) *The National Literacy Strategy Framework for Teaching*. London: HMSO.

DfEE/QCA (1999a) *The National Curriculum: A Handbook for Primary Teachers in England*. London: HMSO.

DfEE/QCA (1999b) *The National Curriculum: A Handbook for Secondary Teachers in England*. London: HMSO.

Donaldson, M. (1978) *Children's Minds*. Fontana/Collins.

Elliott, J. (2000) 'The psychological assessment of children with learning difficulties', *British Journal of Special Education*. 27 (2), 59–66.

Evans, P. (1993) 'Some implications of Vygotsky's work for special education', in H. Daniels (ed.) *Charting the Agenda*. London and New York: Routledge.

Firth, H. and Radley, M. (1990) *From Acquaintance to Friendship*. Kidderminster: BIMH.

Goldbart, J. (1994) 'Opening the Communication Curriculum for pupils with PMLDs', in J. Ware (ed.) *Educating Children with Profound and Multiple Learning Difficulties*. London: David Fulton Publishers.

Harris, J. (1990) *Early Language Development: Implications for Clinical and Educational Practice*. London: Routledge.

Hodapp, R. (1998) *Development and Disabilities: Intellectual, Sensory and Motor Impairments*. Cambridge: Cambridge University Press.

Hohmann, M. and Weikhart, D. (1995) *Educating Young Children*. Yipsilanti, MI: High/Scope Press.

Mitchell, S. (1994) 'Some implications of the High/Scope Curriculum and the education of children with severe learning difficulties', in J. Coupe O'Kane and B. Smith (eds) *Taking Control: Enabling People with Learning Difficulties*. London: David Fulton Publishers.

Nind, M. (1996) 'Efficacy of intensive interaction: developing sociability and communication in people with severe and complex learning difficulties using an approach based on caregiver–infant interaction', *European Journal of Special Educational Need.* 11, 48–56.

QCA (2001) *Developing Skills.* London QCA.

QCA/DfEE (1998) *Design and Technology: A Scheme of Work for Key Stages 1 and 2.* London: QCA.

QCA/DfEE (2001) *Planning, Teaching and Assessing the Curriculum for Pupils with Learning Difficulties.* London: QCA.

Wood, D. (1998) *How Children Think and Learn.* Oxford: Blackwell Publishers.

Chapter 6

The psychoanalytical theorists

Sigmund Freud

Freud's theories have, in the past, been criticised on the grounds that they are 'unscientific'. In particular, Freud used data from the recollections of a limited sample of middle-aged, wealthy, mentally unstable people in Vienna to generate a set of norms describing the development of the personality on a universal scale. Further, the terminology that has found its way into our daily vocabulary, in fact lacks precision or operational definition (Bee, 2000): that is, it cannot be put to the test. Nonetheless, later scientists have reformulated some of Freud's ideas in ways that are testable and they have been able to evaluate specific aspects or hypotheses (for example, Fisher and Greenberg, 1996) to lend further credence to his views on oral and anal personality traits (for an overview of contemporary evaluations of Freudian theory readers are directed to Andrews and Brewin, 2000 and to the special issue on which their paper provides editorial comment). Beyond the level of detail, however, Freud's contribution to our views on the origins of the personality, and to our understanding of human behaviour, is immense.

According to Jolibert (1993), Freud openly expressed a disinclination to explore the educational implications of his views, but expected them to be developed by other psycho-analysts such as his daughter, Anna Freud. Nonetheless, a study of his writings reveals an unambiguous perspective on the role of education, even if pedagogical details are lacking. In particular, he looked to education to uphold and transmit cultural rules and regulations (based on the 'reality principle') that do not allow the expression of immediate instinctual pleasure. Through education, individuals learn how to adapt and re-route their instinctual drives into acceptable activities and agreeable personality traits. However, Jolibert refutes the notion that Freud had identified a repressive role for education; instead, he recognised that educators are necessarily challenged to strike a balance between being repressive and overlenient in order to awaken, in developing children, a drive to establish their own mechanisms for self-regulation. Again according to Jolibert (1993), Freud equated a capacity for education with an intrinsic desire to adjust towards society's values. In other words, Freud saw the child as inherently 'moral' (in the sense of 'capable of making moral judgements') and open to education as the source of moral direction.

Although Freud undoubtedly attributed the moral function of education to its processes, rather than to its content, it is possible to discover and analyse moral directives in the learning opportunities identified in connection with personal, social and health education (PSHE) in England. For example, pupils are encouraged to express feelings, to explore differences between people and to reflect on their relationships. At the same time, this curriculum area aims at helping pupils to become self-confident and to recognise and enhance their own abilities. Many pupils with significant learning needs may bring to the learning situation a poor self-image that does not favour the growth of confidence or a sense of autonomy. A Freudian explanation for this focuses on key figures in the child's life, possibly parents who hold a limited view of her or his potential, which the child adopts through the processes of identification. It then becomes a challenge for educators to work closely with parents so that together they might promote an optimistic and positive view of the child.

Jordan

Jordan was a Year 8 pupil with mild learning difficulties in a mainstream school. He struggled in most subjects except art, which he thoroughly enjoyed. His stepfather was a successful businessman who had great difficulty in accepting Jordan's limitations and could not disguise his contempt for the boy's lack of achievement in almost any area of the curriculum. Consequently, Jordan's self-esteem was very low and he was effectively isolated in many class activities because, as he frequently said, 'I can't do anything.'

Recently, Jordan was asked by a friend of the Special Educational Needs Co-ordinator (SENCo) at their school to provide some line drawings for an information booklet that was to be circulated among parents at a health clinic. Jordan was quite pleased to supply these pictures but his stepfather was ecstatic – at last, Jordan had achieved something of significance and value! The SENCo reported that the effect on Jordan was astonishing: he appeared to grow in stature and he was more confident in interactions with his peers who, for the first time, began to include him enthusiastically in class projects so that he could provide illustrations.

Freud would attribute the initial improvement in Jordan's self-esteem to the change in how his stepfather related to him, because parent–child relationships are seen as crucial to the development of the personality. Peer approval then served to confirm and consolidate Jordan's new image of himself as a person with talents and abilities. The promotion of confidence and responsibility as part of the PSHE curriculum area is discussed in greater detail with special reference to pupils with learning needs in later chapters.

We cannot deny that Freud provoked both lay people and child specialists in Western Europe and North America into adopting a fresh perspective on childhood, when he demonstrated in detail what had previously led William Wordsworth to suggest that 'the child is father to the man'. Similarly, his views inspired a radical reappraisal of the methods by which children are best guided. For example, unlike our predecessors in, say, the early twentieth century, we regard young children's sexual curiosity and some sexual play as healthy. We encourage children to give overt expression to impulses, albeit within the confines of adult-directed activities such as painting, modelling and other outlets of personal expression, because of our belief that 'bottling-up' (repressing) instinctual drives may lead to neuroses.

As emphasised earlier, Freud set out to explain all aspects of human behaviour, and his explanations include those relating to career and vocational choices. For example, people who during the oral stage of development were either overindulged or were not allowed sufficient opportunity to work out oral behaviours will carry over orality into their adult behaviours, a notion for which there is some experimental support (see above). This may explain cigarette and pipe smoking, for example, in which the mouth is regularly stimulated but, at the macro-level, it would, in Freud's view, also explain why people choose careers that allow them to talk uninterrupted, as in teaching and lecturing. The possibility that one works towards a career or vocation that matches emotional needs should be considered seriously when supporting young people to make decisions about further education, training and roles in adult life.

In conclusion, it may be argued that Freud has little to offer practitioners in terms of specific approaches or techniques for teaching pupils of all abilities. While this may be true, it is important that teachers can reflect on the cultural context, which so heavily influences their own thinking, particularly their views on childhood and education. We have set out in this section to indicate the extent of Freud's influence on Western cultures, with a view to providing a basis for informed reflection and analysis.

Erik Erikson

Like Freud, Erikson's theories have been criticised because they do not lend themselves to empirical testing (Miller, 1993; Keenan, 2002), but the stages, and the conflicts which need to be balanced within them, provide rich material for the staff of schools to draw upon. We have chosen to limit ourselves to three main points, based partly on Bee's propositions drawn up in 1989 and detailed in the first section of the book. They relate to the:

- specific developmental pointers within each of the stages;
- importance of society in aiding development;
- reliance of interactions between caregivers and educators, particularly during the early stages.

As many of the pupils we are concerned with are at stages of development that are much earlier than their chronological years, these pointers will be discussed with particular reference to Erikson's initial psychosocial stages. It is important to recognise, however, that these early stages and the ideas embedded in them provide the cornerstone for work in the later stages.

The first point that we want to highlight is concerned with using Erikson's stages to enable the development of pupils who are chronologically at an identified stage, but have not reached it in terms of their maturation. Erikson emphasises that not only is there the capacity for each child to develop within each stage – and he implies that there is a new miracle of vigorous unfolding at every stage (Erikson, 1965) – but he also suggests that pupils may make some steps in development in one or more of the identified stages and then build on them as they get older (see Chapter 3). For pupils with special educational needs, the 'unfolding' will certainly not be 'vigorous' and will need the facilitation of all adults concerned with their education. In his work, Erikson stresses the importance of parents and caregivers in helping their children through each stage, but for pupils with special educational needs, 'facilitators' will extend beyond their immediate family to those involved with their education throughout their lives.

Joel

Joel's 'facilitators' in helping him to build up trust and the recognition of his own capacity to cope include not only his teacher, but also his peers (see Chapter 3). Both teacher and pupils are helping Joel to exercise autonomy, a role that Erikson specifically identified in the second stage. Because of her knowledge of theories of development, the teacher is able to manipulate situations in which her pupils can provide the necessary support for Joel to begin to develop his own identity. Although we have only used her work to illustrate the first of Erikson's stages, as she teaches she draws upon the ideas embedded in at least four, namely:

- trust versus mistrust;
- autonomy versus shame and doubt;
- initiative versus guilt;
- industry versus inferiority.

She does this by regarding diversity as a rich resource in supporting learning and by recognising collaboration with Joel as an important pointer in encouraging independence.

This brings us to the second point we wish to make: the importance of the ethos of the school. A warm, caring school which shares the common goals of positive relationships with both staff and pupils, respects difference and diversity, and values each child's ability to make a genuine contribution to all that goes on within its walls, will certainly aid the process of 'unfolding' and the development of a sense of each pupil's identity.

Although Erikson goes further by suggesting an inner process of maturation, all the children we teach may not ultimately achieve such a process, a point we make in discussing Bruner's theory and Royston's learning needs in Chapter 2. Erikson does, however, suggest that placing an emphasis on meaningful interactions and ensuring that 'institutions are ready' for each child are important steps in facilitating the emergence of different qualities of ego strength at different stages of a person's life.

What might such 'readiness' mean and what are 'meaningful interactions'? Readiness can simply imply that a supportive school will go out of its way to celebrate and value 'difference'. Through its 'culture' (which includes the whole curriculum and approaches to teaching and learning) it can, however, demonstrate to pupils that on the one hand it is alright to be oneself and, on the other, that the experience of the education offered will allow a new 'self' to emerge. As we have already discussed, the emergence of an identity involves others in meaningful interactions and Erikson (1965) regards interactions as being meaningful when adults provide opportunities that 'permit' their pupils to develop. In discussing his theories in Chapter 3, our examples of Joel, Wendy, Raj and John illustrate many aspects of 'permitting', some of which are encouraging pupils to:

- make decisions with support;
- make choices;
- explore (through a range of means including the gradual reduction of support systems);
- listen to others and respond appropriately;
- become confident in their judgements;
- appraise others' actions in relation to agreed criteria;
- help others to take responsibility for their actions;
- widen their repertoire of responses;
- build up self-confidence and self-esteem.

At the same time, adults will also need to prohibit pupils from coming to physical or emotional harm or attempting something that is way beyond their capabilities. If members of staff are 'to grant such permission' they will need to know their pupils well and consequently provide differentiated approaches to learning. In addition all members of staff must work collaboratively by sharing information about their pupils in order to facilitate each child's development through the stages.

The last point we wish to emphasise about Erikson's theories concerns the last statement on the list above: the need for children to develop a positive self-image and to feel good about themselves. The self-esteem of children with special educational needs is particularly vulnerable, the reasons for which can include:

- fear of new situations;
- self-consciousness and shame (of their unusual physical appearance or of their inability to complete tasks or to keep up with peers);
- constantly being labelled and singled out as different.

Alderson and staff (1999) have analysed how they attempted to promote positive self-esteem in their mainstream school, which caters for a wide range of pupils with special educational needs (including some with profound and multiple learning difficulties). Interestingly, as a starting point, they identify strategies that will raise staff self-esteem; a move which illustrates Erikson's theory that his early stages are never fully complete and that the tensions identified in the first stages need to be constantly addressed throughout life. At the time of writing this book, teachers are still feeling vulnerable and undervalued and are reeling from increased administration, responsibilities and bureaucracy. The school, therefore, considers it to be important to develop high self-esteem in adults and children. Two of the principles in its approach ensure that:

- the work of all staff is valued and recognised;
- positive images of staff are presented at all times.

Some of the ways in which adults contribute to the high self-esteem of their pupils are through:

- the implementation of a marking policy that ensures children feel good about their work and enables them to move forward;
- children being praised and their needs discussed constructively;
- the planning of a rich curriculum which counteracts and challenges negative stereotypes.

It is stressed that the children in the school must be:

- made aware that they have rights and that these rights are adhered to both in school and in their lives outside school;
- encouraged to set ground rules with staff and aware of the boundaries;
- aware that making mistakes is part of learning.

(adapted from Alderson *et al.*, 1999, pp.75–6)

More of the educational implications of Erikson's theory will be considered in Part 3.

Erikson's theory and empowerment

What pointers can we find in Erikson's theory that will aid the development of empowerment and self-advocacy? Many are embedded within the stages but some are explicit. Both self-advocacy and autonomy are concerned with empowerment and it is interesting that autonomy is named as part of Erikson's third stage ('initiative versus guilt'). At a basic level, the ability to become empowered requires each of us to make decisions and choices, to take on responsibilities and to form and articulate our views, but such activities cannot be considered without reference to the wider context. We all need the support systems of family, friends and society in order to demonstrate our progress in the process towards empowerment. Certainly Erikson's basic tenet that a struggle for individual identities involves the relationship between people and their culture highlights the fact that autonomy, and ultimately empowerment, is dependent on communicating and socialising with others.

His emphasis on social contexts (the meanings and significances which society provide) is also relevant, as is the importance he attaches to the formation of early relationships. In the early stages of his theory, he highlights the need for the parent/caregiver/teacher to provide, at the very least:

* a warm and loving environment;
* consistency in his or her approach;
* opportunities for children to explore and try things out for themselves in a safe environment.

Throughout the theory, there is a strong sense that children learn to behave appropriately because they are given the opportunity to do so, not because they are forced.

Erikson also believed that each individual's identity has a bearing on the culture. In other words, a person is being shaped by the responses of other people but at the same time is shaping other people's responses. This point is taken up by the multi-authored pack *Index for Inclusion* (Booth *et al.*, 2000) that, amongst other things, is concerned with creating inclusive cultures. One of the questions put to schools is, 'Are all members of the school regarded as both learners and teachers?' (p.59). Such a question relates directly to the impact of one person on another.

A further important aspect of Erikson's work lies in his implied emphasis on the development of self-esteem. Many researchers and writers (Burns, 1982; Stenhouse, 1994; Stevens, 1995, for example) have written about the value of self-esteem in the search for the identity of self, which has been defined in terms of the feelings a person has about the qualities and characteristics that make up his or her self-concept. Lawrence (1996) suggests that a child with high self-esteem is likely to be confident in social situations and in school. He or she is likely to develop a natural curiosity for learning and to be eager and enthusiastic when presented with new challenges. In contrast, the child with low self-esteem will lack confidence in the ability to succeed and may avoid situations that he or she regards as humiliating, difficult or just new. Lawrence (1996) provides a useful bank of activities designed to build up self-esteem, but, as he emphasises, 'no programmes or exercises will make the slightest difference to children's self-esteem unless the teacher conducting them possesses the qualities of acceptance, genuineness and empathy' (p.39). The need to inspire confidence and to teach new skills is seen by Mortimer (2001) as the basis of good teaching, and central to such teaching is a framework of acceptance and respect. The attitudes of others is crucial in allowing the child with special educational needs to resolve the crises that Erikson identified in each of the stages. It is through others that the child will progress towards empowerment and will ultimately, in Erikson's words, 'find his identity'.

References

Alderson, P. (ed.) with staff and pupils of Cleves School (1999) *Learning and Inclusion: The Cleves School Experience*. London: David Fulton Publishers.

Andrews, B. and Brewin, C.R. (2000) 'What did Freud get right?' *The Psychologist*. 13 (12), 605–7.

Bee, H. (1989) *The Developing Child* (5th edition). New York: HarperCollins.

Bee, H. (2000) *The Developing Child* (9th edition). Needham Heights, MA: Allyn and Bacon.

Booth, T., Ainscow, M., Black-Hawkins, K., Vaughan, M. and Shaw, L. (2000) *Index for Inclusion*. London: CSIE.

Burns, R.B. (1982) *Self-Concept Development and Education*. Sydney: Holt, Rinehart and Winston.

Erikson E.H. (I965) *Childhood and Society* (2nd edition). Harmondsworth: Penguin Books.

Fisher, S. and Greenberg, R.P. (1996) *Freud Scientifically Reappraised: Testing the Theories and the Therapy*. New York: John Wiley.

Jolibert, B. (1993) 'Sigmund Freud (1856–1939)', *Prospects*. 23, 3–4 and 459–72.

Keenan, T. (2002) *An Introduction to Child Development*. London: Sage Publications.

Lawrence, D. (1996) *Enhancing Self-Esteem in the Classroom* (2nd edition). London: Paul Chapman Publishing.

Miller, P.H. (1993) *Theories of Developmental Psychology* (3rd edition). New York: W.H. Freeman.

Mortimer, H. (2001) *Personal, Social and Emotional Development of Children in the Early Years*. Lichfield: QEd.

Stenhouse, G. (1994) *Confident Children: Developing Your Child's Self-esteem*. Oxford: Oxford University Press.

Stevens, R. (ed.) (1995) *Understanding the Self*. London: Sage Publications.

Chapter 7

Skinner and the learning theorists

The underlying principle of learning theory is that all behaviour is learned, and that biological or medical causes of disability are not significant: for example, having Down syndrome or cerebral palsy does not prevent the learning of new skills. The basic tenets are an emphasis on observable, measurable behaviour and a de-emphasis of inner states such as intention, desire or reflection on the meaning of the behaviour for the individual.

It is important to stress that in learning theory, behaviour is defined as anything that we do or say which *other people* can *observe* and *measure*. Such behaviour may be a simple event such as picking up a pencil, that can be analysed as:

*   hand–eye co-ordination in locating the object;
*   clarity of movement in touching the pencil;
*   the type of grip used to hold the pencil;
*   the time taken to lift the pencil.

A more complex example is driving a car in which judgements about competence are made (for the official driving test) on the basis of behavioural responses in a number of skill areas. To take one skill area, some of the components of an emergency stop are:

*   looking at road conditions;
*   taking the foot off the accelerator;
*   looking through the rearview mirror;
*   putting the foot on the brake;
*   applying the other foot to the clutch in synchrony while maintaining control over the steering.

It is assumed that 'behaviour' does not occur in isolation, but is influenced by what goes on before it and what follows it. We do not walk or drive a car without a reason; there is always something which occurs immediately before the behaviour in order to prompt us into action (an antecedent). Mostly these reasons are extrinsic and in the case of walking or driving a car the antecedent may be the need to post a letter, or to shop, or to see friends. They can be intrinsic: the reason for the walk is that the action of walking is pleasurable. Other events (consequences or reinforcers) encourage a repetition of that behaviour: the letter is collected, delivered and acknowledged; our friends are pleased to see us; we enjoyed the activity of driving. Readers will be familiar with ABC charts that outline these processes:

A = antecedents

B = behaviour

C = consequences.

Reinforcers or rewards strengthen the behaviour and take various forms. In the case of Jasmin (see Chapter 4), who is learning to use her wheelchair, her reward for effort is food, but many children with special needs will respond to social rewards such as praise or a 'smiley sticker' placed appropriately. Other children, particularly those with complex needs, may find sensory experiences rewarding.

Toby

Although rubella has affected Toby's vision, he enjoys exploring his environment either through the soles of his feet or through touch. His favourite 'toy' is a plastic pop-up figure activated by pressing a switch. It appears that he likes the feel of the hard plastic, but he also uses his limited vision to track the movement of the toy and to find the object when it has fallen. This toy has undergone a number of changes over the years (Toby is now ten) as his first one, a duck, was bought off the shelf at a shop selling pre-school toys. His latest toy is a more age-appropriate spaceman, which is only activated if the moon symbol (a raised symbol system which has similarities to Braille) is found from a choice of switches. His toy has been specifically adapted so that the switches change automatically, and Toby has to work (in the sense of *reading* the right word) to obtain his reward.

Toby finds it difficult to concentrate on many of his normal school activities, and one of the aims identified in his individual education plan (IEP) is to increase his concentration span. When concentration is lost he wanders around the room, usually in bare feet, often bumping into furniture and other children. Such behaviour presents a number of obvious difficulties for staff and pupils, although it is recognised that it is important not to curb his curiosity and his enthusiasm for exploration. At present, he concentrates on most tasks for three to four minutes, and those that he finds more stimulating for five to eight minutes.

The staff have devised a simple timing system which enables them to keep approximate records of his *on-task behaviour* in most situations without the need for stop watches or sophisticated logging devices. If he concentrates on an activity for more than nine minutes, his sensory toy reward is presented to him immediately. On presenting the reward the staff also pat him on the back. At present this is a pleasurable sensation, but it is hoped that, in line with social learning theory, Toby will learn that a pat on the back is *praise*. Toby is therefore learning to work for something he really wants, but he also has to *work* to enjoy the (sensory) sensation of the toy 'popping up' which he finds so enjoyable.

The important point here is that rewards are chosen to suit the pupil and are therefore *powerful*: that is, something that he or she will work for. Second, when first introduced, they must be presented immediately after the desired behaviour has occurred, with an element of enthusiasm so that the learner associates the reward with the response. Later, at a more sophisticated level, access to rewards can be made contingent on the completion of an agreed task and, in some situations, become part of a formal contract and a written agreement. Such a process will inevitably involve some negotiation between teacher and learner.

Anu

Anu was referred to the county psychological service in January of Year 7 because of the continuing concerns about her behaviour. As she was at risk of being excluded from the school, a Pastoral Support Plan was drawn up and a meeting was arranged with her to discuss her behaviour. Anu said she knew that teachers in both her primary and secondary schools often viewed her behaviour as unacceptable and she did not feel that she had a positive relationship with all those who taught her. In discussion with the educational psychologist, it emerged that her relationship with her teachers was directly linked to her like or dislike of a subject. She felt that complaints made by the staff about her behaviour were unreasonable and said that she found it easier to cope in lessons when she could move around and talk to her peers. She complained that the teachers did not give her any opportunities to express her views.

Anu had been 'on report' for bad behaviour a number of times in the past and neither she nor the educational psychologist felt that the report system was a useful way of changing her, or her teachers', behaviour. It was agreed that a reward system with a meaningful incentive should be set up which involved a 'contract'. This was drawn up in negotiation with Anu and agreed to by the head of year and Anu's father.

As part of the preparation for the meeting with the educational psychologist, Anu's teachers had completed a behaviour profile. Their main areas of concern were her incapability to organise herself independently, her lack of motivation, and her inability to concentrate. Their comments included 'does not complete tasks', 'is distractable' and 'unable to sustain attention'. With Anu's help objectives were drawn up which phrased each concern as a target. Examples are:

- I completed an appropriate amount of work in the lesson (this was left open to allow Anu to negotiate the critera and conditions with each teacher);
- I was quiet while the teacher was talking;
- I concentrated on task for a block of ten minutes during the lesson.

Teachers ticked the targets at the end of the lesson if they considered they had been achieved. Anu also had a copy of the targets and rated herself after each lesson, and she and a teaching assistant discussed the records at the end of each day and considered any discrepancies between the two sets.

It was agreed in the initial meeting that Anu's 'reward' for good behaviour should be time on the Internet, something she was very keen on and did not have access to at home. 'Surfing the Net' was built into lesson plans for her on a Friday afternoon and took place in the school library. The time allowed was calculated using the ticks on her record, each tick representing 30 seconds of computer time.

In the first week of the 'contract', Anu earned 11 minutes on the internet; in the second, seven (which she regarded as not worth going to the library for); the third week, 22; and the fourth week, 27. The reward seemed to be working but it was not long before targets and the timing of the reward had to be renegotiated, and eventually the need for a formal contract and any method of recording was not necessary. In this case, Anu's dislike of some subjects was not tackled 'head on' and it was expected that the effect of rewarding her behaviour would be short-lived. It was not, and although she was always considered by many of her teachers to be a 'challenge' throughout her schooling, her relationship with them improved and her behaviour was usually within acceptable limits.

The tangible rewards mentioned above and those of social approval are extrinsic rewards, but rewards can be self-managed and self-generated (intrinsic rewards) and are pursued for the inherent satisfaction they provide (reading a book or writing a poem, for example). Intrinsic rewards are internally driven, and the learner is active in the choice.

In classic behaviourist theory, however, the learner was regarded as passive and responsive only to external forces, and the observations above, about intrinsic rewards and internal drives, would not have been regarded as valid. Moreover, we can see that it might be difficult to attribute the potential for autonomy or self-direction within such a view of learning. Learning theory was developed in order to generate a scientific theory of learning, albeit one which assumed an incremental, vertical progression, through the discovery of laws which could explain the conditions under which learning, or a stable change in behaviour, was achieved. In this way, psychologists anticipated it would be possible to exercise control over what learners learned, how quickly they learned and how much of their learning was retained.

As learning theory developed, psychologists such as Bandura took more account of the meaning of behaviour for the individual carrying it out. Keenan (2002) points out that Bandura's most recent reinterpretation of his own work emphasises the role of self-efficacy (as in the example of Anu). Bandura believes that we acquire our tendencies to persevere, and thus enhance learning and competence, through observing key individuals whom we treat as models. Observing a positive role model who does not give up easily will lead to the adoption of similar attitudes. Conversely, a negative model will induce intolerance or frustration and a weak sense of self-efficacy.

It is against this background that we consider approaches to teaching that exemplify learning theory principles. Learning theory is often regarded as contributing to the elimination of undesirable behaviour through 'time out' for rewards and punishment, and these aspects are considered in Chapter 4. It is often overlooked that learning theory has also been responsible for the development of specific techniques used in building up new skills.

The recognition that complex patterns of behaviour can be established by reference to learning theory principles is reflected in pedagogic practices that, in many cases, involve children with learning difficulties. For example, self-help skills can be taught by breaking the target behaviour into operants and rewarding each one, gradually shaping them into a skill or joining several skills together, again by manipulating the reinforcing conditions. The four most obvious techniques, often used unconsciously by adults to teach new skills in all situations, are: prompting; shaping; modelling and chaining. Let us briefly consider each in turn.

Prompting

Verbal prompting, such as giving instructions, is the most usual way for adults to guide or teach normally developing children above the age of two. Consider how a teacher might 'talk through' with three-year-olds how they should put on their shoes: 'First, straighten your sock on your foot. Good! Now put your foot in your shoe. That's right. Put your heel down. Good. Now bring the strap across and fasten the Velcro. Well done, Aaron.'

For younger children, and older ones who are at early stages of development, physical prompts (where movements are guided by an adult) or gestural prompts (such as pointing or beckoning) may be effective aids to teaching new skills. Martin and Pear (1984) are amongst the many authors who recognised the importance of another form of prompting: that of environmental prompting, where the environment is altered to encourage the learning of, or repetition of, a skill.

Kirsty

Kirsty, who has a profound hearing loss, is the only child in a mainstream class whose special educational needs have been identified. She is finding great difficulty in coping with her hearing aids (which would give her some sound) and has not yet mastered a basic signing or symbol system. As a consequence of her hearing loss, her language skills are extremely limited and she engages in a worrying amount of solitary play (she will, however, play with other children when encouraged). In addition, her fine motor skills are poorly developed in comparison with her normally developing peers. She seems 'clumsy' and, for example, although she is almost four years old she has difficulty with fine motor activities and finds it difficult to build a tower of more than two bricks. The nursery staff try to encourage her to mix more, and to practise and rehearse the motor skills that she is acquiring through informal play with other children.

There are plenty of opportunities throughout the day for children to play together, but Kirsty's lack of hearing means, on the one hand, that she prefers to play alone, and, on the other, that she is not aware of what is expected of her. In order to facilitate her learning, the staff alter the environment (and to some extent the timetable) to provide her with clues which will allow her to build on existing skills. The room is divided into four areas and each area is colour coded. Two areas (blue and green) contain toys and activities that encourage co-operative learning, and those in the green area are particularly suited to the development of fine motor skills. The red and yellow areas contain toys and activities that young children can use either collaboratively or independently. Each child is issued with coloured disks at specific times in the day that indicate the area in which they should work/play for a specified length of time. In addition, some younger children, and Kirsty, are given a specific symbol relating to a particular activity that will either encourage the consolidation of an emerging skill or the development of a new one. In Kirsty's case, the activity is one that encourages fine motor skills. It is hoped that such environmental prompts will strengthen her emerging co-operative skills and help to establish specific fine motor skills.

In this case, not only was the environment altered to facilitate learning, but the prompt was used as an 'object of reference' to cue Kirsty into the event or experience that was happening next. In terms of the Framework for New Learning, Kirsty is moving from 'encountering' experiences to becoming 'aware' of them with the help of the staff. In addition, the staff chose to use the symbols as objects of reference in the hope that she will be encouraged to show an interest in an alternative means of communication.

Objects of reference are often used in a variety of ways with children with complex needs and those who are deaf and blind, including the introduction of tactile symbols, activity boxes, anticipation shelves, calendar systems and timetables. Taken further, these form part of 'reference books' that give pupils clues about the immediate future, the past and the present and allow them the opportunity of a 'history' (Janssen, 2002). This is not to say that objects of reference are used solely to categorise learning experiences and belong exclusively to learning theory. They do not and, as is evidenced in part of the example above, the emphasis is on their use as a cognitive approach to conversation and communication (Janssen, 2001; Van den Tillaart, 2001). Nevertheless, at their most basic, objects of reference do provide environmental clues to learning, in line with the behaviourist technique of prompting.

Shaping

Shaping is the moulding of a simple behaviour into a more complex one. Initially, the behaviour that is as similar as possible to the target behaviour is reinforced and, subsequently, rewards are given for closer and closer approximations. In Chapter 8, we give the example of Ian who was being taught, by moulding one of his existing behaviours (the production of a sound), to create a recognisable word. The reasons for using this approach to teaching are given in the chapter and will not be discussed here, but it is important to state that the emphasis was on providing Ian with a way to articulate a need when he lost a particular object. The second part of the example is given here in order to illustrate the technique of shaping.

Ian

Ian can make a number of sounds: mainly those connected with comfort ('bbb' or 'ba') or those connected with discomfort ('mmm' or 'mu'). Despite his other sensory difficulties, he has some hearing and will turn towards a sound, and he sometimes brings together units of sound: 'mummut' (possibly meaning 'Mummy'). In addition, he occasionally imitates basic sounds, and will 'work' for a reward (an energetic tickle). Building on his existing skills and using the behavioural technique of shaping, he was encouraged to imitate sounds that can be understood by others to mean 'boat'. At first, any approximations to the required sounds were immediately rewarded (by a tickle). As he began to learn what was expected in order to get a tickle, only more accurate approximations were rewarded. After a few weeks Ian's utterances had been 'shaped' to sound like 'buut'. He was then encouraged to produce these sounds immediately he lost his boat. Some years later Ian is still using this utterance appropriately.

Shaping is rarely used to teach communication skills unless, as in the case of Ian, there is a specific reason to do so. It is, however, often used to teach physical skills, such as agility or ball skills.

Modelling

Bandura (1986) maintains that much of our learning depends on imitating others' behaviours and, certainly, in the teaching of new skills it is likely that the adult will model the required behaviour and the child will attempt to copy or imitate it.

Teaching knitting

The son and daughter of one of the authors were both taught to knit by imitating their mother carrying out the task. She also used verbal prompts (such as 'push the needle through', 'wind the wool around') and plenty of social reinforcement ('well done', 'great') in order to ensure that the skills involved were learned. As each child became more experienced and confident, reinforcement became intrinsic, and one at least began to knit for pleasure and leisure. Some 20 years later both are proficient knitters, and regularly practise their skills.

Chaining

An apparently simple task may be too difficult to learn unless broken down into smaller steps; each step connecting with another. Such a process, called 'chaining', enables a highly complex skill to be learned. In teaching knitting to the author's children, forward chaining was used. The children learned, initially through imitation, to carry out a number of steps:

1   pushing the needle into the stitch;
2   winding the wool around the needle;
3   taking the new stitch off the needle.

In this case the first step of the sequence was taught (forward chaining) but, in the learning of some skills, it is often more appropriate for the last step to be taught first: a process known as backward chaining.

> **Jack**
>
> Jack is nine years old and has complex needs, including severe physical disabilities. He has learned to grasp objects placed in his hands using a palmar grip, but he has little interest in using this skill to feed himself, as he has learned that adults will do it for him. He does, however, enjoy pureed food and the staff of the school are teaching him the last step in a chain that will lead to independent feeding: of moving the spoon a small distance to his mouth. The spoon is loaded for him and physical prompts (guided movements) are used to position his arm, and the spoon, a few centimetres away from his mouth. He is then verbally encouraged to complete the last step alone. His independent action triggers his most powerful reward: the food itself. As he masters this final step, the penultimate one in the chain will be added, and so on, until he has achieved the overall target.

One of the criticisms levelled at behavioural techniques is that of 'learned helplessness'. In the above example, Jack had initially come to expect that adults would provide for his every need. He had no expectation of doing anything for himself; a situation that was assumed by his caregivers and he *learned* to rely on them totally. As he began to learn the last steps in the chain of skills for feeding himself, it was easy for his caregivers to calculate the right support at any one step as too little would make him avoid what to him was a very challenging task. If not used sensitively, a technique designed to provide a successful learning experience could erode his fragile sense of his own ability, and confirm for him that 'helplessness is the easiest option'.

The techniques of chaining lend themselves to systematic task analyses: recording and agreeing the schedules of reinforcement in order that all teaching and care staff can achieve the consistency of approach that is crucial to success.

Another criticism of the use of behavioural techniques for teaching new skills is that specific skills taught in one context are not generalised in other contexts. As Farrell (1997) points out, a major concern about the way in which behavioural methods have been applied is that skills are sometimes taught in 'laboratory type' conditions. A quiet room or one-to-one area was often considered an appropriate place to enable a pupil to concentrate on the acquisition of a specific skill. Neither area, however, is appropriate to teach a child how to put on her or his coat first thing in the morning, a number of hours before it is time for outside play. Clearly, skills need be taught in context (Farrell, 1997).

Learning theory and empowerment

There is no doubt that the work of the learning theorists has contributed greatly to the acquisition of new skills, and the elimination of undesirable behaviour by the identification of specific techniques. Such techniques are so successful and straightforward that they are embedded unconsciously into everyday interactions, particularly when those interactions involve adults and children. It would be unusual for any parent or teacher in Western societies *not* to demonstrate a particular skill, to give verbal instructions or to give appropriate rewards. At the basic level of acquiring new learning, the theorists have much to offer. Initially, however, such learning is likely to be under external control and therefore it is difficult to see what learning theory can offer to explain choice and decision-making, for example, or its relevance to empowerment. After all, in its classic form, learning theory dismisses the notion of free will as irrelevant because, according to this perspective, external forces alone shape what we learn and how we act and so determine the course of our lives. Even if the extreme or classic version of learning theory is no longer tenable, however, there is ample evidence that the principles of learning theory can be applied, especially at the acquisition stage of learning, where people need maximum help. As the skill is practised and people become more competent, fewer resources are used so that they can begin to exercise choice and decision-making. Haring, Liberty and White (1981) identified a hierarchy of learning in behavioural terms that involved:

*   acquisition
*   fluency
*   maintenance
*   mastery.

In Chapter 1 we presented the Framework for New Learning on which all learning is based. Although it attempted to encapsulate the process of very early learning, in a theoretical way its final band 'Gaining skills' offers an additional perspective on the hierarchical approach devised by Haring, Liberty and White. In relation to this level of the acquisition of new learning, it is difficult to uphold a purely learning theory approach because both the hierarchy offered in Chapter 1 and that proposed by Haring, Liberty and White suggest active reflection, by the learner, on the process of learning. Knowing *what to do* provides the opportunity for thinking about *how to do it*. In other words, the earlier stages of the hierarchy of learning become the basis for the development of thinking skills, high-level cognitive processes also known as metacognition (see Chapter 9).

In raising considerations of metacognition and thinking skills in general, we have moved away from a learning theory perspective and have begun to identify issues that are emphasised in contemporary views of learning. These will be examined more closely in later chapters. Meanwhile, having discussed the considerable strengths of learning theory principles as demonstrated in approaches to teaching people with special educational needs, it is important to summarise the main criticisms, specifically those identified by Farrell (1997), some of which are:

- the pupil is denied the chance to take an active part in learning;
- behavioural approaches rely too heavily on extrinsic rewards; teaching is undertaken out of context;
- the emphasis is on learning rather than on understanding.

In counteracting the criticisms, Farrell emphasises the importance of the interaction between the 'teacher' and the 'learner'. He stresses the need for the 'teacher' to be a *facilitator* and *enabler* (very different roles to that of 'a controller') and is keen to point out that although the principles of learning theory can be forceful in their own right, they can also be effective when used alongside the work of cognitive theorists.

In fact in much of our teaching we automatically use a combination of approaches that stem from the learning theorists and those which stem from the work of the cognitive theorists. The work of Nind and Hewett (1994) and Hewett and Nind (1998) on developing the basis of communication with people with severe learning difficulties through what they term 'Intensive Interaction' is a case in point. Their work centres on people with learning difficulties who are pre-verbal and it encourages communication and ultimately autonomy and self-advocacy.

The approach is fundamentally concerned with the teacher or caregiver replying to the pupil's signals as if they had communicative significance. In order to do this they contingently respond to the behaviour of the person in *gaming ways* that encourage more interaction. Techniques such as imitation (from learning theory) and turn-taking (from cognitive psychology) are used and 'sensitively adjusted according to the infant's growing repertoire of skills and knowledge' (Nind and Hewett, 1994, p.27). The importance of removing 'scaffolding' (Bruner, 1983) is stressed as the pupil becomes more competent and requires less support (see Chapter 8). The following example shows how the teacher uses a combination of approaches in an 'Intensive Interaction' exchange.

Winston

Winston is nine and has complex learning difficulties. As he is often remote and appears not to be interested in people, it is thought that he may also be autistic, but no clear diagnosis has been made. He has no recognisable communication and will only tolerate adults close to him for a short period. The staff seize every opportunity to respond contingently with him and in this session of 'Intensive Interaction' he and his class teacher are positioned close together, face-to-face, on soft play equipment. Winston appears to like the feel of the equipment and is most relaxed when using it. He makes a movement with his hand which his teacher, Mr Herbert, imitates and their hands touch; the importance of physical contact is one of the features of the approach (see Nind and Hewett, 1994, p.27). The hand movements become part of a brief turn-taking game and at the same time Winston makes some movements with his lips, which again his teacher imitates. After a few seconds Winston makes a sound when their hands touch, which Mr Herbert immediately imitates. The sound-making also becomes a turn-taking game that ends when Winston brings his head forward at an angle almost touching the mouth of the teacher. The teacher blows a stream of warm air on to Winston's cheek. Winston 'stills' and then smiles, makes eye contact, and brings his cheek near again obviously asking for this part of the 'game' to be repeated. The teacher holds back and Winston appears startled. He makes an 'aah' sound, possibly in annoyance that the teacher has not responded in what he regards as 'the right way'. The teacher repeats the sound plus two others that Winston can make, and when the boy brings his cheek forward again blows warm air on to it. A more sophisticated turn-taking game emerges where sounds are imitated and rewarded. This latter part of the activity lasts for no more than a minute, when Winston gets up and wanders off.

Winston's exchanges have been used (with mixed approaches) to foster a positive working relationship between the teacher and the pupil. Elements such as sharing a space, achievement of eye contact, turn-taking and giving and receiving are first steps in the quest for self-advocacy. The techniques used may not be in line with classical learning theory, but some aspects certainly have a behavioural structure which, if used appropriately, are important elements in the process of empowerment.

References

Bandura, A. (1986) *Social Foundations of Thought and Action. A Social Cognitive Theory*. Englewood Cliffs, NJ: Prentice Hall.

Bruner, J. (1983) *Child's Talk: Learning to Use Language*. New York: Oxford University Press.

Farrell, P. (1997) *Teaching Pupils with Learning Difficulties: Strategies and Solutions*. London: Cassell.

Haring, N.G., Liberty, K.A. and White, O.R. (1981) *An Investigation of Phases of Learning and Facilitating Instructional Events for the Severely/Profoundly Handicapped* (Final Report). Seattle: University of Washington College of Education.

Hewett, D. and Nind, M. (1998) *Interaction in Action*. London: David Fulton Publishers.

Janssen, M. (2001) 'Enhancing the quality of interaction'. Fifth European Conference on Deafblind, Noordwijkerhout. Sint-Michielgestel: Instituut voor Doven/Mgr. Terwindtstichting.

Janssen, M. (2002) 'Objects of reference: Objects of conversation'. National Conference on Objects of Reference. Birmingham: University of Birmingham, June 2002.

Keenan, T. (2002) *An Introduction to Child Development*. London: Sage Publications.

Martin, G. and Pear, J. (1984) *Behaviour Modification: What it Is and How to Do it* (2nd edition). New York: Prentice Hall.

Nind, M. and Hewett, D. (1994) *Access to Communication*. London: David Fulton Publishers.

Van den Tillaart, B. (2001) 'Model-based support to improve quality of interaction'. Fifth European Conference on Deafblind, Noordwijkerhout. Sint-Michielgestel: Instituut voor Doven/Mgr. Terwindtstichting.

Part 3

Areas of development

Chapter 8

Communication and interaction

Emile Durkheim (1897), one of the founding fathers of sociology as a discipline, observed that most human characteristics (behaviours and modes of thought) are acquired and practised in social settings. Thus social interaction, and interpersonal communication on which it is predicated, underpins both individual development and the advancement of society. Education has a significant role in the development of the individual and in relation to the wider society, especially, we argue, in creating the circumstances for empowering the individual to assume an active role. It is, therefore, crucial that those who work with children and adults with significant learning needs understand the skills and processes involved in communication and the potential impact on development when communication is compromised.

In providing a framework for thinking about communication and people with learning disabilities, Goldbart (2002) identified four paradigms that she adapted from Burton and Sanderson (1998). Each outlines a different view of learning disability, which, she argues, has implications for intervention aimed at enhancing communication. Briefly, the four models involve the following approaches:

- normalisation;
- functional;
- behavioural;
- developmental.

In our view the four approaches can, between them, offer a positive and productive way of capturing both our aspirations for pupils with severe and complex learning needs and the reality of supporting these pupils to communicate more effectively. Accordingly, we have used Goldbart's framework to formulate our own model which guides the structure and emphases of the present chapter. Specifically, we subscribe to the view that in stressing normalisation, the empowerment of individuals is paramount and we emphasise that the diversity of learning needs must ultimately be recognised by the wider community. In citing a functional approach, we support the need to make interventions relevant to pupils and other learners. The effectiveness of behavioural approaches is acknowledged, discussed and analysed. Finally, we take a developmental approach when we draw on the views of our chosen theorists to explore what is established about typical social and cognitive development and how this knowledge extends our understanding of the processes that underpin communication involving pupils with learning needs.

What is communication?

It is possible to regard communication in a broad sense and to consider examples involving the transmission of information through mechanical means such as traffic lights. We have chosen, however, to emphasise interpersonal communication and to interpret it as joint activity focused on the construction, negotiation or sharing of meaning. Importantly for human beings, it includes language. Communication is achieved when, for example, individual B understands the meaning that A intends B to understand. This presupposes the following:

- A has a reason, a 'meaning', to communicate;
- A understands the aim of communication;
- A has the will or wants to communicate;
- A has communication skills, and the relevant knowledge and understanding of communication;
- B understands the aim of communication;
- B shares modes of communication with A.

Developing communication

When thinking about development we are usually tempted to ask at what age some specified ability or behaviour emerges. In relation to communication, this question may be meaningless because, as argued above, communication is essentially an activity that involves at least two people. According to this view, communication starts directly after birth, when a mother greets her newborn infant for the first time. Nonetheless, it is appropriate to investigate the extent to which the baby already possesses abilities and tendencies that favour and sustain social interaction.

Messer (1994) has reviewed the evidence for an innate, or inborn, disposition for social interaction and has concluded that, by approximately 3 months of age, infants have a firm preference for people's faces over other visual stimuli and are attracted to watch people's movements in preference to non-human activity. The evidence also suggests that this orientation may have either developed *in utero* or is genetically acquired. In either case, as far as researchers can tell, it is present at birth. Similarly, very young infants have been shown to respond more readily to the modified speech that adults employ for talking to children – 'motherese' (see Crystal, 1997, for a brief review of the use of the term) – than to adult-to-adult speech. In summary, the research evidence persuades us that, typically, babies are either innately prepared for social interaction or they are able to demonstrate social responsiveness very shortly after birth.

Early interaction

Although it seems that babies are well prepared for social interaction, they are obviously not endowed with the skills, knowledge or understanding to communicate in the way suggested by the interpretation of communication offered earlier. Certainly, they will not intentionally initiate communication. All the same, their social responsiveness appears to influence others (specifically their caregivers) who, as experienced communicators, adjust their communication strategies and styles in order to elicit responses. Studies of these early exchanges demonstrate the timing, rhythm and repetition of the behaviours of both participants in typical exchanges between an infant and his or her mother (or principal caregiver). In the earliest months, the baby's mother treats almost any of her child's behaviours during these routines as potentially communicative and synchronises her own contributions with those of the child. In this way, these early dyadic (two-person) encounters show many of the features of a dialogue, particularly the phasing of eye-contact to signal turn-taking, and the maintenance of mutual gaze (joint action) to identify the object of joint attention. Bruner (1983) emphasised the role of intersubjectivity in the development of social interaction, with primary intersubjectivity a feature of the first year, developing into secondary intersubjectivity when the two conversation partners focus their joint attention on some feature beyond themselves. However, the early 'conversations' are more correctly pseudo-dialogues (Schaffer, 1977) because the adult, as the competent partner, takes responsibility for sustaining them. Nevertheless, a key aspect is the evident pleasure that infant and caregiver share. Enjoyment, we may assume, provides reinforcement for both partners to return to the same conversation time after time, but in attributing a major role to the adult partner it becomes important to review the demands on that partner when the child is not developing typically in certain respects.

Early communication and children with special needs

It is obvious from what is known about the format of early 'conversations' that, for development to proceed along typical lines, sight and hearing must be functioning normally. When children have impairments that affect either modality, the usual patterns of interaction as described above do not always appear. For example, Lewis (1987), describing the behaviour of infants who are born blind, draws attention to the tendency for them to appear less communicative than sighted babies. She explains that babies who cannot see, 'still' in response to sound and direct their faces towards the source of the sound even if this means turning away from the parent or caregiver. They are less likely, in these circumstances, to initiate any vocal exchange. Parents may interpret such responses as a rejection of their communicative efforts, particularly when they are trying to engage the baby in order to talk about the sound. Lewis also reports that parents tend to talk less to babies who are blind than to infants with normal sight, possibly because the range of conversation topics is narrower when objects in the environment cannot be pointed out. This observation has led professionals to make recommendations about the early support of parents when visual impairment in infants is confirmed, in order that appropriate communication skills might be fostered in what could be, for the parents, a challenging situation (McLinden, personal communication).

   Although it might be tempting to assume that deaf babies are at greater risk than infants with severe visual impairment of failing to develop communication skills, this is not necessarily the case. As we describe elsewhere, deaf babies demonstrate extraordinary persistence in their communication attempts but, as far as developing useful communication skills is concerned, there may be an advantage for deaf babies if they have deaf parents. For example, deaf parents using sign language are well placed to teach it to their infants and Hodapp (1998) describes how such a specialised application of intuitive parenting includes modified sign-language that is equivalent to motherese.

   As explained in Chapter 5, interventions to promote social relationships and the behaviours that sustain them when children have severe difficulties in this area take the format of naturally occurring exchanges and extend their learning opportunities, as in Intensive Interaction (Nind and Hewett, 1994). Specifically, during Intensive Interaction, caregivers and teachers echo back, to the child or adult, their spontaneously produced vocalisations and other behaviours that could have a communicative function, much as parents do with young babies. However, for children with profound and multiple learning difficulties there is a need to be selective about the behaviours that are copied, choosing those that appear to have some meaning for the child. The teacher's objective in copying them is to promote an understanding that the meaning behind the behaviour can be shared.

> **Sally**
>
> Sally, a pupil with complex needs, is said to be at an early stage of developing intentional communication and is increasing her skills in expressing her needs and preferences.
>
> In a one-to-one teaching session her teaching assistant is facing Sally who quickly establishes eye contact and begins to smile. The assistant maintains eye contact and smiles back. Sally then makes several 'mmm' and 'aaa' sounds which the assistant imitates. Sally smiles and laughs and a turn-taking game follows in which Sally and the assistant imitate each other. Sally quickly takes the lead and other sounds are made which are reinforced as the assistant copies them. The session lasts for about four minutes and for most of the time Sally holds eye contact, maintains interest, co-operates and appears to find the activity pleasurable.

Intentional communication

As the baby matures the conversation changes and, with the recognition that she or he is becoming more physically, socially and cognitively competent, the adult imputes intentionality more selectively. Issues of intentionality in relation to interpersonal communication come sharply into focus where individuals have disabilities or learning difficulties and Coupe O'Kane and Goldbart (1998) provide a taxonomy for describing a progression towards intentional communication functioning. For example, they identify three levels of pre-intentional behaviour: reflexive, indicating an involuntary response to some internal state or external stimulus; reactive, suggesting a voluntary response; and proactive, the earliest indications of goal-directed behaviour.

Piaget accounts for developments during the sensori-motor period by asserting that motor behaviour that is initially spontaneous and unplanned, gradually becomes goal-directed when associated with positive sensory experience. That is, having accidentally discovered the consequences of certain behaviours during the stage of secondary circular reactions, the baby purposefully initiates the behaviour to achieve desirable goals. This confirms the baby's 'contingency awareness' (an understanding that a certain sensation is contingent upon a specified motor activity), which in turn is linked to her or his increasing ability to co-ordinate physical activity with sensory feedback. Contingency awareness is accompanied by demonstrations that the infant has established rudimentary meanings: for example, she or he will indicate that 'spoon' is 'understood' by showing how one is used. At this point in development, therefore, the baby is co-ordinating schemes that are refined or differentiated versions of primary schemes.

A differentiation of schemes to include the effect of intentional actions on inanimate features of the environment is paralleled by an awareness of goal-directedness or intentionality towards other people. Specifically there is awareness, on the baby's part, that one's own communicative behaviour creates an effect in someone else. This is a primitive notion of causality in relation to other people, providing the child with the opportunity to influence others and to exercise choice.

Yvonne

Yvonne is 16 and is developmentally delayed. She loves to bounce on a beanbag on the trampoline. When the activity ceases, Yvonne 'stills' and her face is sad and serious. On one occasion, Yvonne lifted her hand towards the teacher who immediately began to bounce her again. This occurred several times and now Yvonne uses the gesture to communicate 'more' when she's on the trampoline.

It is debatable, in the case of Yvonne, whether she is aware that her hand movement indicates 'more' to her teacher or that she understands that her action is causing her teacher to repeat the activity. In behaviourist terms, Yvonne has forged an association between the action of raising her hand and the continuation of a rewarding activity. Nonetheless, this chance discovery can be developed for teaching some notion of causality; at the same time, it can become a signal for 'more' in other contexts.

We have seen that the adult's communicative behaviour towards the child has a facilitative effect on the infant's developing social behaviour. In turn, however, adults take their cues about how to engage the infant in interaction from evidence of his or her increasing social and cognitive understanding and we have discussed possible challenges to the usual parenting styles when infants have impairments of sensory, intellectual or physical functioning. Piaget's view of development indicates the cognitive foundations for social interaction, but de-emphasises the role of other people. By way of contrast, as we explained in Chapter 2, Bruner stresses the interplay between biology and culture to account for developmental progression and he addresses the social-cultural aspects quite explicitly, providing a framework for considering the emergence of intentionality (Bruner, 1981). Coupe O'Kane and Goldbart (1998) describe the three elements of Bruner's taxonomy of early intentional communication: initiation for behaviour regulation; initiation for social interaction; and initiation for joint attention. As explained by Coupe O'Kane and Goldbart, where the aim of the encounter is to share a common focus, communicative acts are often directed towards regulating other people's behaviour.

But it is often too easy to assume that children with complex difficulties affecting their ability to communicate will restrict themselves to goal-directed behaviour.

Bel

Bel is a wheelchair user and has very severe learning difficulties. Concerns about possible diabetes were raised because Bel repeatedly indicated her cup (which is distinctive because it is decorated with a 'Barbie-doll' transfer). Support staff interpreted this as a request for drinks and noted the frequency with which this 'request' was made. When the concerns were shared with Bel's mother she was able to enlighten the staff: Bel wasn't asking for a drink, she simply wanted to share her enjoyment of the special cup with other people.

Before leaving the issue of intentional communication, it is important to consider how Vygotsky interpreted this important aspect of human activity. In Chapter 2 we emphasised that Vygotsky located the origins of all development in the social context; according to this view, caregivers assign intention to the infant who, as a consequence, learns that certain activities elicit responses from other people and, therefore, that he or she has powers of communication. For Vygotsky, unlike Piaget or Bruner, social and cognitive development is fundamentally due to the child's internalisation of culturally-given meanings, a view that has important implications, for example, for the deaf children of deaf parents. These parents can be expected to mediate, for their deaf children, a deaf culture that encompasses a different world-view to that held by their peers with hearing parents. For the purposes of planning teaching and learning, the population of children with hearing impairments should not therefore be regarded as homogenous but should be seen as varied and heterogeneous, as with any other group of pupils.

The differing emphases of the theorists, on whom we have chosen to focus, should not be seen as mutually exclusive but as complementary, as each assumes significance in the practical issues of how to promote communication and interaction in educational settings. For example, Affective Communication Assessment (ACA) (Coupe O'Kane and Goldbart, 1998) is a tool for use with people who have complex learning needs, including those needs arising in connection with sensory and physical impairments and whose ability to communicate is very restricted. The authors describe the application of ACA in terms of providing a framework for detailed observation and the recording of both the incidence of closely specified behaviours and the context in which each behavioural element most often arises. Observation and recording provide a baseline for intervention. As the name implies, it is expected that, at the outset, the behaviour of the child (or adult) does not suggest any intention to communicate, but can be reliably interpreted as registering affective states such as likes and dislikes; thus communication is at the level of reflexive behaviour.

Promoting functional communication

At a school for learners with a range of profound and multiple learning difficulties (PMLD), all students with communication needs have 'communication profiles', comprising laminated sheets that either hang on the back of their wheelchairs or walkers or, for those who are fully mobile, are on display in the classroom. These profiles record individual levels of communication skills and techniques for every member of the school staff and more able students to use, throughout the school day, to promote functional communication. The profiles stress the importance of all staff offering students the opportunity to indicate preference, to make choices and thus to be enabled to work towards making their needs and wants known. Post-16 students with PMLD are integrated fully with more able students of the same age with physical disabilities, on one day each week. The more able students have also quickly become aware of the importance of giving students with PMLD options, and of taking their needs and preferences into consideration when the whole group makes decisions about activities and other aspects of shared learning.

It is, therefore, important for teachers, caregivers and indeed any communication partners to treat spontaneously produced affective behaviours as if they are communicative signals and to steadily shape them in the direction of purposeful communication. Coupe O'Kane and Goldbart (1998) describe the approach in some detail and interested readers are directed to their publications for examples of recording sheets. For present purposes, it is sufficient to note the authors' emphasis that caregivers must be sensitive to very subtle changes in behaviour and should be consistent in their own responses in order to establish those behaviours as routine. In this respect, we can see that, although Bruner's model for explaining the development of communication skills provides a framework for ACA at one level, the principles of learning theory are also reflected in the notion of shaping purposeful communication out of reflex behaviour. In drawing attention to conditioning as the basis of learning in the ACA context, it is appropriate to point out that a major weakness of such learning may be that the behaviour acquired in one context does not necessarily transfer to other contexts.

Leanne

Leanne is 17 and has severe and complex difficulties in learning. Although she has no apparent hearing or visual impairment, she has scoliosis (curvature of the spine) and very limited mobility, and needs to use a wheelchair. Leanne is at the early stages of intentional communication. By sensitive and skilled monitoring of her limited behaviours, staff at the school are confident that they can interpret her attempts at communication. Specifically, they have noticed and responded to her attempts at 'eye-pointing', that is, visual fixation on people or objects. Her teachers therefore claim to know that she wants a cup of tea when she eye-points the kettle, the tea-mugs and then members of staff. In the same way she signals her desire to have her jewellery box by eye-pointing (in the presence of a teacher) the tray containing the box and the table in front of her. Leanne is also on a toileting programme and on several occasions she has made eye contact with a member of staff, vocalised and looked at the door, signals that have been interpreted as a desire to be taken to the bathroom.

Leanne has lived with her foster mother, Marie, for two years. In a recent discussion with Leanne's teachers, Marie expressed a wish to be able to communicate better with her foster daughter and, in particular, her desire to understand Leanne's needs and wishes. When staff reported that they felt that they were able to understand some of Leanne's needs and described her communication attempts through eye-pointing, Marie was very surprised: she hadn't noticed this visual behaviour and therefore was not primed to explore its significance and value.

The development of language

So far we have concentrated on communication that does not, in terms of the developing child, involve producing words. To some extent this is because, developmentally speaking, non-verbal communication precedes spoken language. Additionally, of course, it features importantly and routinely in all human interaction but, finally, it has particular interest in the present context because, as we have shown, it can become the focus for intervention for some groups of learners.

We may assume that, in the normal course of development, children are relatively sophisticated communicators by the time they utter their first words. To describe typical development and clarify what components develop, the subject of language can be divided in many different ways. For the purposes of this book, development in the following areas is seen as significant:

- *Phonology* refers to the speech-sound systems of individual languages.
- *Semantics* is the linguistic term for meaning negotiated through words and utterances. In studying semantics, linguists also consider the way in which words are chosen and utterances structured. The construction of meaning is discussed in greater detail in Chapter 9.
- *Grammar* is concerned with the way words are modified and combined to signal different meanings. Thus, 'morphology' refers to the use of morphemes or the smallest units of meaning in language; 'syntax', to the rules governing how speakers order words to change meaning.
- *Use* has two dimensions in relation to communication: function and context. The 'function' of communication refers to the reasons why individuals communicate and the 'context' to how individuals choose a particular form for achieving the goal. 'Pragmatics' is the term to describe this aspect of language but it can also refer to the non-verbal aspects of language.

Building up a vocabulary

We focus on the building of a vocabulary in order to return to the notion of a developmental progression. Phonology is concerned with the system of sounds that make up a person's native language. Although the range of possible speech sounds is immense, any one language makes use of relatively few and it is the task of the developing speaker to acquire an understanding of the combinations and patterns of sounds that signal differences in meaning in the language that surrounds her or him. Typical patterns in the development of speech, from early reflexive sounds such as crying and fussing through to the production of conventional words, are charted in developmental schedules, such as those by Stark (1986). These also acknowledge the significance of variations in pitch and stress in conveying meaning.

Phonological development is supported by the child's increasing control over speech mechanisms, but it also depends on interaction with a community of native language-users. There is ample evidence that, around the age of eight months, the language that he or she is hearing influences the child's babbling. For example, it is around this age that the vocalisations of infants with normal hearing start to differ from those of congenitally deaf babies. Feedback seems to be important in maintaining babbling at this stage and, lacking such feedback, deaf babies start to use pointing and to devise their own manual signs.

At this stage, it is appropriate to consider how infants acquire their receptive and expressive vocabularies. Clearly, these are culture-specific and therefore must somehow be learned. Skinner and others, adopting a behaviourist approach, emphasise the part played by reward in establishing verbal behaviour (Skinner, 1957). We can imagine how this might work, in a very simplistic form: a baby sees a biscuit, points to it and articulates a word that sounds like 'biscuit'. He or she is then given the biscuit. This provides the reinforcement to retain that set of behaviours for future use. In other words, language performance is explained by reference to the progressive reinforcement of learned responses to stereotypical environmental events.

The behaviourist perspective with its focus on steadily rewarding approximations towards conventional words has informed approaches with individuals who have limited spoken language.

Ian

Ian, the pupil already discussed in Chapter 7, is eight years old and has complex learning difficulties, including some visual impairment. He has a favourite toy (a colourful plastic boat) that he sucks, bangs and holds in one hand. Because of poor eyesight and limited mobility he often misplaces it and becomes upset when he cannot find it. His parents and the staff who teach him everyday understood that his screams and head banging probably meant that he had lost his boat, but he also used these extreme behaviours to indicate other needs, and members of staff not working closely with him had trouble in interpreting them. Ian's epilepsy often means admittance to hospital where the nursing staff find great difficulty in knowing what he wants. It was decided, therefore, to teach him to provide a more positive response when he lost his boat, a response which could easily be understood by other people.

As shown in Chapter 7 he can make a number of sounds and it has proved possible to build on his existing skills by using the behavioural technique of shaping. He was encouraged to imitate sounds which could be understood by others to mean 'boat' (the syllables presented by the teacher sounded like 'buut', but the utterance could easily be understood) and any resemblance to the target sound was immediately rewarded. Later, only the more accurate approximations were accepted and he was encouraged to use these sounds whenever he lost his boat.

However, it has been argued that many aspects of language cannot be learned in this way. Noam Chomsky (1965), in particular, vigorously opposed Skinner's view, saying that the samples of speech which surround children are inadequate as models. Under normal circumstances, people do not speak in perfectly constructed, grammatically formed sentences yet most children become competent speakers. He also asserted that the key characteristic of language is its infinite variability which means that most utterances are unique and therefore cannot have been copied. Chomsky proposed, instead, that humans are biologically disposed to develop language and are endowed with a language acquisition device (LAD) that is, in structural-functional terms, separate from other cognitive processes, thus contrasting with Piaget's view that language development is a part only of general cognitive growth. The LAD is, according to Chomsky, a processing system that enables the developing speaker-hearer to extract from samples of speech certain regularities or grammatical rules via access to a universal grammar. The universal grammar is 'hard-wired' in the language centres and it somehow characterises the fundamental aspects of all languages. Views on innate linguistic capacities have recently been elaborated and interested readers are referred to Dockrell and Messer (1999) for an overview.

Bruner's theory about the origins of language reflects his commitment to a social inter-actionist view of development. While acknowledging the existence of a powerful biological drive for processing and producing language, he attributes an important role to the strategies that parents provide as well as other mechanisms that promote language use in the child's cultural environment. Bruner coined a collective term for the mechanisms, somewhat tongue-in-cheek in view of the acronym coined by Chomsky: a language acquisition support system (LASS), in 1983. In summarising the views of Chomsky and Bruner, it is important to note that both would oppose the view that language is steadily built up from the reinforcement of single words or phrases, as learning theory would suggest. Instead, there is, in both theories, a clear indication that the child processes corpora (more commonly, chunks) of spoken language to deduce single words; a view with which most language specialists today would concur. More important, however, than the acquisition of single words, the child acquires language along with a social identity.

Moving on from single words

Once the child is producing single conventional words, or close approximations to them, she or he is able to signify meaning with some degree of sophistication. This brings indications of developments in the child's use of spoken language, particularly her or his capacity for regulating interactions with other people. For example, holophrastic speech, in which a single word uttered with varying inflections can convey a variety of meanings, opens up new communication horizons. Parents or principal caregivers are now better able to attribute meaning to their babies' utterances, but it is evident that meaning is still heavily dependent, for interpretation, on the context with which both adult and child are familiar.

It is widely observed that some children with Down syndrome do not progress beyond the 'one-word' stage of language development, although it must be added that 'one word' covers phrases that actually comprise more than one word. In these cases, the salient point is that the phrases are learnt and produced as one item. Dockrell and Messer (1999) review the research into language competence in this group of learners, which interestingly reveals that their speech comprehension exceeds what might be predicted on the basis of language production. According to Dockrell and Messer there are a number of likely explanations for this phenomenon. For example, one element of the syndrome is the difficulty that such children have with speech articulation because of a disproportionately large tongue. The more competent conversation partner may respond to poor articulation and slow responses, from a child with Down syndrome, by reducing their expectations of what the children can say and answering for them. As a result, conversations are often initiated and dominated by the other speaker and the child is not encouraged to produce long or structurally complex utterances in order to elaborate topics of her or his own choosing. The clear message for teachers and caregivers is to allow more time for any child with expressive language difficulties to plan and produce speech and to investigate, in conjunction with language specialists, how to support language production.

Evidence that young children are attempting to assemble a rule-based system for understanding and generating language comes when they have been producing words for some time and have been combining them into two- and three-word utterances. In addition to 'prosody' – that is, the variations in pitch and stress that help to convey meaning and are crucial in holophrastic speech – utterances involving more than one word require the application of grammar and syntax for meaning to emerge. That is, the speaker needs to know and use the rules linking structure and meaning. Consider the following exchange in which Rory, aged three, is looking at the brand-name label in a pyjama jacket:

Rory (pointing):	What that says?
Adult:	It says 'St Michael'.
Rory (wide-eyed):	St Michael weared those jamas?

From this example, it seems that Rory's understanding of syntax, or the way in which the word order helps to carry meaning, is not fully developed, specifically in relation to questions. All the same, the adult understands what Rory means and responds appropriately. Rory then generates a new word, 'weared', in place of the conventional form, 'wore'. This confirms that he has abstracted, from the language that surrounds him, a rule that says: to put a verb into the past tense you add the morpheme '-ed'. It is unlikely that Rory copied 'weared' from another speaker. It is for reasons such as this that linguists reject the behaviourist view as a complete explanation of how language is acquired.

Semantic-pragmatic developments

Although it is interesting and enlightening to examine each aspect of language development separately, space does not allow for attention to such detail here. In Chapter 9 we look at how meaning and thought emerge in relation to language use, but now we revisit the emergence of intentional communication to consider how the pragmatic aspects of spoken language develop, referring to *The Pragmatics Profile of Everyday Communication Skills* (Dewart and Summers, 1995).

Tools such as the Pragmatics Profile provide a schedule based on the notion of a 'normal' developmental pathway, against which the skills of children whose development is causing concern can be assessed. Other developmental schedules (for example, Sheridan, 1997) provide a descriptive overview of typical development in all areas. These screening devices are used as a preliminary step when some deviation from the norm is suspected and they identify where more detailed examination is required. In relation to language use, the Pragmatics Profile identifies communication intentions, response to communication and interaction/conversation. Within each of the three areas, the progression from birth to mature levels is charted, describing typical communicative behaviour associated with developmental 'milestones' along the way. Readers are directed to the Pragmatics Profile for details, but we will be using its broad framework to discuss and compare the pragmatic skills of learners who have difficulties in communicating.

The correlates of semantic-pragmatic development

Piaget's theories about development suggest that the child first establishes certain conceptual distinctions, to be reflected later in spoken language. These include self-awareness or the understanding that 'I' am a person whose identity is distinct and separate from that of other people and who can initiate activity voluntarily and, therefore, exercise personal autonomy. Conversely, things and people separate from the self share with the self a common space, with each having a spatial relationship to the other. Further discoveries about the world include the notion of causality and the role of people (self and others) in causing events and changes. Finally, in using objects to stand for other things or ideas, the child demonstrates the capacity for symbolic thinking which is essential to the use of language for constructing and communicating meaning.

Bruner, of course, considers the centrality of symbolic thinking in establishing effective language, and we have outlined his views in Chapter 2. This aspect of language use has special significance for the development of cognition and learning and therefore is discussed again in Chapter 9. In the meantime, reflect again on the example of Sally, aged 10, and her teaching assistant in the early part of this chapter. The turn-taking game described is part of an 'Intensive Interaction' session and we can speculate about the emergence of several features of language use, linking them to theoretical frameworks.

What does the exchange reveal about Sally's language and communication abilities and her knowledge of her environment? As she smiles and laughs when her assistant imitates her sounds, Sally clearly recognises that her teaching assistant is responding to her vocalisations. She is *causing* the adult to do something. In taking the lead in the turn-taking game which follows, Sally is also establishing the rules of dyadic exchanges whereby one person contributes and the other responds, and she understands what imitation involves. Turning to the question of intention, it seems that Bruner's notion of initiation for joint attention underpins Sally's intention as she seems to be striving to share a focus with the adult for the purpose of enjoying a game, just as very young children enjoy peek-a-boo games. As far as the assistant is concerned the purpose of the exchange is to use Sally's pleasure as a reinforcer to establish the use of vocalisations. It is easy to see how the principles of behaviourism underpin the assistant's practice and how the approaches that learning theorists advocate, such as shaping (discussed in more detail in the example of Ian and his lost boat) could bring about elaborated purposeful verbal behaviour.

In proposing the extension of the teaching assistant's efforts to shape Sally's attempts in the direction of purposeful communication, it is necessary to refocus on the question of Sally's intentions. In these contexts Vygotsky maintained that the child, initially, has no intention but that this is imputed by her or his communication partner so that intention is negotiated on the interpsychological plane (between the communicators) before it is available intrapsychologically (in the mind of the developing child). Put simply, the teaching assistant assumes that it is Sally's intention to have fun through the exchange and she manipulates the encounter accordingly. Sally learns from this that she, Sally, is having fun. Through Affective Communication Assessment techniques (Coupe O'Kane and Goldbart, 1998), which were described earlier, practitioners and parents exploit these principles to shape intentional communication.

In the example above, it seems that Sally *wants* to share a focus with the teaching assistant. This situation contrasts with that of learners with autistic spectrum disorders who appear to lack the will to share and negotiate meaning. Their learning needs and the responses to them are of a totally different order.

Communication difficulties associated with autistic spectrum disorders

In the present context, the term autistic spectrum disorders (ASD) refers to a wide range of learners: that is, it is not restricted to those with severe autism. For example, it may refer to children and adults with semantic-pragmatic disorder. In all people with ASD, communication shows unusual or deviant patterns, but not necessarily delayed language development as observed in individuals such as Sally, where there is an expectation that language development can follow typical patterns, albeit at a very early stage. In many cases this deviance is attributed to the individual's inability or unwillingness to share in joint action formats at a very early age. For example, at the earliest levels young children who go on to demonstrate ASD may fail to use signals such as eye-gaze and seem not to understand finger-pointing. This means that the foundations for sharing meaning through the usual patterns of mother–child interaction are not established. Lacking experience of early pseudo-dialogues, many children with ASD do not develop language. The problems are compounded by an ongoing apparent lack of motivation to enter into the social processes that usually draw heavily on, and contribute so richly to, verbal and non-verbal language. In other cases, language does emerge but communication is nonetheless impaired because individuals with ASD fail to adopt the essential features of dialogue which relate to *sharing* meaning. Consequently, the opportunity to create and differentiate meanings is also constrained. In the most severe cases, this leads to a total inability to use language and there is often a noticeable impact on receptive and expressive vocabulary growth. Alternatively, children develop idiosyncratic uses of vocabulary that obscure, rather than facilitate, communication and it becomes a challenge for communication partners to discover the meaning that words and utterances have for children with these difficulties.

Edward

Edward is four years old and has ASD compounded by severe difficulties in learning. One day he lost something in his bedroom and when asked where it was by his mother he replied, correctly, 'Under my bed'. He was praised for finding the missing article.

A couple of days later he was asked a question. In reply, he said, 'Under my bed' and for the next four months, his reply to any question, for example, 'What would you like for tea?' or 'What did you do at nursery today?' was 'Under my bed.' Edward not only used this as a standard response to all questions but chanted it as a mantra wherever he went.

According to the Pragmatics Profile devised by Dewart and Summers (1995), language use, at its most sophisticated, involves being able to express a range of communicative intentions and to respond to increasingly complex and subtle communication behaviour in other people. Additionally, mature language use implies skills in initiating and terminating conversational exchanges and the timing of these exchanges. Further defining features include demonstrations of understanding the need for adjustment to ensure that one's communication partner is participating fully in the exchange, and the use of social conventions: for example, those that acknowledge the status of the communication partner. Given our understanding of ASD, it is obvious that these individuals lack the skills to achieve successful communication at any level of sophistication. A typical scenario is that of people with ASD pursuing a topic without checking the understanding or interest of their conversation partners. In educational settings, children with ASD may indicate their difficulties in understanding subtle or meta-phorical language or humour, particularly that based on word-play or sarcasm. At extreme levels their rigidity of thinking, in relation to language, challenges teaching staff, as the competent conversation partners, to produce language that is devoid of metaphor and transparent in meaning.

William

William is in Year 4 of the local mainstream school and has autistic spectrum disorders. His teacher asked him to take the register to the office of the school secretary, and William returned, still carrying the register. Further questioning revealed that William had understood that he should take the register to the office. What he failed to grasp was that he was expected to leave it there and come back without it.

On another occasion the teacher asked William, 'Are you going to move house soon?' William replied, 'We're not moving house, it's staying where it is. We're going to live in another one'.

Support for language development

Earlier in this chapter we stressed that communication and language behaviour do not emerge spontaneously from babies and young children, although the drive to communicate is strong in most, apart from those with autistic spectrum disorders. Instead, there seems to be a complex interplay between the biological dispositions of the developing child and a strong desire, on the part of more competent communicators, to involve that child in a community. Therefore, when communicating with typically developing children, caregivers in many cultures modify their adult-to-adult language forms and delivery of speech in order to elicit social responses from the child. As the child matures and becomes more competent (cognitively, socially and linguistically), child-directed speech changes.

When a child's potential for developing effective communication and language skills is compromised, the demands on the adult speaker increase, as pointed out earlier. It was proposed, for example, that teachers of pupils with ASD should examine their own language styles, vocabulary and use of metaphor for potential areas of confusion. In line with a theme of this book, it seems that teachers and other professionals concerned with pupils who have complex learning needs that could affect communication and interaction should maintain a focus on fostering language skills that are generalisable to situations beyond the classroom. Underpinning this suggestion is a recognition of the role of communication in empowering the learner to become an active participant in the wider society. However, balanced against the requirement of schooling to prepare pupils, in some general sense, for citizenship is the need to create optimum conditions for broadening their learning capacity and providing them with access to a curriculum of learning. In this section we consider the special challenges that face the communication partners of people with severe and complex learning needs, in supporting all their communication needs, and some of the resources that might help them to meet those challenges.

Decisions and choices

A central theme of this book is an emphasis on the empowerment of the individual to make decisions and exercise choices. Communicating one's decisions and articulating expressions of choice are clearly an essential part of the process and in earlier sections of this chapter the notion of intention was explored in some detail. Accordingly we have already highlighted the significance of being capable of having some intention, of signalling that intention, and of having that intention understood by others.

In the normal course of development children become progressively more competent at articulating their desires and needs and get better at communicating their feelings, knowledge and understanding. As teachers and education professionals, we may fully accept Vygotsky's views that both the content and the mode of a child's thinking are a product of social interaction rather than her or his spontaneous reflection on society. Nonetheless, we usually accept that children will, on an individual basis, negotiate for themselves a world-view through which they will ultimately exercise personal autonomy. This final position represents the highest order of choice or decision-making: Guess (1985), quoted by Caldwell (2000), provides a hierarchy for exploring the emergence of these processes in people with complex learning needs, starting with choice as a preference. This might be expressed as a response to the question, 'Do you want juice?' where the answer would be indicated as a positive or a negative. At the next level, decision-making involves selection from a number of alternatives where another person presents the alternatives. At the most mature level, decision-making impacts on the course of one's life: that is, it is the exercise of self-advocacy.

It is when adopting a caring role towards people with severe and complex learning needs affecting communicative competence that professionals feel keenly the responsibility for interpreting the communicative endeavours of their pupils or adult students. When people are not adept at using the methods of communication favoured by the wider community, misinterpretations are ever possible, as with Bel whose story was told earlier. Misunderstandings of the intention behind communicative behaviour may be genuine or they can reflect the wishes, desires or prejudices of the people surrounding the person who has communication difficulties.

The possibility of misinterpretation of the intentions or decisions of a person with learning difficulties is increased because of the tendency of this group of people to acquiesce to decisions made on their behalf. That is, they are more likely to agree than disagree with a proposition from a teacher, for example, simply because they lack the competence to evaluate the proposition or do not develop a self-concept that includes themselves in a decision-making role. Erikson's view is that competence in decision-making emerges naturally as the child is encouraged to experience new and challenging situations within the security of warm, trusting relationships. When children have, for example, physical disabilities or sensory impairments, caregivers may be tempted towards excessive caution, thus restricting opportunities for exploration. Similarly, the children may be fearful of new situations because of their difficulties. It follows then that situations must be manipulated so that children can *safely* experience some dissonance that calls for a decision, as in the case of Wendy described in Chapter 3.

In order to reduce the potential for misinterpretation, approaches have been developed whereby staff can check the consistency of an individual's response to certain situations in order to provide a means of assessing her or his decisions or feelings concerning that situation. Grove (2000) has produced a set of guidelines in which she emphasises the importance of introducing checks to ensure objectivity in interpretation, which include looking for consistency of responses when locations and personnel change. Ian's way of interpreting his need to retrieve his boat was to produce challenging behaviour which in the main could be interpreted by those close to him. In the context of the wider community, however, his responses were not easy to 'read', and by building on his existing skills, he was taught strategies which were more likely to be understood by more people. The purpose of Grove's guidelines is to facilitate communication; they are, therefore, concerned with promoting the communication competence of teachers and caregivers, by bringing intuitive skills to an explicit level.

Alternative and augmentative communication

Children whose learning needs restrict their ability to use speech in order to communicate may require an entirely different means of communication, or some additional form. The term 'alternative and augmentative communication' (AAC) covers both these circumstances. Clearly, the first part of the term is used to imply that the child or adult does not have access to speech-based communication, as in the case of some members of the deaf community who rely exclusively on sign language. The second part, 'augmentative communication' suggests that the learner can use speech, but that some additional form is needed, either to clarify their own speech or to support their understanding of speech.

Forms of AAC might comprise plastic markers which are used to symbolise, or stand for, ideas, manual sign systems, or different applications of assistive technology – for example, computers. In assessing their value, it is important to ask whether the AAC adopted can be used by all potential communication partners or whether it fails to empower the user in some circumstances. Still focusing on the potential restrictions of AAC, we need to consider whether it provides users with the freedom to express a range of desires, decisions and feelings or whether it restricts them to a menu of pre-programmed symbols and functions. It may be that AAC has an important role in extending the cognitive skills of people whose language competence is restricted and this aspect is explored later in relation to objects of reference in Chapter 9.

Conclusion

In this chapter we have emphasised that the ability to communicate with other people is crucial for developing and exercising personal autonomy. Further we have indicated that the success of any interpersonal exchange, the means by which communication is achieved, lies with both parties. However, where difficulties or disabilities restrict communication skills and strategies, there is a need for the more competent partner to value, support and facilitate the other's communication attempts. In any intervention aimed at providing support or facilitation, the empowerment of the individual must be a primary consideration.

References

Bruner, J. (1981) 'The social context of language acquisition', *Language and Communication.* 1, 155–78.
Bruner, J. (1983) *Child's Talk: Learning to Use Language.* Oxford: Oxford University Press.
Caldwell, P. (2000) *You Don't Know What It's Like.* Brighton: Pavilion Publishing.
Chomsky, N. (1965) *Aspects of the Theory of Syntax.* Cambridge, MA: MIT Press.
Coupe O'Kane, J. and Goldbart, J. (1998) *Communication before Speech: Development and Assessment* (2nd edition). London: David Fulton Publishers.
Crystal, D. (1997) *The Cambridge Encyclopaedia of Language* (2nd edition). Cambridge: Cambridge University Press.
Dewart, H. and Summers, S. (1995) *The Pragmatics Profile of Everyday Communication Skills.* Windsor: NFER-Nelson.
Dockrell, J. and Messer, D. (1999) *Children's Language and Communication Difficulties.* London: Cassell.
Durkheim, E. (1897) *Rules of Sociological Method.* New York: Free Press Edition, 1950.
Goldbart, J. (2002) 'Communication and severe learning difficulties'. Paper presented at Penhurst School Conference.
Grove, N. (2000) *See What I Mean.* Kidderminster: BILD.
Hodapp, R. (1998) *Development and Disabilities: Intellectual, Sensory and Motor Impairments.* Cambridge: Cambridge University Press.
Lewis, V. (1987) *Development and Handicap.* Oxford: Basil Blackwell.
Messer, D.J. (1994) *The Development of Communication from Social Interaction to Language.* Chichester: John Wiley & Sons.
Nind, M. and Hewitt, D. (1994) *Access to Communication.* London: David Fulton Publishers.
Schaffer, H.R. (ed.) (1977) *Studies in Mother–Infant Interaction.* London: Academic Press.
Sheridan, M. (1997) *From Birth to Five Years: Children's Developmental Progress* (2nd edition). London: Routledge.
Skinner, B.F. (1957) *Verbal Behaviour.* New York: Appleton-Century-Crofts.
Stark, R.E. (1986) 'Pre-speech segmental feature development', in P. Fletcher and M. Garman (eds) *Language Acquisition.* Cambridge: Cambridge University Press.

Chapter 9

Cognition and learning

Imagine that, without preamble or preparation, you are snatched away from your familiar surroundings and deposited in an alien environment. The physical properties of the environment are different from anything you have previously experienced; the sounds that assail your ears are incomprehensible; the sights that meet your eyes make no sense. What are your first reactions to the event? Think about your response in the face of awesome incomprehension. Imagine, if you will, your sense of impotence. But, even as the experience threatens to overwhelm you, do you feel the drive to grapple with the unknown, gradually bringing this new environment within your power?

You have, of course, already experienced an event like this. In 1890, William James, one of the first scientists to be recognised as a psychologist, described the moment of birth as a 'great blooming, buzzing confusion' for newborn infants arriving in the world with, as he saw it, no knowledge or understanding. Since James (1890) published his views, advances in the methods of enquiry and the technology to support them have allowed us greater insights into the capacities of neonates (newborn infants). We now believe that certain dispositions are inborn and that we are biologically prepared to process information received through the senses in specific ways.

In this chapter we explore the processes through which we come to understand our environment and to build up a fund of knowledge about it. We begin by briefly considering primary sensory experience and perception; look at concept formation, memory and problem-solving; and review the relationship between language and cognition. As we focus on cognition, we attempt to account for diversions from the typical course of development and revisit the theoretical perspectives outlined in the opening chapters. First, however, it is appropriate to make some general comments on how intellectual, or cognitive, variations within any given population have been categorised in mainstream psychology.

Psychometrics is a branch of psychology that is concerned with measuring individual characteristics and it was within this field that intelligence testing and the notion of the IQ (intelligence quotient) first assumed prominence in Europe and North America during the early twentieth century. Intelligence tests were originally conceived to identify children whose learning capacities were significantly restricted and the results were used to legitimate arrangements for alternative schooling for these children, away from ordinary classrooms where their presence might challenge the homogenous teaching approaches that were favoured in the early days of mass education. Since then, the use, and sometimes overuse, of intelligence testing has been well documented, and accounts of its history make fascinating but disturbing reading (see, for example, Kamin, 1974). In particular, spurious 'evidence' about racial differences in measured intelligence was used to justify practices that we would today find indefensible. However, these accounts provide a powerful reminder that any tests must not be culturally biased towards or against any group of individuals. Indeed, Elliott (2000) notes that some education authorities no longer use IQ testing for this reason, but instead advocate the dynamic measures, discussed in Chapter 5, as an alternative.

The principal argument against intelligence testing stems, in part, from the lack of a clear view of what intelligence is and from the unsupported assumptions that have emerged around its concept. For example, it has been regarded as a unitary characteristic that is genetically determined, therefore fixed. Contemporary views on intelligence, however, acknowledge the complexity of cognitive processing and some support the idea of multiple intelligences (see Gardner, 1999). These views acknowledge within-individual variations in cognitive competence depending on the nature of the problem-solving domain: for example, music or language.

Notwithstanding the arguments against their use, intelligence tests can, and do, support the assessment process by providing a profile of learners' strengths and needs in specified, if limited, areas of intellectual functioning. Moreover, the original formulation of intelligence tests provided for the concept of *mental age*, that is, the level at which an individual can problem-solve. Accordingly, a ten-year-old who solves intelligence test items at a level commensurate with his or her chronological age has a mental age of ten, whereas a ten-year-old who can solve problems that are usually only achievable by the typically developing 12-year-old is said to have a mental age of 12. Intelligence quotient (IQ) is then calculated as a ratio between mental age and chronological age (and multiplied by 100 to remove values that would otherwise be expressed by decimal places). Thus, in the examples given, the first child would have an IQ of 100; the second, an IQ of 120.

These developments in psychometrics have provided a means of testing or, more accurately, sampling intellectual competence, and of quantifying the outcomes in terms of mental age and then IQ. The classification of people with learning difficulties (for the purposes of research, for example) depended on their IQ scores so that those with a score of between 51 and 75 were identified as 'mildly retarded', whereas those with a score of 50 or below were deemed 'severely retarded' and those under 20 were considered to be 'profoundly retarded'. While labelling in this way might have been defensible for allocating individuals to categories for research purposes, we would argue that such generalisations cannot inform educational intervention nor offer guidelines for supporting individuals with learning difficulties towards personal fulfilment and independence.

Similarly, however, theorists have attempted to make generalisations about the underlying reasons for variations in measured intelligence; specifically what creates difficulties in learning for some individuals. The purpose of categorising *aetiologies* or causes is to provide a framework for exploring such aspects as the rate of development in different groups; patterns of development; or the structure of intelligence in people with learning difficulties. Hodapp (1998), acknowledging the work of Zigler, distinguishes two forms of what is called, in the USA, 'mental retardation'. The first is believed to have an organic basis and includes genetic disorders such as Down syndrome, Fragile X syndrome, Williams syndrome and Prader-Willi syndrome (for more information, see Worthington, 1999). Also included are those that arise in connection with brain insult caused, for example, by prenatal exposure to rubella, accidents during birth, postnatal head injuries or diseases such as meningitis. The other category is generally known as cultural-familial, where there is evidence that low intelligence is a characteristic of the whole family. In this case, it is not known what role genetic factors play or whether the major determinant could be discovered in the family environment.

Another issue that theorists have tried to uncover relates to patterns of development, either in the whole population of people with learning difficulties or within the categories described above. Two views are the 'similar structure hypothesis' that maintains that, at any given level of development, typically developing and atypically developing children will evidence the same cognitive processes underlying their problem-solving behaviour. The other is the 'similar sequence hypothesis', according to which children with learning difficulties will move through the same developmental stages as their typically developing peers. Together, these hypotheses represent a developmental delay view of learning difficulties, which maintains that children with learning difficulties progress in the same way as their normally developing peers, but at a slower rate. It contrasts with the defect/difference perspective that attributes one or more defective components in cognitive processing as the cause of learning difficulties. The former view is more optimistic, allowing, as it does, a role for education in enhancing learning opportunities and the subsequent advancement of cognitive competence.

The developmental approach

Intellectual differences, either across the whole population or within groups of individuals who have learning difficulties with specified aetiologies, assume significance principally in psychological studies where scientists are interested to establish why some individuals perform better on certain intellectual tasks than others. Our concern here is with exploring aspects of cognitive functioning with a view to understanding why some individuals may experience difficulties with learning. As suggested above, we see no advantage in focusing on a deficit view of learning difficulties and therefore adopt the developmental approach that stresses the similarities between children with learning difficulties and their typically developing peers. However, the developmental perspective does not overlook the obvious differences, and the approach that we take in the Framework for New Learning proposes views of development that value attainments in all groups of learners.

Perceptual development

Although it is important to consider perception because of its primacy for the cognition process, it is difficult to draw a line indicating where perception ends and cognition begins. Certainly, understanding, knowing, remembering and problem-solving are cognitive processes, but perception itself requires that information about a stimulus, fed through the senses (the visual system, for example), should be processed, or acted upon, in order to produce apprehension of the stimulus. The first level of perception involves stimulation of one or more of the senses when, obviously, any dysfunction will change the course of development significantly; this is given a special focus in Chapter 11.

For the moment it is necessary to return to the enigma outlined earlier: when does perception become cognition? Most recently, psychological enquiry has chosen not to dwell on the question but to regard the former as part of the latter. The conflation of the two levels of processing sensory information into one is particularly apparent when we examine the acquisition of the object concept as a classic example of concept formation.

Concept formation

Thinking back to the adventure described at the beginning of this chapter and to James's observation about a 'blooming, buzzing confusion', it is evident that sensory input must somehow be organised so that understanding can crystallise. Without mechanisms for categorising experience and making broad generalisations, we would be overwhelmed by the fluidity and diversity of the external environment, unable to predict, plan or control. It is therefore essential that we 'make sense' of our experiences by treating them, or aspects of them, as having something in common with other, similar experiences. The process of conceptualisation is considerably extended by the use of language to label and qualify concepts. For example, we have a concept that is labelled 'cat' so that we know what to expect when we encounter 'cat' and we can predict how we will behave in response to this particular experience. This concept can be qualified as 'the big cats' to change the expectations so that we would not attempt to stroke a 'big cat' or feed it a saucer of milk. However, for the moment, the role of language is not explored: concept formation also takes place in the absence of language.

Certain concepts are prerequisites to the formation of other concepts and have therefore become a focus of study and research (see Meadows, 1993). For example, the concept of 'sameness' would seem to underpin the process of categorisation that accompanies concept formation but we have to understand what it is that is the 'same' in multiple objects or events in order to link them and we also need to understand that 'same' does not usually mean 'identical'. Although, in important respects, every experience is unique we organise our initial responses to each experience on the basis of aspects that are not unique.

As indicated above, one concept that could be regarded as crucial to all understanding is the object concept, studied in detail by Piaget. The object concept is closely linked to the notion of egocentricity and the steady move away from egocentricity ('decentering') that was described in Chapter 2. In the earliest days, when the infant is profoundly egocentric, she or he has no understanding of the existence of objects (people or things), unless they are within her or his current field of perception. That is, for an infant at this stage of development, any object that is no longer stimulating sensory activity and therefore cannot be directly experienced has 'gone out of existence'. Similarly, as an outcome of development, children only gradually come to understand *invariance*, or the unchanging nature of physical phenomena despite changes in appearance, as a result of different orientations or presentations as illustrated in conservation experiments. The classic view of the infant developing towards a mature object concept, encompassing the permanence and invariance of objects, characterises the progress of the sensori-motor stage of development, a key component of Piaget's cognitive developmental theory.

Piaget was persuaded that although young children are genetically prepared to process information in characteristic ways as they mature, the experiences that come to them through their senses and their motor exploration of the physical world trigger new ways of understanding that world. Hence the term *sensori-motor* thinking. How different, then, might be the conceptual development of children whose sensory awareness or motor development is, in some way, restricted or different?

Studies of babies affected *in utero* by their mothers' use of the thalidomide drug provide a natural if tragic demonstration of the effects of motoric disabilities on cognitive development (Decarie, 1969). These studies show that where physical exploration of objects and their surroundings is very limited because of missing or deformed limbs, but vision is functioning normally, the object concept develops as in children with no motor difficulties. In contrast, research strongly suggests that development of the object concept in infants who are born blind (Warren, 1994) is likely to be delayed. In the latter case, opportunities to experience or, in the terminology of the Framework for New Learning, *encounter* the object in the first place are greatly reduced. Furthermore, once the object has been removed beyond their touch, or once it ceases to make a sound, these babies cannot scan their surroundings; more fundamentally, perhaps, as Warren explains, they lack an understanding that they *have* surroundings. The findings about the importance of sensory exploration are consistent with Piaget's explanation of the growth of intelligent thought. Meanwhile, demonstrations of understanding object permanence emerging in the absence of physical exploration cast doubts on his assertions about the need for motor activity.

Such findings must, however, be interpreted with caution: Warren (1994), for example, points to the considerable variations in the developmental progress of the object concept within one population of children (those with a severe visual impairment). To some extent, he suggests, variations can be explained because any visual function, however restricted, can produce a different outcome depending on when an infant became blind. Within the very small population of infants who are blind from birth, variations have also been found and these are sometimes attributed to the ways in which tasks are presented by investigators. This explanation links into a more comprehensive analysis of variations and possible causative factors that underpin Warren's approach to developmental differences. The latter: '... draws our attention to the dynamic interplay between the child's capabilities and the circumstances provided by the environment' (Warren, 1994, p.6).

The approach resonates with that of Piaget because it emphasises the role of adaptation. In short, the child brings to any task personal resources (for example, skills, understanding, physical capabilities) and the environment, in turn, presents circumstances with certain opportunities and challenges. It is the child's task to adapt to features of the environment: first to understand them, then to change that understanding in response to changes in the features, thus bringing them, theoretically at least, within her or his control. Piaget elaborates his view, describing the twin processes of assimilation and accommodation (see Chapter 2). Thus, the child who is blind brings knowledge and abilities with which to act upon the environment, but he or she does not bring visual skills. When the child is also immobile, because of immaturity, objects and other physical surroundings may not be immediately apparent to her or him and as a result opportunities for encountering external reality will be limited. According to this deficit view, the child will be delayed in progressing to the next stage of learning that has been identified as *awareness*.

Another perspective on the conditions for development is provided in the central tenets of Vygotsky's theory (see Chapter 2). Whereas Piaget sees the child as the 'lone scientist' struggling to make sense of reality, Vygotsky emphasises the part played by other people in interpreting reality in order to bring it within the growing child's realm of awareness. Warren (1994) draws attention to the quality of parent–child relationships and the opportunities for appropriate experiences as key factors in determining progress towards an object concept. We may assume that sensitivity to a child's needs arising out of a warm parent–child relationship leads to the creation of imaginative experiences through which the child builds the conceptual structures for understanding object permanence and invariance.

Teachers and other professionals can therefore support the process of concept formation in children for whom development *could* be compromised. Bruner also strongly advocates that adults must be proactive in supporting the conditions for cognitive development and he identifies the importance of training in this respect (Bruner, 1996). In England, the focus of professional training to support pupils' conceptual development is made explicit by the Teacher Training Agency (TTA, 1999). In general terms, it is to be expected that appropriately trained professionals will manipulate the circumstances so that pupils can initially encounter objects in highly specific ways on a number of occasions. Through repeated encounters it is intended that pupils should become aware of the objects and all their properties in a variety of contexts.

The reflections of Temple Grandin

Temple Grandin is a scientist with an international reputation for designing livestock equipment, a subject on which she publishes widely. She has written extensively about her firsthand experiences of autistic spectrum disorders and she provides penetrating insights into the difficulties of concept building. These may be created by a failure to integrate information received through different modalities but she also notes the impact of being unable to think in language. In the extract below her reflections allow us to speculate on possible reasons for a poorly developed understanding of object invariance:

I have conducted an informal little cognitive test on many people. They are asked to access their memory of church steeples or cats. An object that is not in the person's immediate surroundings should be used for this visualization procedure. When I do this, I see in my imagination a series of 'videos' of different churches or cats I have seen or know. Many 'normal' people will see a visual image of a cat, but it is a sort of generalized generic cat image. They usually don't see a series of vivid cat or church 'videos' unless they are an artist, parent of an autistic child, or an engineer. My 'cat' concept consists of a series of 'videos' of cats I have known. There is no generalized cat. If I keep thinking about cats and churches I can manipulate the 'video' images. I can put snow on the church roof and imagine what the church grounds look like during the different seasons.

Some people access their 'cat' knowledge as auditory or written language. For me, there is no language-based information in my memory. To access spoken information, I replay a 'video' of the person talking. There are some brilliant people who have little visual thought. One totally verbal professor told me that facts just come to his mind instantly with no visual image. To retrieve the facts, I have to read them off a visualized page of a book or 'replay the video' of some previous event. This method of thinking is slower. It takes time to 'play' the videotape in my imagination'.

(www.grandin.corm/inc/visual.thinking.html)

This account suggests that some people with autistic spectrum disorders may not easily form concepts: that is, generic ideas that encapsulate the essential features of separate aspects of their experience. Instead they focus on specific examples. Thus, a child may fail to acknowledge a cat because it is not identical in every respect to the cat he or she already knows. Alternatively, the cat may undergo some subtle change: for example, it may have a bandage on its paw. Again the child may judge that this is not the same cat because the visual appearance has altered.

Contingency learning

A fundamental concept that typically starts to emerge in the early months of life is the notion of cause and effect. By the time we are able to reflect explicitly on our understanding of how things happen, we have adopted, unquestioningly, the expectation that every event is somehow *caused*, leading us to explore ways of controlling aspects of the environment once we can attribute the causes. Pupils and older students with learning difficulties may not have reached this level of understanding.

Adults with difficulties in learning

Many years ago, when adults in the UK with learning difficulties traditionally lived in large institutions, a new initiative was trialled for more able people to live together in groups of four or five in semi-independent settings. Training in basic living skills was given ahead of the move to their new homes, and staff were confident that they had covered everything that someone would need to know in order to live without close supervision. During the first evening, a member of staff called at the home of one group to find them sitting in total darkness. When he queried this situation one person said, 'But it got dark and the lights didn't come on!'. Ahead of the move, staff had failed to appreciate that no one in this group would have ever considered the association between nightfall and the activation of artificial light.

A first step in acquiring the concept of causality is achieved when an individual recognises that certain of her or his personal actions are regularly associated with particular events and that the events appear to be contingent upon the actions. In the case of people with profound and multiple learning difficulties (PMLD) the associations will need to be forged over a period of time before contingency awareness is established. Its centrality to concept development has led practitioners and researchers to investigate ways of promoting it, often with the support of technology. For example, switches can be adapted for use by people with very limited physical capabilities, who may, in important respects, be considerably empowered and liberated when they can control the environment in a multi-sensory room by operating a switch or a series of switches.

Ratna

Ratna is a teenage pupil with complex learning difficulties and is a wheelchair user. She has frequent episodes of distressed and self-mutilating behaviours and a significant degree of visual impairment. Thus opportunities to exert control over her immediate environment and to make choices are limited. Ratna loves music and being in the multi-sensory room. She has recently been using a new piece of equipment, the kaleidoscope, which transforms visuals in front of it and also music and other sounds into kaleidoscopic images. Ratna has been able to control the kaleidoscope and the music input by operating a Big Mac switch; she has become aware that when she presses the switch the music comes on and images rotate on the wall in front of her. Ratna can concentrate on this activity and shows obvious pleasure and enjoyment for periods of up to 20 minutes. Initially she became agitated when the music stopped, but she has learnt that if she presses the switch again she is able to access the music and the moving images.

It is tempting to overestimate the value of technology alone in bringing about cognitive development in this group of learners. This is a major theme of Bozic and Murdoch's (1996) book in which it is suggested that the child, the teacher and the technology (in collaborative activity towards specified goals) form 'a functional system' (p.2). The collaborative activity is planned around the identified needs and strengths of individual children and it derives its theoretical basis from Vygotsky's view of the zone of proximal development (ZPD). Accordingly, the teacher must select goals and relevant technology that will extend the learner's capabilities but not challenge him or her beyond his or her current ZPD. Initially, the teacher will mediate learning activities but the clear aim is that the learner should eventually be able to work independently, supported only by the technology.

By using the Bozic and Murdoch model of functional systems to conceptualise the dynamic relationship between teacher, pupil and supportive technology, we can analyse some key issues. First, as shown in the example below, it is imperative that the teacher or intervener plans an approach that is firmly based on the needs and capacities of the pupil.

Trevor

Trevor is 14 and has complex learning difficulties including very limited useful hearing and vision. His intervener, using equipment to assess his potential to exert control over events in his immediate environment, observed him in the multi-sensory room. She noted that he had a strong preference for yellow objects and he loved watching the yellow bubble tube in the dark area. At first Trevor worked with the intervener to operate the large switch that activated the tube, but he is now able to reach out independently and bang the switch and laughs, vocalises and watches the bubbles intently.

This necessarily demands insightful assessment, and we suggest that Vygotsky's dynamic assessment is appropriate (see Chapter 5). The principles of dynamic assessment enmesh closely with those of *scaffolding*, a process of providing support only when needed. In scaffolding, the teacher continually assesses the pupil's responses, checking that she or he is working within her or his ZPD and gradually phasing out support as the pupil's competence increases.

Second, a functional systems approach acknowledges the role of technology but also its limitations: teaching and learning, particularly as viewed through a Vygotskyan lens, are essentially processes that involve social interaction. Switches, computers and other technological support systems are tools that Bruner refers to as 'amplifiers' but approaches to ensuring support for learners should not be driven by the capacities of the technology. Therefore, when teachers come under pressure to set targets that justify the purchase of expensive equipment and specify them in terms that are most easily quantified, it will be necessary for them to assert their professional judgement of a child's needs over organisational and administrative considerations. In the following scenario, it would be tempting to identify targets for Kylie in terms of more talking books as she responds so well to them. In order to promote lateral development in self-advocacy skills, however, it might be more appropriate to think about what she has gained cognitively and to seek opportunities for transferring these gains.

Kylie

Kylie is 11 years old and her learning difficulties are considered to be severe. Her receptive language is good but her expressive language is limited. She likes using a computer and her class teacher has found that she particularly enjoys using interactive talking books. These software packages read the text of an illustrated story, the user clicks to turn the pages and to activate additional sequences within each page. Initially Kylie needed one-to-one support to use the packages but with help and tuition the amount of input required has slowly decreased and she is now able to click the icon to turn pages and to click on parts of the pictures to activate additional animation sequences.

Finally, we can look critically at the shift in power within the functional system over time. The intention is, of course, that the process leads to the greater empowerment of the learner. Crucially, it should create opportunities for the exercise of choice, and therefore allow the learner to choose whether or not to pursue an activity. This approach contrasts with scaffolding where there is an expectation that the learner achieves some highly specific goal of the teacher's choosing. Instead, by reviewing the progress that has been made in the personal development of the learner, opportunities for generalising skills and knowledge will become apparent. Re-focusing the discussion on contingency learning, it would be expected that, from learning how to operate a switch that activates a coloured light, the learner might demonstrate an awareness that it is her or his activity that initiates the coloured light; a rudimentary understanding of causality.

Memory

There are many ways of conceptualising memory and memory functions. In Freud's view, for example, memory operates selectively to repress material that the individual does not want to recall and so psychotherapy is concerned with uncovering 'forgotten' experiences. For the purposes of understanding the role of memory in learning, an information-processing approach is adopted. Memory is regarded as a system comprising three interrelated processes: *registration* is the process in which sensory information is selected for long- or short-term *storage*, and *retrieval* relates to the recall of stored information for conscious deliberation. The storage of selected information has attracted a great deal of research interest and is particularly significant for understanding learning needs.

Once incoming information has been selected for attention, it passes to short-term memory (STM), one component of which is working memory, a workplace for processing material, in coded form, that is to be memorised. Working memory comprises a central executive function that, continuing with the analogy of a workplace, is the station where the information is sorted and resources are allocated, depending on whether it requires mainly visual or phonological processing. Information then passes to two 'slave' systems: the phonological loop for extending the short-term memory of speech and the visuo-spatial sketchpad that holds images. Material can pass directly to long-term memory (LTM) from STM or it may stay for longer than the normal 30-second storage time in STM owing to the operation of working memory (see Gathercole and Baddeley, 1993, for a full account).

In addition to understanding the components of memory it is important to be aware that LTM is believed to process differentially three different types of information, giving rise to the notion of three long-term memories:

- *Procedural memory* underpins the capacity to remember *how* to carry out certain activities. This makes extensive (but not exclusive) use of 'muscle' memory and is best illustrated in connection with producing a signature, which may be achieved without any recourse to imagery (remembering what the signature looks like) or a semantic code (remembering the names of component letters, in sequence). Instead, signing one's name seems to be an activity that is controlled by the muscles of the hands and arms 'remembering' how to make appropriate movements.

- *Episodic memory* records personal experiences and is likely to make use of imagery: that is, 'pictures' (visual or auditory) of events, places or people.
- *Semantic memory*, as the name suggests, refers to the memory storing material that has been built up and categorised largely through symbolic representation, outlining our knowledge of the world.

As suggested above, each of these 'memories' helps to support the recall of different types of information but there is also evidence that they emerge developmentally, with semantic memory as a system that is based on verbally encoded material developing last of all. As Goswami (1998) points out, memory structures and functions are closely associated with other cognitive processes. It is therefore to be expected that, if there is delay or divergence in the developmental pathways of intellectual growth, memory will be affected. At the same time, memory can be separately affected – for example, by damage to the frontal regions of the brain – in which case it is poor memory that restricts learning and negatively affects cognitive development.

It is probably more important to investigate ways of supporting memory function than to attempt to establish the direction of causality with regard to memory and other aspects of cognition. First, we should examine claims that some children with special educational needs (SEN) have poor memories. For example, it is widely believed that memory impairment is a core characteristic of children with Down syndrome, as is language impairment (Laws *et al.*, 2000). Laws, Byrne and Buckley reviewed research investigating both areas of impairment and they found evidence that the specific locus of impairment is in phonological memory and phonological and syntactic aspects of language, suggesting that the working memory component underperforms. Basing their own study on these findings, Laws, Byrne and Buckley compared memory and language development, over a four-and-a-half-year period, in children with Down syndrome in mainstream and special schools. They found that pupils in mainstream schools showed significantly greater improvement (initially at least) in grammar, comprehension and measures of short-term memory function that make demands on the phonological loop. It was suggested that there could be factors associated with mainstream but not with special schools that create the conditions for promoting language and memory, but do not make any difference to non-verbal aspects of cognitive development. It was not the aim of the study to establish what these factors were, but the authors proposed that there is more teaching–learning time in mainstream schooling because less time needs to be dedicated to the physical care of individual pupils. However, significantly for the issues we are emphasising here, the authors suggest that the focus of further research might be the increased opportunities for participation with typically developing peers and greater expectations of pupils' abilities on the part of the teachers who, as a result, use more sophisticated language.

It is not only children with Down syndrome who have related memory and language impairments. Some children have severe but specific memory difficulties with unknown causes although many may also have a history of spoken language problems that, in the preschool years, required speech and language therapy. Children in this group typically experience difficulties in remembering strings of instructions, in dealing with sequentially presented symbols, and with mental arithmetic. They are also likely to struggle with reading and spelling and it is probable that they have phonological processing weaknesses or visuo-motor difficulties that affect working memory function. Whereas the underlying processing weakness cannot be corrected, the way in which information is presented can substantially change the nature of tasks, notably by reducing the cognitive demands placed on learners.

Abigail

Abigail is a Year 11 pupil in a mainstream school, who is well motivated but has struggled with learning for many years. When she was about ten years old it was felt that her problems were mainly grounded in reading and writing weaknesses, described by the school as dyslexic in nature. Intervention then took the form of one-to-one support with reading and spelling. Abigail's literacy skills showed an initial improvement in response to specialist support but, by Year 10, her form tutor expressed concern that her written work was again deteriorating and that she was struggling to read texts. Further testing identified severe difficulties in visual short-term memory function and visuo-motor co-ordination. Additionally, it was discovered that Abigail had developed a form of epilepsy that is known to seriously affect learning through its impact on concentration and attention. The continuing effect of underachievement, combined with difficulties created by epilepsy, was undermining Abigail's sense of self-worth and consequently her capacity for learning was further restricted.

The school's response has been to offer a broader system of support than if the difficulties had been entirely attributed to dyslexia. Instead of focusing solely on aspects of written language, her individual education plan emphasises that instructions directed to Abigail should be presented singly, her understanding should be checked and her memory of the instructions supported with visual aids. Series of tasks are written down and she works to lists. However, even managing the lists has become challenging and currently Abigail has study lessons for three hours each week in which a learning support teacher helps her to process and condense the lists. An essential part of the learning plan is the support that Abigail gets at home where she usually completes her work.

An example from geography illustrates how the system of support operates: as part of a settlement study Abigail had to complete a map showing the location of a village; to write a paragraph explaining how to find the nearest major shopping area; and to make a list of the shops in the village. Abigail and her teacher studied each part in turn, wrote out the order in which each element should be tackled, together with further helpful hints. Abigail completed the work at home and took it back to school where it was incorporated into her coursework.

In Abigail's case it is evident that there are many facets to the system of support offered to her. For example, parental participation is crucial not only to help Abigail to complete the work that she takes home, but to monitor the situation for signs that pressures are mounting or that Abigail's self-esteem is being eroded in some way. In England, the SEN Code of Practice (DfES, 2001) reminds education professionals about the role of parents in supporting children with special educational needs and requires systems to be in place to facilitate parental participation.

Meanwhile, it is important to view the support that Abigail receives, not simply as a means of helping her to 'get by' but as teaching mechanisms that promote her cognitive skills. One outcome is likely to be the reduction of anxiety which, as Riding (2002) explains, limits working memory capacity. Another outcome of the techniques described above is likely to be the emergence of 'metamemory'.

The term 'metamemory' refers to the capacity for reflecting on the operation of one's own memory, usually with a view to improving or supporting its functioning. For example, most mature thinkers are aware that memory capacity is limited and therefore they must take deliberate steps to store crucial information, say, by writing it down. Metamemory is part of a wider capacity known as metacognition or 'thinking about thinking'. In the terms of the Framework for New Learning, metacognition is developed from 'gaining skills and understanding'. That is, having gained skills and understanding, the learner reflects on his or her capacity to use them. Metacognitive awareness is then more often associated with typically developing learners, but there is no reason why their spontaneously adopted strategies should not also be actively taught to people with SEN. Watson (1999; 2001) gives examples of teachers modelling metacognition for pupils with moderate learning difficulties and the same approach can be used for promoting memory strategies.

Powell (2000) acknowledges that teachers might model, for most pupils, the techniques she or he regularly uses to support memory. For example, she or he might write down stages of a learning task or, for non-readers, represent these in pictures. However, Powell points out that, because of the rigidity of the thinking characteristic of people with autistic spectrum disorders, pupils in this group should select pictures or other mnemonics for themselves. In this way, the act of choosing, signals for the child some control over his or her own learning and, Powell suggests, sets up notions of him- or herself as an active learner.

Problem-solving

Young children do not spontaneously alight on the correct strategy for solving specific problems. They will experiment during the later stages of the sensori-motor period but, as would be expected, this involves physically rehearsing a range of solutions, and, through trial and error, the correct solution is discovered. Once the child is capable of symbolic thought, she or he can mentally rehearse strategies and explore their potential before enacting a limited range in order to discover which are successful. At this stage children may have a range of strategies at their disposal, but as their approach to using them is not systematic, problem-solving is still lengthy and inefficient.

By applying some of the issues that have been identified in relation to typically developing children to those whose development is atypical, it is possible to see how the latter might be supported in order to problem-solve independently. Lacey (1991) offers scenarios where pupils with severe learning difficulties are gradually encouraged to take responsibility for solving problems and one of the examples, together with some of her observations, is examined here to explore possible approaches and how they reflect certain theoretical positions.

Lacey describes a situation in which a pupil is introduced to strategies for crossing the road. By reference to the Framework for New Learning we might say that the first step is to arrange for the learner to *encounter* the road and become *aware* of its implications for pedestrians. It is then necessary for the learner to direct her or his *attention* to the essential features of the road. Lacey suggests that, at this point, the teacher will hold the learner's hand, which will not only secure the learner's safety but will help her or him to orientate herself or himself to the direction of the traffic flow. She further suggests that, on the next occasion, the teacher again holds the hand of the learner, talking through the process and the features of the task. We would interpret this as again drawing attention to its key aspects. On the next outing the teacher walks alongside the learner, providing a running commentary of what they are doing and what is significant for crossing the road safely. Lacking physical contact with the teacher, the learner must attend fully to what they are both doing and must participate in the task. *Participation* is further enhanced at the next stage when the teacher questions the learner about the sequence of events. Finally, the learner's active *involvement* is assured when she or he takes responsibility for directing the teacher. Lacey suggests that when this stage has been successfully achieved the learner is ready to attempt the task independently.

The process of scaffolding and Bruner's view on the role of the teacher are evident in the teaching–learning situation described by Lacey (1991). Specifically, the teacher:

> … serves the learner as a vicarious form of consciousness until such a time as the learner is able to master his [sic] own action through his own consciousness and control.
>
> (Bruner, 1985, p.24)

It is significant, however, that the analysis we have provided here stops short of acknowledging *gaining skills and understanding*. In order to recognise this level of achievement it should be clear that the learner can cross any road under any conditions. It is possible that the learner develops, as Lacey observes, 'self-regulatory behaviours in a variety of contexts' (1991, p.93). Self-regulation involves reflecting on what one is doing and why, with a view to problem-solving and, as Vygotsky (1962) emphasises, language has an important role in supporting self-regulation. Writers (Zarkowska and Clements, 1988, for example) discuss the challenges of encouraging some learners to generalise the strategies that they have acquired in one context to another that is similar but not identical.

Many techniques for teaching people to generalise strategies to solve new problems owe their theoretical basis to learning theory. In brief, a problem represents a stimulus for a new behavioural response, which, if successful, solves the problem. Success reinforces the correct response that is then established and applied each time the identical problem situation arises. Effective problem-solvers can recognise when fresh situations are sufficiently similar to the original to make the same response appropriate. That is, they can overlook variations that are irrelevant to the resolution of the present problem. The converse situation requires the problem-solver to discriminate between the features of the original stimulus (problem) and a new problem to discover that a change in behaviour is needed for its resolution.

The approaches that are described here demand a facility for using language or some other form of symbolic thought to self-question, self-instruct and self-regulate. However, cognitive psychologists recognise that all individuals vary in their cognitive styles and that cognitive style influences the strategies that they adopt for any specific problem or type of problem. Cognitive styles are usually viewed as varying along two dimensions: the wholist-analytic dimension and the verbal-imagery dimension (Riding, 2002). The former represents the tendency for people to view a problem either as a whole or as components leading towards a whole. The second refers to the disposition of people either to verbalise problems or to reflect on them in terms of mental pictures or images. Additionally, it is known that there may be typical patterns of cognitive style associated with certain medical conditions: for example, Fragile X syndrome (Saunders, 1999). Thus, these dimensions are believed to have their origins in an individual's neurological organisation and are, therefore, not responsive to training. What can be changed is the way in which tasks are presented. That is, in modelling approaches to problem-solving, teachers can take account of the two dimensions and imaginatively create opportunities for each type of thinker to respond to the task. We may therefore assume that just as in the population of people without special needs, there is a sub-group that prefers not to have problems presented in words or symbols. Individuals with limited language abilities may respond better to imagery – for example, pictures – to show a sequence of steps.

Language and thought

In the preceding section, it was argued that most learners tend towards particular learning styles. Nonetheless, all typically developing learners make some use of language to support problem-solving and other intellectual activities. It follows, then, that it is often a restricted facility for language use or comprehension that gives rise to learning difficulties. Before continuing with a discussion of approaches or techniques that have attempted to compensate for the impact of language-based difficulties on learning, rather than on communication, it is necessary to look briefly at possible relationships between language and thought.

Long before questions about language and thought became the topic of psychological enquiry, philosophers argued about how far language determines thought or, the opposite view, reflects the products of thinking. These broad questions have since been reformulated to enable their closer examination and we have already represented one set of opposing views: Piaget regarded language as the outward expression of thought, whereas a Vygotskyan perspective holds that thought only becomes possible through internalised language. For the purposes of considering how learning can be supported in the absence of language competence, we take the view, with Vygotsky, that reality is constructed for the developing child who usually gains access to it chiefly by means of language. As an outcome of life experiences the child interprets reality and represents this back to other people and her/himself principally through language, in line with Piaget's view. In this way, individuals adopt culturally relevant ways of thinking, but assert their individualism so that societies and cultures themselves develop. This model allows us to consider the effects of language difficulties at different levels.

In Chapter 8 it was proposed that infants come to acquire a sense of meaning during interactions with primary caregivers, usually with a parent who imputes meaning even to very early reflexive behaviours. If interaction breaks down for any reason, the development, not only of communication, but also of language itself and its role in cognitive development, is compromised. In the most extreme circumstances, the child fails to develop intent or meaning and it becomes a challenge for other people to provide the means whereby the child can signal her or his apprehension of stimuli, however limited this might be. Objects of reference are widely recognised as indicating an individual's understanding that one object can stand for another, just as words stand for ideas. Park (1997) discusses objects of reference in relation to communication and provides a framework for analysing object reference use. In thinking about objects of reference as tools for thinking that are a precursor to language (Bruner, 1996), it is important to be sure that the object is linked to a specific representation in the mind of the individual concerned. The learner must be able to signify that some object is meaningful for her or him in relation to another object, person or event that is not immediately present. Without evidence for this, teachers cannot assume that the learner has made the connections that might be exploited as the basis for further learning.

Throughout this chapter, we have taken the view that teaching should strive to reduce the negative impact of within-child factors on learning potential. In this final paragraph we summarise our views by focusing briefly on specific language difficulties. Difficulties are said to be specific when they appear as anomalous to a pupil's normal facility for learning, although it is no longer widely considered appropriate or helpful to use an IQ score in order to assess the anomaly. The term 'specific language difficulties' is often used to suggest that the difficulties are restricted to language and that other areas of learning are unimpaired. The reality is, however, that any language delay or impairment has the potential to interfere with *all* learning because of its dual roles as a tool for thought and as the medium for communication. Moreover, in relation to learning in the narrower sense of activities pursued in a dedicated learning context – for example, a school – a facility for language is highly valued. It follows that the learning needs of pupils with language delays or difficulties may challenge conventional teaching approaches, particularly when the delays, difficulties or impairments also compromise the acquisition of fluent and effective reading, writing and spelling skills. As Garton and Pratt (1998) emphasise, teachers should examine their language use carefully, particularly when they teach children whose language development is not yet complete, children for whom the language of instruction is not their home language, or those with specific language difficulties.

Miss Thomas

Miss Thomas is the Year 3 teacher in an inner-city school. In her class of 30 children about half are from a range of ethnic minority groups and some are only now learning to speak English. Most of the children come from neighbouring housing estates that bear all the signs of social disadvantage. Two children (whom Miss Thomas identified as 'Jack' and 'Jill') have educational statements confirming specific language impairments: one, 'Beth' has specific learning difficulties (dyslexia) and another, 'Billy', has Down syndrome. Recently Miss Thomas has started studying for a qualification in teaching children with language and communication difficulties and delays. She was required to tape a lesson with Year 3, then analyse and critically evaluate her own use of language. Here is an extract from her project report:

Monday, April 14 (Literacy Hour: Group Work)
9.15–9.17 'Now, children, you're to go into your groups … and, Yellow Group, remember, Mrs Godwin is in hospital so you must be especially grown-up and I'll come to you in a moment … but first, everybody listen: I want someone to take the register to the Office [pause] … Jack, don't you want to take the register … I thought you liked going to see Mrs Blake?'

COMMENTARY There are too many ideas and commands and no pupil input. The key instruction about moving into groups was to happen last but it was given first and in an incomplete sentence. Yellow Group (to which Jack, Jill and Billy belong) have information which will only become significant after they have started work in their group. Jack obviously failed to understand the implicit request about the register and I didn't give him enough time to respond to my first question.

9.43–9.44 'Jill, is that pencil sharp enough or should you have asked me to sharpen it for you? It's OK? Then get weaving, you're not going to sit there all day, are you? Which words have you chosen to put into interesting sentences?'

COMMENTARY The first question comprises two parts, the second of which is structurally complex. The instruction to 'get weaving' and the reference to sitting there 'all day' make use of the type of non-literal language that confuses Jill. The final question is closed, it doesn't give Jill an opportunity to reflect on her own thoughts or practise her emerging expressive language skills.

SUMMARY   I have noticed that I tend to use language that will lose the children with language impairments and difficulties. It will also benefit the rest of the class, particularly those who aren't yet fluent English language users, if I:

- use less non-literal language;
- keep questions and instructions syntactically simple;
- allow pupils the time and opportunity to respond verbally;
- provide the means for my pupils to show me how they are thinking and what they are thinking about so that I can modify my teaching approach;
- don't use spoken language as the *only* means of communication in the classroom.

Through her professional development programme, Miss Thomas has gained skills and understanding that enable her to work more effectively with all learners, but particularly those whose development could be compromised by language difficulties when they are competent in all other aspects. She now recognises that the 'problem' for these children does not reside in them, but in the interactive context of the classroom and it is within her capability, as the more able language user, to manipulate this. She acknowledges that she must identify individual children's zones of proximal development. At the same time, she must look for ways of assessing and enhancing their intellectual skills that do not rely exclusively on teacher–learner talk or – where it is reading, writing and spelling that challenge children – written language. Working in collaboration with the speech and language therapist, Miss Thomas uses signing and symbols but also drawings and role-play. Importantly for children with *specific* difficulties, she has recognised that they are fully capable of metacognition, which, in turn, leads them to devise their own learning strategies and reveal their preferred learning styles.

Many of the factors that are significant in teaching children with specific language difficulties will also apply to those with severe dyslexia as a language-based disorder (Layton and Deeny, 2002). Additionally, however, it is worth remembering that dyslexia is primarily a difficulty with acquiring fluent and effective reading and spelling skills. As such, some of the difficulties that characterise dyslexia will respond to skills training. The principles of learning theory require that each skill, competence or knowledge domain to be acquired should be represented as a series of components. For behavioural approaches this creates a clear framework for the application of reinforcers. In the case of learners with dyslexia, the same principles serve to provide a basis for the analysis of task demands in order to identify written language demands and to address them, again according to the profile of strengths, weaknesses and learning styles that individual learners present (Thomson and Watkins, 1998).

Conclusion

The focus of interest in this book is children and young people learning in schools. Educational provision is increasingly determined by external agencies such as governments that set their own aims and content. However, learning is a lifelong process of gaining skills and understanding that lead to personal fulfilment and, in this chapter, we take the view that the primary responsibility of teachers is to promote learners' access to the learning process. This becomes crucially significant when those individuals are less likely to acquire learning skills spontaneously and are said to have special educational needs. Teachers have a role in mediating a reality that is meaningful to all children, but especially those with severe and complex needs. For these children it may not be appropriate to conceptualise progression in terms of a vertical 'ladder' towards the attainment of curriculum targets. Instead lateral progression will be evident whenever children indicate that they have generalised their learning to apply it in novel situations. With their knowledge and understanding teachers are uniquely placed to recognise the capacities of their pupils and to manipulate the teaching–learning situation accordingly in order to give *all* children the opportunities to develop as self-determining citizens.

References

Bozic, N. and Murdoch, H. (1996) 'Introduction', in N. Bozic and H. Murdoch (eds) *Learning through Interaction: Technology and Children with Multiple Disabilities*. London: David Fulton Publishers.

Bruner, J. (1966) *Towards a Theory of Instruction*. Cambridge, MA: Harvard University Press.

Bruner, J. (1985) 'Vygotsky: a historical and conceptual perspective', in J.V. Wetsch (ed.) *Culture, Communication and Cognition: Vygotskian Perspectives*. Cambridge: Cambridge University Press.

Bruner, J. (1996) *The Culture of Education*. Cambridge, MA: Harvard University Press.

Decariel, T.G. (1969) 'A study of the mental and emotional development of the thalidomide child', in B.M. Foss (ed.) *Determinants of Infants' Behaviour* (Vol. 4). London: Methuen.

DfES (2001) *Special Educational Needs: Code of Practice*. London: DfES.

Elliott, J. (2000) 'The psychological assessment of children with learning difficulties', *British Journal of Special Education*. 27 (2), 59–66.

Gardner, H. (1999) *Intelligence Reframed*. New York: New Books; Basic Books.

Garton, A. and Pratt, C. (1998) *Learning to be Literate: The Development of Spoken and Written Language*. Oxford: Blackwell Publishers.

Gathercole, S.E. and Baddeley, A.D. (1993) *Working Memory and Language*. Hove: Lawrence Erlbaum Associates.

Goswami, U. (1998) *Cognition in Children*. Hove: Psychology Press.

Grandin, T. (2003) Available online at www.grandin.com/inc/visual.thinking.html.

Hodapp, R. (1998) *Development and Disabilities: Intellectual, Sensory and Motor Impairments*. Cambridge: Cambridge University Press.

James, W. (1890) *The Principles of Psychology*. New York: Dover Publications.

Kamin, L. (1974) *The Science and Politics of IQ*. Potomac, MD: Lawrence Erlbaum Associates.

Lacey, P. (1991) 'Managing the classroom environment', in C. Tilstone (ed.) *Teaching Pupils with Severe Learning Difficulties: Practical Approaches*. London: David Fulton Publishers.

Laws, G., Byrne, A. and Buckley, S. (2000) 'Language and memory development in children with Down syndrome at mainstream schools and special schools: A comparison', *Educational Psychology*. 20 (4), 447–57.

Layton, L. and Deeny, K. (2002) *Sound Practice: Phonological Awareness in the Classroom* (2nd edition). London: David Fulton Publishers.

Meadows, S. (1993) *The Child as Thinker*. London: Routledge.

Park, K. (1997) 'How do objects become objects of reference? A review of the literature on objects of reference and a proposed model for the use of objects in communication', *British Journal of Special Education*. 24 (3), 108–14.

Powell, S. (2000) 'Learning about life asocially: the autistic perspective on education', in S. Powell (ed.) *Helping Children with Autism to Learn*. London: David Fulton Publishers.

Riding, R. (2002) *School Learning and Cognitive Style*. London: David Fulton Publishers.

Saunders, S. (1999) 'Teaching children with Fragile X syndrome', *British Journal of Special Education*. 26 (2), 76–9.

Thomson, M.E. and Watkins, E.J. (1998) *Dyslexia: A Teaching Handbook*. London: Whurr Publishers.

TTA (1999) *National Special Educational Needs Specialist Standards*. London: TTA.

Warren, D.H. (1994) *Blindness and Children: An Individual Differences Approach*. Cambridge: Cambridge University Press.

Watson, J. (1999) 'Working in groups: social and cognitive effects in a special class', *British Journal of Special Education*. 26 (2), 87–95.

Watson, J. (2001) 'Social constructivism in the classroom', *British Journal of Special Education*. 16 (3), 140–7.

Worthington, A. (ed.) (1999) *The Fulton Special Education Digest*. London: David Fulton Publishers.

Zarkowska, E. and Clements, J. (1988) *Problem Behaviour and People with Severe Learning Disabilities: A Practical Guide to a Constructional Approach*. London: Croom Helm.

Chapter 10

Behavioural, emotional and social development

As we stressed at the beginning of this book, the process of development is inextricably linked to the influences of growth and maturation and to factors external to the child. External factors (the family, the environment, the culture and community, together with the many experiences encountered as he or she develops and matures) affect him or her. It is usual to refer to the process as 'going through stages of development', although Bee, in a 1989 edition of her book on child development, uses the term 'system of development' rather than 'stages'. The term is broad in extent and is concerned with two distinct elements, rather akin to those referred to by Erikson as 'dilemmas' (Erikson, 1965).

The first element is the importance of recognising that the child is a 'joined-up person' and that all aspects of development are interlinked and closely associated. Although the chapters in Part 3 are concerned with four distinct areas of development based on the Teacher Training Agency's (TTA's) 'Extension Standards' within the National Specialist Standards for Special Educational Needs for England (TTA, 1999), readers will see that *all* facets of development are intertwined and that each area interrelates and interacts with all the others. As we stress throughout the book, cognition is closely related to language and communication and will influence the behaviour of the child and the formation of his or her social relationships; similarly, sensory experiences, or a lack of them, will have an impact on physical development. Lack of mobility will also affect the formation of social relationships, and may determine the child's behaviour and his or her emotional development.

The second element within Bee's 'system' is a consideration of the external factors identified above. The child develops within a structure that involves other people (the family, the community and society) and this structure entails adapting to different environments. The environment of the school may be very different from that of the home, and the environment and ethos of one school may be very different from that of another. Bee's ideas take into account the emphasis Vygotsky places on the socio-cultural aspects (see the discussion on Vygotsky and empowerment in Chapter 5). The different environments make varied demands upon the growing child and either support or hinder his or her emerging skills, knowledge and understanding and, equally importantly, particularly in relation to the themes within this chapter, the development of relationships and the fostering of a good self-image. Naturally they all impinge on the lifelong process of empowerment as outlined in Chapter 1.

This chapter is entitled 'Behavioural, social and emotional development' and, as in the two previous chapters in this section, these themes reflect the strands of the TTA Extension Standards. It is not our intention to highlight specific aspects of the Standards (which are an audit tool for teachers in England only), but it is interesting that in a document that is designed to enhance professionals' understanding of pupils with a wide range of special educational needs, behaviour is placed as the first of the three strands. Our viewpoint, however, is that a child's behaviour results from his or her social and emotional development.

As we have seen in Chapters 4 and 7, learning theorists often refer to behaviour as everything that a child does, but our definition of behaviour is more in line with dictionary definitions which highlight certain attributes, such as a person's:

*   treatment of others;
*   consideration of 'self';
*   ability to conform, and contribute, to the formation of rules;
*   conduct in a range of social situations.

With the possible exception of the last attribute, they all arise from an individual's ability to form relationships and to establish a good self-image. We, therefore, regard the child's social development as being of central importance.

Becoming a social being

A normally developing infant has a number of genetically acquired patterns or rules which govern the way that he or she behaves in the early days of life. These reflexes quickly become what Bee (2000) refers to as 'the dance of interaction and attachment' (p.320), and consequently she and other writers (Flavell, 1963, for example) challenge Piaget's early writing in which he suggests that the infant remains a passive individual for some weeks. As will be seen in the example of Amy, who is only a few weeks old, the interactions between her and her mother are reciprocal and each is influenced by the other.

Amy

Amy is feeding and her basic rooting, sucking and swallowing reflexes have extended into the acquisition of other skills such as:

*   visual focusing (initially on the source of food and, later, on her mother who is providing it);
*   sensitivity to the sounds around her (particularly to the caressing sounds made by her mother at the time of feeding).

Very quickly, however, Amy becomes an *influencer* of the social environment, rather than a passive recipient. She and her mother become mutually involved as Amy:

*   maintains eye contact for longer periods;
*   touches her mother's skin during the feeding process;
*   begins to smile (or is it wind?);
*   alters her facial expression to one of contentment at the feeding process;
*   distinguishes the nipple from other objects;
*   makes sounds of enjoyment;
*   turns her head to the source of food.

Her mother alters her responses by:

- returning her gaze;
- providing warmth, tactile experience and movement (rocking Amy as she feeds);
- smiling at her;
- speaking slowly and caressingly;
- watching her.

Chapter 8 gives details of the development of early communication, but what is important here is that Amy's and her mother's conduct and treatment of each other alter as they interact, and they also become more 'attached' to each other through their individual and collective responses or behaviours. Freud considered the child's emotional attachment to the mother as the foundation for the formation of all relationships (Freud, 1960) and many psychoanalysts regard the early behaviours of the mother (or caregiver) and child during feeding as the basis for building close emotional bonds.

The psychoanalyst John Bowlby (1965), however, did not take this view. His theory of attachment is not based on behaviours during feeding, but on the biological survival of the species that ensures the infant's safety in a warm and loving environment. In his view, Amy's initial signals of visual focusing, grasping and smiling (as described above) are innate and help to ensure that other humans respond to her needs. Bowlby calls this the *pre-attachment* phase (birth to six weeks), when babies do not mind the presence of an unfamiliar adult as long as their needs are met.

However in the next stage, the *attachment in the making* phases (six weeks to six months) the infant displays 'different' behaviour with an unfamiliar adult, and greater pleasure when in the company of the mother or major caregiver. This phase is replaced by the *clear-cut attachment* phase (six months to approximately two years) where there is likely to be separation anxiety on the part of the child when a familiar adult leaves. Bowlby postulated that the infant can then reason that the adult continues to exist out of sight. Berk (2003) links this aspect of Bowlby's theory to Piaget's theory on the development of object permanence, and suggests that babies who are not anxious when separated from their major caregivers are unlikely to have acquired object permanence; a point made by Warren (1994) and referred to in the last chapter.

In the *clear-cut attachment* phase infants actively seek contact with the major caregiver that in turn leads to the last of Bowlby's phases: the formation of reciprocal relationships (from 18 months onwards). Berk (2003, p.419) writes of this phase:

> By the end of the second year, rapid growth in representation and language permits toddlers to understand some of the factors that influence the parent's coming and going, and to predict her return ... Now children start to negotiate with the caregiver, using requests and persuasion to alter her goals rather than clinging to her.

Whether or not one agrees with Bowlby's theory of the survival of the species, he, along with the cognitive developmental theorists, stresses that the formation of reciprocal relationships are essential for interpersonal communication and stable emotional development. Erikson, arguing from a psychoanalytical perspective, also emphasises the importance of such relationships (see Chapter 6) in each person's search for his or her own identity.

In contrast to Amy's and her mother's mutual involvement and interaction when feeding, Bryony and her mother are having greater difficulty in responding to each other in the same way.

Bryony

Bryony is a passive baby who readily goes to sleep during feeding. Her rooting, sucking and swallowing reflexes are slower than Amy's and, consequently, she is not gaining weight; a major concern to her mother. She has been advised by the Health Visitor to bounce Bryony up and down to waken her when she sleeps in the middle of a feed (a procedure which makes her protest) and to stroke her daughter's throat in an attempt to encourage her to swallow. Bryony's tiredness and passivity means that she is not entering into 'the dance of interaction and attachment' with her mother and is neither providing eye contact, nor touching her, nor making sounds of enjoyment. Consequently, Bryony's mother is not encouraged to alter her behaviour in response to her daughter and the rapid mutual learning (seen in Amy's case) is not happening. Her mother is taking the initiative and is learning that maternal commitment and infant need are not well synchronised. Feeding is becoming a battle, rather than an activity that fosters reciprocal social interaction. This is not to say, of course, that such behaviour will not allow close emotional bonds to develop eventually and that Bryony will not grow into a social being. Instead the 'system of development' emerging at present is not an easy one for either mother or daughter.

At the end of the first year it became clear that Bryony had not passed many of the developmental milestones usually established by a child like Amy, and a diagnosis of developmental delay was made. Naturally, growth rates are unpredictable in young children, but Bryony appeared to be behind other so-called 'normally developing' children in major areas such as mobility and communication. All those who are concerned with the education of children with special educational needs will recognise that it is important not to become preoccupied with what children *cannot* do, but to consider and build upon what they *can* do. At the end of the first year Bryony had achieved the following:

In *mobility*, she could:

✓   lift her head when lying on her tummy;
✓   sit if her back was supported;
✓   kick when lying on her back.

In *social development (early communication)* she could:

✓   make cooing and throaty sounds;
✓   make noises when talked to;
✓   turn to loud sounds;
✓   smile.

Bryony's mother had learned that in becoming a support for her daughter she had to provide the opportunities to practise and build on her physical and mobility skills. In doing so, she began to recognise that physical capacities have a major effect on social development.

As Bryony was not ready to sit alone or to crawl she could only explore objects if they were brought to her and put into her hands. In the mother's attempts to provide experiences that extend her daughter's motor capacities she became what Bruner calls an 'amplifier', and in Chapter 2 we discussed this aspect of Bruner's theory in terms of teaching children who have complex needs.

As can be seen by her achievements, Bryony's social development was at an early stage and her slowness in responding to her mother's attempts to communicate with her were often aborted. For example, her mother would make cooing noises, but Bryony took some time to respond and, when she did, the sound she made often coincided with the mother's next sound. Turn-taking was therefore difficult to establish and her mother, not knowing how to proceed, became less inclined to communicate in such a way. In learning theorists' terms, there was a lack of reward or reinforcement.

However, the mother slowly recognised that she must give more time for her daughter to respond and, consequently, the pace and pattern of interaction was gradually adjusted. Over time, their interactions became reciprocal and they learned from each other, but it is important to recognise that the growing awareness by Bryony's mother of the part *she* must play in her daughter's development formed the culture of learning that is discussed in the section on Bruner in Chapter 2. As Bryony matured, her mother altered the quantity and quality of her support, and offered an adjustable 'scaffold' that fitted Bryony's level of performance (Bruner, 1996; Vygotsky, 1962). One outcome of close, repeated encounters with Bryony was that her mother had intuitively made use of operating within Bryony's zone of proximal development (see the discussion on Vygotsky's work in Chapter 2) and gradually, as Bryony became more competent, her mother was able to turn some of the responsibility for social interaction over to her daughter. Since Bruner and Vygotsky published their views, other cognitive psychologists have used a range of terms to illustrate 'scaffolding' which broadens and extends the concept. Rogoff (1990), for example, uses the term 'guided participation', which goes beyond the physical prompting techniques referred to in the chapters in this book concerned with learning theory, and suggests greater co-operation and collaboration from the pair.

As a child's social development extends, he or she may become wary of strangers. Such a reaction gradually lessens as he or she enters into more complex and reciprocal relationships with a range of people including peers. Social learning theorists (Bandura, 1977 and Sullivan, 1953, in the USA) have emphasised the importance of peers and early friendships in the development of the child as a social being. These theorists, along with Erikson albeit from a rather different perspective, also highlight how early relationships help to shape both personality and behaviour.

Learning takes place *directly* by direct teaching of the child, but also *indirectly* by providing a focus of observation for the child (a model). Bandura (1977) believes that observing and imitating adults, and also other children, teaches the child to behave morally and socially, and such models exert their strongest influence in the preschool years. Repeated observations of others allow children to internalise rules of good conduct and to select behaviours that they regard as appropriate or inappropriate, and adults and other children are, therefore, agents of behavioural and social control. The emphasis on *indirect* modelling by the social learning theorists is slightly different from the *direct* modelling put forward as a technique for teaching and learning by the classic learning theorists, but the importance of observation to both groups of theorists cannot be denied.

The function of play

Play has often been regarded as a way of exercising skills that will be required in later life: a sort of rehearsal. Piaget was, however, more concerned with the development of cognition through the content of play as was Vygotsky, who regarded play as the means by which the child built mental structures that involved the use of language and other aspects of the culture. Keenan (2002) points out, however, that: 'play also allows children to explore their social world by adopting various roles and interaction patterns thereby promoting social development' (p.202).

He identifies the following milestones in the social development of normally developing children:

- birth–6 months: awarenessof and interest in other people;
- 6–12 months: clear interest in, and response to, peers;
- 12–14 months: engages in parallel play, understands the rules of exchange, evidence of pro-social behaviour such as empathy;
- 3 years: engages in co-operative play, dominance hierarchies are observed (rankings within the group based on a characteristic such as toughness or bossiness);
- 4 years: engages in associative play, some conflicts occur;
- 6 years: more time spent with peers, group sizes increase, goals of friendship are defined by shared interests;
- 7–9 years: peer acceptance is the goal of friendship;
- early adolescence: friendships centre on intimacy and self-disclosure, peer groups form cliques;
- late adolescence: friends are seen as a source of social and emotional support.

(adapted from Keenan, 2002, p.202)

In order to understand the development of children with special educational needs it is important to explore some of these milestones, which may not correspond to the chronological ages of normally developing children. Such milestones are better thought of as 'signposts'.

If we consider the first two signposts together, we can see in the example of Bryony that she had certain social limitations that made it difficult for her and her mother to interact. Amy, on the other hand, became an influence on the reciprocal interaction between mother and daughter in the first few weeks of life. As the children developed, both passed the signpost of becoming aware of other people, although Bryony did not seem to be aware of others until she went to school. 'Other people' included other children, and Amy began to show a fleeting interest in peers from about the age of two months. By the age of six months she was watching them carefully, returning their gaze and gradually responding to their play. In the following example, two junior-age boys with complex needs were responding to each other, possibly in a similar way to that of Amy in her first year of life. The boys had passed the 'signpost' of just being interested in each other, and had devised a sophisticated, social, co-operative game, which to the uninitiated could be considered outside their capabilities.

Thomas and Danial

Thomas and Danial, who have profound and multiple learning difficulties and limited movements, were lying on parallel mats during a rest period from curricular activities. They each had a toy, in this case a toy lawnmower, within their grasp. They began using their limited movements to push the lawnmowers towards each other, in what could be interpreted as an effort to exchange them, but the game became more complicated as each child responded to the other. After rolling towards each other they appeared to try to take each other's toy whilst keeping a hand on their own. Later they returned to actions which could be interpreted as an 'exchange'. Danial for example, pushed his toy towards Thomas and let go of it and Thomas attempted to poke his toy into Danial's stomach. Each child displayed enjoyment.

(adapted from Eason *et al.*, 1992, p.322)

Danial and Thomas have built on many of the learning opportunities outlined in the Framework for New Learning in Chapter 1 (QCA/DfEE, 2001) and are *gaining new skills and understanding* through their play. Their play became sophisticated as they *encountered* playful experiences, became *aware* of toys as vehicles for interaction, *attended* and *responded* to each other and became attuned to each other's movements. They have *engaged* in a social activity that requires *participation* and *involvement*. Their learning is more than gaining cognitive skills, but is equally concerned with the development of social understanding and competence.

Despite an interest in other children and people, some children may show a fear of unfamiliar adults (and children); a reaction often referred to as 'stranger anxiety'. Not all children show this response, but it is not unusual for such fears to emerge in the second half of the first year. A child being picked up by someone he or she does not know, for example, may cry and become agitated. Erikson stresses the importance of a healthy sense of mistrust in the first of his psychosocial stages (trust/mistrust, see Chapter 3). The ways in which babies and young children regulate their reactions depend on the social context in which the stressful reactions are handled. If a caregiver overreacts to a situation by, for example, not intervening in a supportive way, then it is likely that the child's distress will be reinforced and emotional development may be affected, in that the child could become more anxious and overreact to out-of-the-ordinary events. At this stage, children only portray their feelings through primitive means, such as crying or drawing away, but as they develop language or learn to communicate, there is a greater possibility that they will be able to describe their emotional states and to talk about their feelings and the feelings of others. From the discussion it is easier to see how social development underpins emotional development.

Using words or gestures to communicate opens up new prospects for interactions, which become more and more complex as motor skills also increase and, as the child becomes confident, understanding is established. A signpost (usually within the first 18 months) is that the child moves from playing alongside others, or in parallel to them, to an understanding of simple rules. Children co-ordinate their responses in more sophisticated way – 'your turn' – and pretend play begins to emerge.

Feeding giraffes

At the age of three and a half, the son of one of the writers and his younger sister insisted on taking a bucket of 'food' to the bottom of the garden to feed their 'giraffes'. They pretended that there was food in the bucket and in their world, the trees in the garden became the symbols for giraffes. They invented simple names for their 'pets', and talked about them (and even fell out over them) at other times in the day. Make believe, pretence and imagination had become part of their social play.

Over 20 years ago, Jeffree *et al.* (1977) outlined the importance of imaginative play for children with learning difficulties. Their suggested functions for imaginative play can, of course, apply to both normally developing children and those with special educational needs. Their proposals are listed below.

Imaginative play helps to develop thought and language

In Piagetian terms the ability to allow one thing to stand for another, to picture something which is not there, and to talk or communicate about it to another, contributes importantly to the development of cognition as discussed in the previous chapter.

Imaginative play helps children to understand others

Children learn to put themselves in the place of others, and they construct a naïve 'theory of mind', which Berk (2003) describes as 'a coherent understanding of their own and others' mental states' (p.439). As Happe (1994, p.38) reminds us:

> ... normal children from around the age of four years, understand (however implicitly) that people have beliefs and desires about the world, and it is these mental states (rather than the physical state of the world) which determines a person's behaviour.

In Piagetian terms, they are no longer egocentric.

Children with autism, however, often lack the ability to put themselves in the shoes of another person and 'theory of mind' has become a significant tool in the assessment of autism. Important work has been carried out by researchers (led by Simon Baron-Cohen) who have devised a classic false belief test, widely known as the 'Sally-Anne' test. The test has become a standard tool in the identification of autism and therefore it is important to highlight it here.

The Sally-Anne test

Baron-Cohen (1995) explains that the test involves children seeing 'Sally' putting a marble in one place, and later when she is away, 'Anne' moves it to another location. Children without autism understand that since Sally was not there when her marble was moved, she will still believe that it is where she put it. On being asked 'Where will Sally look for her marble?', normally developing children of around three or four years will give the right answer, but a significant number of children with autism will point to where the marble is in its new location.

The test has been widely used and 'proven', but researchers offer different explanations for the reasons why children with autism have this lack of understanding. They range from difficulties with interpersonal relationships at early stages of development (Tager-Flusher, 2001; Baron-Cohen, 1995), to difficulties in planning behaviour (Russell, 1997), to an inability perceptually to link information together to form a whole (Happe, 1994). For an overview of these discussions, the reader is recommended to consult Lewis's seminal work on disability, which includes a chapter on 'How do children with autism develop?' (Lewis, 2003, p.249).

Imaginative play helps creativity

As we can see from the example of 'feeding the giraffes', imagination and inventiveness go hand in hand. Around 20 per cent of the free play of children of about four and five years involves complicated imaginative play, and Bee (1989) reminds us that children who exhibit a great deal of such play are regarded by nursery staff as being generally more socially competent, more popular and less egocentric. This view is supported by Bruner (1996) who considers play as fundamental to the development of the child.

Imaginative play helps children to come to terms with themselves

Jeffree *et al.* (1977) emphasise that imagination can become a safety valve for stressful and difficult situations. Children are able to escape from themselves into other roles and they – particularly only children or those who are being bullied – often invent imaginary friends, or project themselves into more powerful positions.

Paul

Paul, a pupil with athetoid cerebral palsy in a mainstream middle school, although appearing to be accepted by his immediate peer group, is often a target for bullying by other (particularly older) pupils in the school because of his 'different' mobility patterns and slurred speech. Such bullying usually takes the form of name-calling ('spaz' – a 'street cred' version of spastic – is commonly used) and blatant imitations of his uncontrolled movements. On the surface, Paul appears to take this in good part, although he does confess to the Special Educational Needs Co-ordinator (SENCo) that he finds such behaviour hurtful, and has been found shedding a few tears in private. To an outside observer, he seems well integrated into the life of the school and appears to get on with his classmates, many of whom he knew in his first school. His parents, however, have become concerned that he does not want to invite friends home, as their other children do, and are worried that his interaction with his peers is at a superficial level.

From their knowledge, obtained through a support group, they are aware that children with cerebral palsy may not make close friends easily and can become socially isolated as adults. Paul readily articulates that he has not got a best friend, or a close circle of friends, at school to share his interests and problems (a point confirmed by his teachers). Most children of his age take an active interest in sport, but because of his physical disabilities Paul cannot take part and therefore is not interested in sporting activities.

His parents note that as a younger child he developed a close imaginary friend, 'Ali', to whom he talked openly. As he has matured, Paul has been overheard conversing with 'Ali' in the privacy of his bedroom. His parents recognise that it is very unusual for a child as old as nine to have an imaginary friend, and are worried that he is emotionally insecure. On the other hand, they recognise that 'Ali' may provide the emotional support needed by Paul at times that may be more stressful and difficult than is generally thought. They shared their concerns with the SENCo and Paul's teaching assistant at a recent parents' evening.

This example illustrates a number of dilemmas for Paul's parents and the school staff:

- Does Paul's dependency on an imaginary friend stem from emotional immaturity, or is there cause for concern in terms of Paul's mental health?

- Should there be a close monitoring of his conversations with 'Ali' in order to find out if his imaginary friend is proving an outlet for a deeper problem (is this a strategy for coping or a way of regulating feelings?) or whether it is just part of late development in one area?
- Is there a connection between Paul's inability (or reluctance) to make close friends and his maintenance of an imaginary friend?
- Does his slightly slurred speech really discourage or inhibit communication?
- Should Paul be made aware of these concerns, and his views sought?

In the interests of empowerment the answer to the last question is 'yes', but at the time of writing this book the other questions remain unanswered. These are, however, the questions that the professionals dealing with Paul need to raise and, of course, there are no easy answers.

It is important, however, to reflect upon why Paul's peers may not wish to become close friends. Although children's social skills (which include their ability to communicate with others) are important in the acceptance by a peer group, other less rational characteristics also have an effect. Unfamiliar factors, including fear of human difference such as strange names, unusual accents, and physical unattractiveness, can set children apart (Keenan, 2002). As Paul's disability results in unusual facial expressions, it may be that his peers are wary and embarrassed, and therefore more likely to judge Paul to have other negative characteristics that he does, in fact, not possess: often termed the 'spread phenomenon' (Wright, 1974). Frances (2000) found that such reactions to an unusual facial appearance by school children often resulted in staring, teasing, bullying and name-calling. Paul has an additional disadvantage of not being interested in the 'accepted' sporting interests of his peer group.

It seems that his immediate peers acknowledge that Paul is a member of their class, but true friendships have not developed. The distinction between acknowledgement or *acceptance* and *friendship* is an interesting one (Asher *et al.*, 1996), and it fits in with Keenan's 'signpost' for normally developing children around seven to nine years when it is suggested that peer *acceptance* is the goal of friendship and the beginning of more intimate relationships. Paul's peers' good-natured recognition of him could be a positive indication that close friendships will emerge.

The notion of 'difference', however, will also have an effect on how Paul views himself. His knowledge of himself is being formed through his interaction with others, and his relationships play an important part in the development of his personality and character. Freud's view of emotional development suggests that felt emotions can result in inner conflicts which the child represses because they are unacceptable. It is possible in Paul's case that his superego is compelling him to repress his feelings of hurt and anger at the way in which he is being treated because these feelings might lead him to 'lash out' in an aggressive response. Instead he resorts to behaviour usually associated with a younger child.

Opportunities to make warm and satisfying friendships are related to emotional well-being and stable behaviour throughout childhood and adolescence and into adulthood. Younger children are naturally influenced by the adults around them, but older children care more about what their peers think about them, and research by Rosenberg (1979) showed that adolescents are more concerned with their best friends' opinion of them than that of their parents as they enter Erikson's fifth psychosocial stage of identity/role diffusion. When young people with learning difficulties have left school their 'best friends' are often those with similar difficulties in learning. One reason for this can be attributed to the fact that, through choice, their educational and leisure activities may only include those with similar disabilities. Another reason could be that, as part of the move to maturity, people without learning difficulties are likely to leave home and establish an existence that is, on the one hand, self-reliant, and, on the other, encompasses a wide and varied circle of friends (Lindon, 1996). Many of these friends may not find it easy to accept someone with a disability, which may be due to lack of confidence or negative perceptions. In order to counteract such attitudes strategies have been devised which help young people to recognise the personal qualities and inherent abilities of their peers with learning difficulties. The *Fast Friends Programme* is one such strategy that has proved effective (Shevlin, 2003; Shevlin, 2001). Mainstream pupils view videos of pupils with learning disabilities achieving in different situations and then take part in structured curricular activities with them. Viewing the videos has helped many mainstream pupils to establish positive expectations towards developing relationships with their peers with learning difficulties. Shevlin (2003, p.96) reports that the following comments, made after the experience, are typical of the mainstream pupils' reactions:

> 'I learned how easy it is to get on with them if you give them a chance';
> 'I learned you could become real friends with someone with a disability.'

Berk (2003) lists four ways in which close friendships help emotional development through:

* an exploration of self in relation to another (a process that supports the development of self-concept and identity);
* the provision of a foundation for future intimate relationships (through, for example, the emotion-laden discussions between best friends in adolescence on romance, sex and love relationships);
* support in dealing with the stresses of everyday life (in supportive friendships, anxiety and loneliness are reduced and self-esteem is fostered);
* better adjustments and more positive attitudes towards school (interacting with friends made at school encourages children and young people to view school more positively).

The development of self-esteem and its place in emotional development

Berk's first point leads us to consider the development of the self and the importance of self-esteem. In Chapter 3, we mention the importance of a 'self-scheme' in the overall development of the child. This 'self-scheme' or understanding of him- or herself will alter as the child matures, and it is generally thought of as a process which involves the self as a *subject* of experience, often referred to as *existentialist* self (Lewis, 1990). In this early process, the child learns that he or she is an agent of change.

Erikson has shown through his psychosocial stages that the way in which people feel about themselves influences their achievements in all areas of development, and there is considerable evidence to show the correlation between self-esteem and academic achievement (see, for example, Lawrence, 1996). How others respond to children will inevitably influence their ideas about them, as the following writing of a pupil in year 10, taken from an article written by Indoe *et al.* (1992; p.151), reveals:

> School ain't much fun
> When all the teachers do is

Tell you off
Couldn't do better
Just average all they say
Well I'm special mate, unique,
Might not be brilliant at sport
Maths, English or any of those things
Though I can do 'em
Yer there isn't another me is there?
I'm unique
You aint seen nothing yet.

Certainly this could have been written by any one of us, and it reveals, at a basic level, the notion of 'self' as being different to others, but at a more sophisticated one, the fragility of the concept of 'self'. This pupil is angry, resentful and hurt that his 'performance' is constantly being evaluated as inferior alongside his peers. The work illustrates that our understanding of ourselves is intertwined with social development and consequently influenced by others' reactions to us. The pupil, in terms of Erikson's theory, is likely to be at the stage of experiencing the tension between 'industry versus inferiority', and unfortunately, the balance is tipped towards the feeling of inferiority (see the hazards associated with this psychosocial stage in Chapter 3).

The first step in understanding 'self', however, is an awareness of a separate identity. In Piaget's view, the extreme egocentrism that characterises the thinking of the very young infant is only gradually replaced by the 'self-scheme'. In Freud's view, separation from the primary caregiver does not occur until the ego begins to develop and only with the emergence of these phases does self-'awareness' become evident. The classic test of self-awareness was the 'rouge test' (Lewis and Brooks-Gunn, 1979) in which a red spot was placed on the noses of young children who were then encouraged to look at their reflection in a mirror. It was found that children around 15 to 20 months would touch the red spot on their own nose when they saw their image. The researchers concluded that if the children knew what they looked like (were 'self-aware') then they would be surprised by an addition to their image and would want to explore it by touch. It is suggested that people brought up totally isolated from others do not have this self-awareness, which again highlights the importance of social interaction in the development of the 'self'.

From this basic awareness of 'self' emerges a more sophisticated understanding based on important qualities or characteristics such as gender, name and size. This development is often referred to as the 'self as an object' or the 'categorical self' (Lewis, 1990). A further development occurs as social interactions increase and the 'self' begins to take into account the reactions of others. As far back as 1902, Cooley introduced the term 'looking-glass self', meaning that other people reflect back to us their perceptions of us. Our self-concepts may then change to accommodate the reflected view. This process is particularly potent when the reflection comes from 'significant others' (Mead, 1934): people whom we are close to or have regular contact with. As children mature and take on board more and more information from a range of 'others', they may reject or filter information if it does not fit with their views of 'self'. The people who become meaningful to them, and to whom they look for support, change as they mature. Research carried out by Rosenberg (1979) showed the expected: that young children relied heavily on adults for their evaluations, but older children cared what their best friends thought about them. These evaluations of the 'self' (particularly in terms of others' perceptions of our own achievements and competences) become the basis of 'self-esteem'. It is likely that the older pupil who wrote the words above has low self-esteem and, for all his bravado, the fact that he mentions certain areas of the curriculum (sport, maths and English) indicates that these are important to him. Despite his comment 'Though I can do 'em', it is likely that he is constantly being told by his teachers that his performance is poor and, as already emphasised, in Erikson's terms he is experiencing the crisis of industry versus inferiority; it is possible that, unless his 'significant others' change towards him, inferiority will win.

It is not just negative comments that fuel negative perceptions of difference. In the case of Micheline Mason (quoted by Miell in Barnes, 1995), who has a physical disability, her own realisation of the enormous hurdles ahead of her assumed massive proportions and were likely to have had a bearing on her self-esteem at that time.

Micheline

Micheline wrote:

> The first time the doubt that I belonged to this particular planet struck me, was a glorious, calm, blue-skied day when I was about twelve years old. Lying flat on my back in the garden, staring at the sky I was thinking about growing up. Until that moment I think I had somehow believed that when I grew up I would become normal, i.e. without a disability. 'Normal' then meant to me, 'like my big sister', pretty, rebellious, going out with boys, doing wonderful naughty things with them, leaving school and getting a job, leaving home, getting married and having children. That momentous day I suddenly realised that my life was not going to be like that at all. I was going to be just the same as I had always been – very small, funnily shaped, unable to walk. It seemed at that moment the sky cracked. My vision expanded wildly. My simple black and white world exploded into vivid colours which dazzled and frightened me in a way in which I had never been frightened before. Everything took on an ominous hue. At that point I saw life as a tremendous competition and I believed that I was just not equipped to cope.
>
> (Miell, 1995, pp.205–6)

In this example, Micheline's beliefs, attitudes and values pertaining to herself (her self-concept) have been challenged. An evaluative component modified the way in which she saw herself, and her self-worth or self-esteem were threatened. Early research undertaken in the 1970s and 1980s on the self-esteem of children with physical disabilities suggested that it was difficult for them to maintain high self-esteem as they were constantly contrasting themselves with the able-bodied (Richardson *et al.*, 1964; Henker, 1979). Since writing this, Micheline Mason has developed her ideas and sees one of the main problems for people with a disability as the attitude of others and the lack of resources. Now, as a parent of a child with a disability, she is dedicated to helping educationalists to embrace full equality for *all* in all aspects of the community life.

In considering the attitudes of others, Fox (2002, p.7) emphasises that:

> … this social model of disability suggests that the problems of the child with a physical disability do not reside in their disability but rather are located within their social world, for example, the lack of facilities at school or the attitude of their teachers.

Lack of facilities and 'set' attitudes of the staff at schools to pupils apply to all children (but particularly to those with difficulties in learning), and the need for acceptance, love and approval in order to foster self-esteem is stressed by both the psychoanalytical and developmental theorists.

It would be wrong in a chapter with emotional development as part of its title not to make explicit reference to the development of emotional expression and understanding. Keenan (2002), in an excellent chapter encompassing all aspects of emotional regulation, takes a functionalist view of emotional development. Such a view stresses that emotions are adaptive processes that are influenced by development in other areas, particularly in the social, cognitive and perceptual domains. As the child matures, emotion becomes the regulator of social and cognitive behaviour; a point that we will return to later. He provides a succinct summary of the milestones in the development of emotional expression and understanding and his milestones for social development have already been discussed in this chapter. It is easy to see how the two areas overlap.

Some of the early emotional expressions, such as stranger distress, have been discussed already. Envy, guilt and embarrassment, however, have their roots in the evaluative component we made reference to when discussing Micheline Mason's writing. At around two to three years, a child begins to evaluate his or her behaviour against a perceived standard. He or she may feel embarrassed if the behaviour does not match up to the standard or, in the case of becoming envious, if the behaviour does not match up to another person who is held in high esteem. As the child matures, there is the realisation that two emotions can occur together. In normally developing children at around adolescence there is the recognition that different 'sets' of emotions can occur from a single event and these can disrupt or disorganize functioning. If we are happy as a result of something, but at the same time a little nervous (for example, being given an award and having to make a speech in recognition of it), we will experience a range of emotions during a block of time: pleasure, pride, embarrassment, fear and relief are just some of the possibilities of emotions felt during the award ceremony.

Table 10.1 Keenan's milestones

Age	Emotional expression	Emotional understanding
0–3 months	Startle, disgust, distress, the social smile	
3–6 months	Laughter, anger, interest, surprise, sadness	
7 months	Fear	
7–9 months	Stranger distress	
12 months		Social referencing
18–24 months	Shame, pride	
2–3 years	Envy, guilt, embarrassment	
3–5 years		Emotional display rules
6–8 years		Awareness that two emotions can occur in sequence
9 years and beyond		Awareness that two emotions of the same valence can occur simultaneously
11 years		Awareness that one event can elicit a range of feelings

In Paul's case (described earlier in this chapter), the name-calling by his peers evoked feelings of both anger and distress, but his apparent nonchalant attitude could be a product of his ability to regulate his emotions. His emotional arousal is controlled by his capacity to cope. The research into the regulation of emotions suggests that a number of factors come into play, some of which are intrinsic, others extrinsic. The development of the central nervous system, the changes in cognitive functioning and the growth of linguistic skills are some of the *intrinsic* processes which aid regulation. *Extrinsic* processes can be identified as those influential 'outside' factors, such as the love and understanding of parents and other key individuals, opportunities to talk about feelings to a 'best' friend, and the expectations of society (or in Bruner's term 'the culture'). From a basic regulation of both the intrinsic and the extrinsic factors comes an understanding of an emotional self that is shaped by the reaction of others. A person may perceive herself or himself as quiet or diffident and therefore bring conscious strategies into play in order to confirm his or her beliefs. As we mature, a complex network of self-belief systems is incorporated into our 'self-awareness'.

Behaviour

Our development as a social being and the way in which we deal with our emotions, and establish a self-image, to a large extent determines our behaviour. Some children exhibit behaviours which are out of the ordinary, or difficult to interpret, and are therefore regarded as 'challenging'. Such an expression is important as it implies that difficulties arise because of the way in which the child and the 'system' interrelate. The system may be the application of 'standards' by parents, school or society, which are ill-matched to the child's abilities and understanding.

David, discussed in Chapter 4, struggles to understand what is expected of him and, therefore, exhibits 'challenging' behaviour as a protest against his inhibiting learning environment. In an effort to allow him to 'cool down', the staff often send him out of the room, which gives him an opportunity to escape from the work he does not understand, and offers them some respite from his behaviour. In David's case the responsibility for his behaviour is placed on his shoulders ('conform or else') without taking into consideration the responsibilities that staff have to differentiate experiences and to provide pupils with the opportunities to learn and to achieve. For him, the seemingly inflexible system is likely to be a major reason for the increase in challenging behaviour. The *Index for Inclusion*, which has been sent to all maintained schools in Britain, provides materials to support staff in building on their own knowledge about what impedes learning (Booth *et al.*, 2000). Below are some of the examples of questions (taken from a variety of sections of the materials) that the staff teaching David may wish to consider.

David

- Is the achievement of students valued in relation to their own possibilities rather than the achievements of others?
- Do staff attempt to counter negative views of students who find lessons difficult?
- Is there an emphasis on celebrating difference rather than a single 'normality'?
- Do students feel that teachers like them?
- Do staff understand their potential for preventing student difficulties?

- Do staff observe lessons in order to reflect on the perspective of students?
- Are difficulties of behaviour related to strategies for improving classroom and playground experience?
- Are the connections recognised between devaluation of students, and disaffection, disruption and disciplinary exclusion?
- Do all students share responsibility for helping to overcome the difficulties experienced by some students in lessons?
- Are the attempts to remove barriers to learning and participation of one student seen as opportunities for improving the classroom experience of all students?

Embedded in many of these questions is an emphasis on the development of the individual and, for David, his teachers and his peers, attempting to answer questions such as these will encourage a consideration of each person's individual strengths, feelings and preconceptions. Putting the answers into practice will also bring about change in the social and emotional development of the 'group'. These reflections can also lead to the building of a web of interrelated support systems (ecosystems) that enable children to feel valued, safe and important partners in the structure of the learning and teaching environment.

Schools often use *Circle Time* to encourage pupils to explore their own feelings and conflicts in a non-blaming, non-punitive way. Such a process can enhance self-esteem and encourage self-worth but, at the same time, help to develop a better understanding of the feelings of others. Circle Time is used in primary and secondary schools and the structure varies depending on the age of the pupils and their experiences of working together. The pupils sit in a 'circle' which ensures that everyone is in the best position to be seen and heard. The school rules on bullying presented in Chapter 3 were devised by Year 7 pupils in this way. Curry and Bromfield (1994) provide useful activities for the development of the personal and social education of primary age pupils, including those whose behaviour is disruptive. Circle Time, however, can also be an effective way of helping pupils with other forms of 'challenging' behaviour: the withdrawn child and the pupil who is isolated from his or her peer group, for example.

It can be said that *all* children who present challenging behaviour are trying to 'communicate' something. David was 'communicating' his concern about the inappropriate, possibly unstructured, learning activities that were often presented to him. Ranjit, detailed below, communicates in a similar way, but his 'challenging' behaviour is more intense and has the potential to hurt others.

Ranjit

Ranjit, a pupil with complex needs including severe limitations in the development of language, is taught in a small group of 12 children in a special school. He does not use a recognised communication system, but takes part in curriculum activities if he has the individual help of a learning support assistant. When the assistant is not available, he makes few demands on his teacher and does not attempt to interact with the other children. Recently, however, Ranjit has, for no apparent reason, forcefully overturned the table he is working at. Such a behaviour is dangerous to the other children, some of whom are wheelchair users and cannot easily move out of the way. Members of staff are shocked by the outburst and their reactions are often rather extreme which makes the other children anxious. Naturally, members of the staff are very concerned about the aggressiveness and intensity of Ranjit's behaviour and are keen to find out what message he is trying to communicate. Some of the questions they are considering are, 'Is he asking for more attention?' 'Is he bored?' 'Is he feeling unwell?' In order to obtain answers, they are starting to analyse the problematic behaviour using an ABC chart (discussed in Chapter 7). Such a behaviourist technique has the potential to provide answers, and it is possible that the analysis will lead to the following strategies of intervention:

- a more structured programme of activities reflecting Ranjit's learning needs and ensuring success;
- a reward system associated with the structured programme;
- predictable one-to-one teaching systems set within a timetable that have clear boundaries to each learning activity;
- a whole-school approach to the reduction of the behaviour, including agreed strategies of intervention.

It is likely that the latter will involve a consideration of the development of a communication system that is recognised by all staff. In a survey on the identification of the challenging behaviour of pupils with severe learning difficulties in special schools (Harris *et al.*, 1996), it was found that a possible reason for the challenging behaviour of many children was a lack of a recognisable system of communication for each child. Such a finding is surprising when considerable research has been carried out into the development of alternative and augmentative systems of communication. The staff of the special schools taking part in the research (considered to be good schools) were aware of developments in these areas, but had made little attempt to establish such systems for all pupils. Harris *et al.* (1996) emphasise that when pupils are provided with the skills and opportunities to make their needs known, there is always a considerable reduction in the levels of challenging behaviour. Ian, in Chapter 8, was given the skills to make his needs known when he lost his favourite toy, and consequently his challenging behaviour was reduced.

For some children, however, there may be physiological or neurological reasons for specific behaviours which challenge the system. Pupils with Prader–Willi syndrome, for example, are prone to excessive eating, which can present health problems. Girls with Rett syndrome develop 'hand-wringing', which inhibits the development of fine motor skills, and a high proportion of children with Lesch–Nyhan syndrome self-injure. It is also important to emphasise that social and family difficulties contribute to emotional disturbance and have a direct effect on the way in which the child behaves, and on his or her social development.

Emotional and behavioural difficulties

'Emotional and behavioural difficulties' (commonly referred to, as we write, as EBD) is a term that is often used to describe a specific group of children with special educational needs whose 'needs' are often thought best met by special provision. But how do these children's needs differ from those of David and Ranjit described earlier in this chapter? In 1994 a DfEE Circular described such difficulties as those that: 'lie on a continuum between behaviour which challenges teachers, but is within the normal, albeit unacceptable, bounds and that which is indicative of serious mental illness' (p. 7, para.2).

Such a definition is socially constructed; a label of EBD will evoke a different response in each adult involved with the child and, as Cole *et al.* (1999) stress, 'the lively youngsters in one setting can be deemed a major problem in another' (p.22). EBD does not arise from committing certain acts, but arises when other people define the act as serious. Visser and Rayner (1999) point out that the term draws on 'societal, cultural and individual histories and perspectives' (p.14). Such individual histories may, of course, involve difficult family backgrounds or physical or sexual abuse and, as Cooper *et al.* (1994) emphasise, acts of antisocial behaviour, violence and aggression may be the norm in a pupil's family or social subgroup and may consequently result in disruptive behaviour in school. However, they also state that matters of individual and family pathology have often been overplayed in attempts to understand the cause of emotional and behavioural problems and attention should now turn to a consideration of how schools exacerbate, and sometimes cause, such problems. Historically, terminology used to describe pupils with EBD ascribed blame to the pupils only. Terms such as 'maladjusted', 'disturbed', 'disruptive' or 'psychiatric' imply that the child is at fault and by focusing the blame on the pupil the need to consider the structure and regimes of the school does not arise. Only a small proportion of children labelled EBD require therapeutic or medical help. The rest are locked, with their family and the staff of their schools, into an inescapable chain of negative reactions: the disruptive behaviour of pupils results in negative reactions from adults; such negative reactions produce more disruptive behaviour in the pupils. Research shows that pupils who are deemed to have emotional and behavioural difficulties often underachieve and have some difficulties in sustaining concentration, which results in difficulties in learning. These pupils are often acutely aware of their 'failures' (Daniels *et al.*, 1998; Cole and Visser, 2000) and are often concerned that their peers also recognise them in such a way. In order to be considered 'hard' and 'cool' by other pupils they resort to even more 'disruptive' behaviour. Another cause of action is that of 'flight', and pupils with EBD often resort to truanting as an escape mechanism.

In the past, three separate ways of intervening with such children, which are directly related to the theorists we have considered, have been documented by writers such as Wolfgang and Glickman, 1986; and Cooper *et al.*, 1994. Put simply these involve:

RULES/REWARDS AND PUNISHMENTS   Draws on behavioural principles where external rewards (which are reviewed and changed) shape and alter behaviour. Intervention requires a controlled environment 'which shapes the academic skills required by society' (Cooper *et al.*,1994, p.118).

CONFRONTING AND CONTRACTING   Stems, according to these writers, from the work of Bruner and the notion that development is based on a relationship between individual growth and the influences of society. Intervention is different from the examples of behavioural contracting that we have given in Chapter 7, which rely on rewards to change behaviour. In the views of Wolfgang and Glickman and Cooper *et al.* the 'confronting and contracting' perspective involves a consideration of the development of the child alongside the external forces of 'the culture', and when challenges arise teacher and pupil have a shared responsibility to find a mutually acceptable solution.

RELATIONSHIP-LISTENING   Based on Freudian psychoanalysis where the expression of feelings is seen as crucial to development and staff provide an environment which encourages pupils to take control of their own emotions. Intervention includes listening, reflecting feelings, and avoiding judgements.

Rather than considering these interventions as separate from each other, staff of schools will bring into play aspects of each in their interactions with pupils. Indeed, as Cole (2003) emphasises, where staff are seen as coping well with 'difficult' children a climate of 'listening' is evident. Cole (2003) suggests that staff do not 'need to be masters of psychoanalysis or of therapies'. Like all teachers, 'they should be well-organised, consistent, humorous, calm, enthusiastic; skilful in delivering their curriculum subjects; set clear boundaries; (and be) flexible …' (p.70). In addition, they should be positive in their approach and willing to consider the behaviour of their pupils from different perspectives, and above all they should be good listeners. Cole (2003) gives an indication of what *pupils* are looking for in their teachers in this description given by a Year 10 girl with a statement of EBD from research undertaken by Daniels *et al.* (1998): '… teachers who understand you and take an interest in you. After you have finished your work they ask you who you are. They socialise. You get to like them …' (p.70).

Such teachers will undoubtedly analyse the behaviour of their pupils in context and consider such questions as whether he or she is:

* protesting about uninspired and boring teaching;
* not understanding the content of the lessons;
* making a political or personal statement;
* reflecting models of behaviour which are the norm in his or her family or circle of friends;
* communicating distress because of disturbing experiences;
* displaying behaviour which is being 'modelled' by members of staff (for example, verbal aggression).

(adapted from Upton, 1992)

The staff of the school are well aware that these are only *some* of the questions that need considering, but it is important to stress that they are seeking to understand the behaviour in terms of the interactions of all involved, either within the school or in the community. They will then be concerned to break the chain of negative reactions described above. Specific programmes may be brought into play. One such programme is Stop, Think, and Do (Petersen, 2003) which combines the development of cognitive problem-solving with the learning of new behavioural skills to help pupils to improve their relationship with people and to make, and keep, friends.

Whatever specific strategies are used, it is clear that theory and practice are giving out messages that schools will only be successful in alleviating the challenges brought about by children who are considered to have emotional and behavioural difficulties if the ethos of the establishment encourages members of staff to listen and talk to children in order to seek greater insights into the behaviour and actions of *all* involved.

Dean

Dean is a Year 8 pupil in a mainstream school. His performance in most curriculum areas was significantly below that expected of a 13-year-old and his attainments in reading, spelling and writing were particularly low. His behaviour was giving cause for real concern: he would deliberately distract other pupils and disrupt the class by interrupting, arguing with teachers to create confrontational situations wherever possible. Some of his behaviour seemed deliberately planned to get himself removed from the classroom; at other times he would remove himself, storming out of the room and slamming the door. He was threatened with exclusion on several occasions.

Dean was selected for an intensive period of one-to-one specialist help with his literacy problems. This took the form of a multisensory approach to tackle the underlying problems that have prevented Dean from gaining independent decoding skills. At the same time, Dean's teacher investigated his learning style and allowed Dean opportunities to practise emerging skills in ways that suited his modes of learning. Although Dean made good progress in reading and writing, his skills in literacy-related areas remained low. Nonetheless, his teacher was able to engage his interest in texts and writing tasks that were age-appropriate. The effect on Dean's self-esteem has been dramatic: he now participates fully and enthusiastically in the one-to-one sessions by contributing his own ideas. Other teachers have commented on the improvement in his behaviour and a visitor to the school who had met Dean early in the one-to-one teaching programme has remarked on the visible change in his demeanour when she revisited the school recently.

Conclusion

A central theme running throughout this chapter has been the importance of social interaction and its bearing on the development of the emotions and behaviour. Pupils with special educational needs require, more than others, an environment which encourages and supports social development, and also encourages them to take responsibility for their own actions. They also need to be given clear messages that they are valued as individuals in their own right, and that their achievements in all areas of development are of significance. Poor skills of interaction can be seen to be a cause of rejection which, in turn, leads to the development of poor self-esteem and possible antisocial behaviour.

Our examples in this chapter highlight the need for staff and caregivers to provide targeted help in order to address the developmental needs of pupils with a range of difficulties in learning. As we have emphasised, the work of the theorists in the promotion of behavioural, emotional and social development provides a firm foundation for the consideration of such specific and appropriate support. In no way are we suggesting that one theorist (or group of theorists) can provide all the answers in every area, and obviously the views of some theorists are of greater help in one area of development than another. Used sensitively, and inter-changeably, the work of each theorist makes a valuable contribution to providing the targeted support needed to ensure the development of behaviour, emotion and social interaction. As we have stressed in relation to the emotional and behavioural difficulties experienced by some pupils, targeted support needs to be placed within an ecosystemic approach where *all* interactions, negative and positive, of those involved (pupils, peers, caregivers and school staff) are seen as influencing behaviour and fostering social development. Such an approach requires a degree of self-analysis by all parties where personal constructs and perceptions are considered against the perceptions of others within the social system (Stakes, 1999). Only then can mutual respect be encouraged and a foundation for mutual support be established which provide sound foundations for the process of empowerment.

References

Asher, S.R., Parker, J.G. and Walker, D.L (1996) 'Distinguishing friendship from acceptance', in W.M. Bukowski, A.F. Newcombe and W.W. Harup (eds) *The Company They Keep: Friendship in Childhood and Adolescence*. Cambridge: Cambridge University Press.

Bandura, A. (1977) *Social Learning Theory*. Englewood Cliffs, NJ: Prentice Hall.

Baron-Cohen, S. (1995) *Mindblindness: An Essay on Autism and Theory of Mind*. London: MIT Press.

Bee, H. (1989) *The Developing Child* (5th edition). New York: HarperCollins.

Bee, H. (2000) *The Developing Child* (8th edition). Needham Heights, MA: Allyn and Bacon.

Berk, L.E. (2003) *Child Development* (6th edition). Boston, MA: Allyn and Bacon.

Booth, T., Ainscow, M., Black-Hawkins, K., Vaughan, M. and Shaw, L. (2000) *Index for Inclusion: Developing Learning and Participation in Schools*. Bristol: Centre for Studies on Inclusive Education (CSIE).

Bowlby, J. (1965) *Child Care and the Growth of Love* (2nd edition). Harmondsworth: Penguin Books.

Bruner, J. (1996) *The Culture of Education*. Cambridge, MA: Harvard University Press.

Bruner, J., Jolly, A. and Sylva, K. (eds) (1976) *Play: Its Role in Development and Evolution*. Harmondsworth: Penguin.

Cole, T. (1998) 'Understanding challenging behaviour: prerequisites to inclusion', in C. Tilstone, L. Florian and R. Rose (eds) *Promoting Inclusive Practice*. London: Routledge.

Cole, T. (2003) 'Policies for positive behaviour management', in C. Tilstone and R. Rose (eds) *Strategies to Promote Inclusive Practice*. London: Routledge.

Cole, T., Daniels, H. and Visser, J. (1999) *Patterns of Educational Provision Maintained by Local Educational Authorities for Pupils with Behaviour Problems* (Report sponsored by the Nuffield Foundation). Birmingham: University of Birmingham.

Cole, T. and Visser, J. (2000) *EBD Policy, Practice and Provision in Shropshire LEA and Telford and Wrekin LEA*. Birmingham: University of Birmingham.

Cooley, C.H. (1902) *Human Nature and the Social Order*. New York: Scribner.

Cooper, P., Smith, C.J. and Upton, G. (1994) *Emotional and Behavioural Difficulties: Theory to Practice*. London: Routledge.

Curry, M. and Bromfield, C. (1994) *Personal and Social Education for Primary Schools through Circle Time*. Tamworth: NASEN.

Daniels, H., Visser, J., Cole, T. and de Reybekill, N. (1998) *Emotional and Behavioural Difficulties in the Mainstream* (Research Report RR90). London: DfEE.

DfEE (1994) *Pupils' Behaviour and Discipline* (Circular 8/94). London: HMSO.

Eason, P., Gleason, J.J., Hull, R. and Pye, J. (1992) 'Close observation', in T. Booth, W. Swann, M. Masterton and P. Potts (eds) *Learning for All No. 1: Curricula for Diversity in Education*. London: Routledge.

Erikson, E.H. (1965) *Childhood and Society* (2nd edition). Harmondsworth: Penguin Books.

Flavell, J.H. (1963) *The Developmental Psychology of Jean Piaget*. Denmark: Van Nostrand.

Fox, M. (2002) 'The self-esteem of children with physical disabilities: a review of the research', *JORSEN*. 2 (1), available online at http://www.nasen.uk.com.

Frances, J. (2000) 'Providing effective support in school when a child has a disfigured appearance: the work of the Changing Faces School Service', *Support for Learning*. 15 (4), 177–82.

Freud, S. (1960) *A General Introduction to Psychoanalysis*. New York: Norton.

Happe, F. (1994) *Autism: An Introduction to Psychological Theory*. London: UCL Press.

Harris, J., Cook, M. and Upton, G. (1996) *Pupils with Severe Learning Disabilities who Present Challenging Behaviour: A Whole School Approach to Assessment and Intervention*. Kidderminster: BILD Publications.

Henker, F. (1979) 'Body-image conflict following trauma and surgery', *Psychosamtics*. 20, 812–20.

Indoe, D., Leo, E., James, J. and Charlton, T. (1992) 'Developing your self and others the EASI way', *Educational Psychologist in Practice*. 8 (3), 151–5.

Jeffree, D.M., McConkey, R. and Hewson, S. (1977) *Let Me Play*. London: Souvenir Press.

Keenan, T. (2002) *An Introduction to Child Development*. London: Sage Publications.

Lawrence, D. (1996) *Enhancing Self-Esteem in the Classroom* (2nd edition). London: Paul Chapman Publishing.

Lewis, M. (1990) 'Social knowledge and social development', *Merrill Palmer Quarterly*. 36, 93–116.

Lewis, M. and Brooks-Gunn, J. (1979) *Social Cognition and the Acquisition of Self*. New York: Plenum.

Lewis, V. (2003) *Development and Disability* (2nd edition). London: Blackwell Publishing.

Lindon, J. (1996) *Growing Up: From Eight Years to Young Adulthood*. London: National Children's Bureau.

Mead, G.H. (1934) *Mind, Self and Society*. Chicago: University of Chicago Press.

Miell, D. (1995) 'Developing a sense of self', in P. Barnes (ed.) *Personal, Social and Emotional Development of Children*. Oxford: Blackwell Publishers, in association with the Open University.

Petersen, L. (2003) 'Learning to stop and think', *Special!* Summer issue, 20–3.

QCA/DfEE (2001) *Planning, Teaching and Assessing the Curriculum for Pupils with Learning Difficulties*. London: QCA.

Richardson, S., Hastof, A. and Dornbusch, S. (1964) 'The effects of physical disability on a child's description of himself', *Child Development*. 35, 893–907.

Roggoff, B. (1990) *Apprenticeship in Thinking*. New York: Oxford University Press.

Rosenberg, M. (1979) *Conceiving the Self*. New York: Basic Books.

Russell, J. (1997) *Autism as an Executive Disorder*. Oxford: Oxford University Press.

Shevlin, M. (2001) 'Preparing for contact between mainstream pupils and their counterparts who have severe and profound multiple learning disabilities', *British Journal of Special Education*. 30 (2), 93–9.

Shevlin, M. (2003) 'Establishing and maintaining contact between peers with and without severe or complex learning difficulties', *JORSEN*. 1 (1), available online at http://www.nasen.org.uk.

Stakes, R. (1999) 'The matching process: key factors influencing pupil behaviour in schools', in J. Visser and S. Rayner (eds) *Emotional and Behavioural Difficulties: A Reader*. Lichfield: QEd.

Sullivan, H.S. (1953) *The Interpersonal Theory of Psychiatry*. New York: W.W. Norton.

Tager-Flusher, H. (2001) 'A re-examination of the theory of mind hypothesis of autism', in J.A. Burack, T. Charman, N. Yirmiya and P.R. Zelazo (eds) *The Development of Autism: Perspectives from Theory and Research*. London: Erlbaum.

TTA (1999) *National Special Educational Needs Specialist Standards*. London: TTA.

Upton, G. (1992) 'Emotional and behavioural difficulties', in R. Gulliford and G. Upton (eds) *Special Educational Needs*. London: Routledge.

Visser, J. and Rayner, S. (1999) *Emotional and Behavioural Difficulties: A Reader*. Lichfield: QEd.

Vygotsky, L.S. (1962) *Thought and Language*. New York: Wiley.

Warren, D. (1994) *Blindness and Children: An Individual Differences Approach*. Cambridge: Cambridge University Press.

Wolfgang, C.H. and Glickman, C.D. (1986) *Solving Discipline Problems: Strategies for Classroom Teachers*. Boston, MA: Allyn and Bacon.

Wright, B.A. (1974) 'An analysis of attitudes and dynamic effects', *New Outlook for the Blind*. 68, 108–18.

Chapter 11

Sensory and physical development

Historically, the effects of sensory and physical impairments have often been studied in order to extend our understanding of typical development. For example, it has been argued that research on the effects of blindness on language and communication development provides fresh insights into language acquisition (Lewis, 2003). As we have shown in the other chapters, our intention in writing this book is to reverse this trend: we believe that we should explore the developmental progression of children with special educational needs within the frameworks that seek to explain development in *all* children. Our commitment to including all children within the same explanatory frameworks is linked to our conviction that, regardless of physical capabilities or the status of sight and hearing, all individuals strive towards personal autonomy.

We recognise that developmental processes are complex and it is often difficult, and indeed in many cases impossible and not desirable, to determine which area of development causes changes in other areas. For example, what prerequisites are necessary in the area of vision and hearing for physical development to occur, and vice versa? In the previous chapter we emphasised the need to understand the 'signposts' children encounter as they grow and mature, and we stressed the importance for professionals to have knowledge of the patterns of normal development in order to take appropriate action. In the areas of development discussed in this chapter, in particular, 'appropriate action' relates to the management of, and the provision for, the functional and educational difficulties that can result from sensory impairments and physical disabilities. However, as we demonstrate, other effects, apart from those of the physical disabilities themselves, influence the way in which the individual grows and adapts. For example, the way in which modifications are made or the manner in which possible aids are presented may have profound implications for the development of learning abilities or for personal development. Similarly, as we point out, the manner in which other people build on the person's spontaneous response to a lack of ability in some areas will shape (or inhibit) the development, not only of physical skills, but also of conceptual understandings in relation to that area.

Throughout the book we have illustrated the overlaps in areas of development and have shown that each has an impact on another. Sharman *et al.* (1995, p.93), in offering the following 'signposts' (which they refer to as milestones) for gross and fine motor skills, highlight the interweaving of physical and sensory development. For example, the following are some of the abilities infants between the ages of one and six months have usually acquired:

✓ lift his or her head to change position;
✓ wave arms and hands;

✓   kick legs alternately when placed on his or her back;
✓   watch main caregiver;
✓   follow movements;
✓   absorb visual stimuli.

And some of the abilities usually acquired by children between 18 months and five years are:

✓   run safely;
✓   ride a tricycle;
✓   stand on tiptoe, hop, jump and skip;
✓   enjoy music and movement;
✓   show hand preference;
✓   build a tower of bricks;
✓   use scissors;
✓   thread beads.

People use a range of headings in order to highlight patterns of development. Sheridan (1997), for example, chooses to describe *posture and large movements* and *vision* and *fine movements*, and Griffiths (1967) uses the terms *locomotor* and *eye and hand co-ordination*. The descriptors, or targets, within the various categories demonstrate the close relationships between one area and another, although we are not advocating a 'tick list' approach to recording development. *All* children vary at the age at which they acquire the same skill or piece of knowledge, or understand a particular concept, and it is not unusual for activities highlighted by 'experts' as *important* to be missed out altogether. We regard *detailed* charts of developmental progress of limited use, but 'signposts' illustrating broad bands of development can provide important guidelines for:

•   considering appropriate teaching and learning experiences regardless of chronological age;
•   utilising information on what may be achieved in order to plan accordingly;
•   a focus for the application of the Framework for New Learning;
•   the identification of *marked* differences.

To help children with sensory impairments and physical disabilities to become empowered, staff, parents and caregivers will need to carefully consider appropriate aids and adaptations to the learning environment to support development. For pupils with physical disabilities, wheelchairs, standing frames and prostheses are important amplifiers for motor capabilities, and glasses and hearing aids can assist the development of the senses of those with vision and hearing losses. Detailed analysis of the physical environment will also be necessary in order to reduce the impact of the disabilities. For example, Wendy, a pupil with visual impairment and a physical disability, referred to in Chapter 3, needs to be placed in the best possible position to ensure that her limited vision is used to good effect and that she is given every opportunity to extend her fine motor skills. At present, a standing frame, with bright light coming from the right-hand side, is her best 'aid' for the acquisition of knowledge, skills and understanding. As she matures and develops physically, other 'aids' for learning will become important. Although Toby, in Chapter 7, has vision and hearing impairments, he enjoys exploring his immediate environment through touch using the soles of his feet and his hands. The examples of Kirsty in the same chapter, and Jasmin in Chapter 4, illustrate the importance of adaptations of classroom equipment, furniture and the environment. The adapted volley ball (a balloon filled with dried pasta) allows Tom, in Chapter 3, to take part in a game with his peers that would otherwise not be accessible to him. Ramps, uncluttered corridors and wide doors with handles at a convenient height need to be considered if Jasmin is to travel independently in her wheelchair.

It might appear that the issues surrounding the physical development of children whose special educational needs stem from physical disabilities are different from those we have discussed in relation to other aspects of development. For example, access to buildings is of crucial concern, as are the correct positioning of pupils and the administration of passive movement regimes in order to maintain good body posture and to prevent contractures. In addition, specific physiotherapy may be required for particular conditions (chest physiotherapy for children with cystic fibrosis, for example) and staff may need to be trained to move and handle children in certain ways (Jackson, 2000). However, in presenting and examining the case studies we return to the main theme of this book, which focuses on self-advocacy. When physical abilities are compromised there may be a tendency for physically able people to assume the role of advocate for the child or adult who has a disability. By effectively denying people the opportunity to negotiate a position from which they can take control, even in limited ways, over their own lives, well-meaning parents, professionals or peers can prevent the child or adult from encountering certain experiences. These, as the Framework for New Learning emphasises, are crucial to ongoing development in all areas. In relation to physical disabilities, as we will show, encountering experiences is often perceived as 'facing challenges' but, we assert, it is necessary if all concerned are going to maximise and consolidate the physical potential of the child or adult with the disability.

Physical development

As already stated at the beginning of this chapter, knowledge of basic patterns of gross and fine motor development help to identify differences that may become apparent in the developmental patterns of children who have specific disabilities, particularly those with motor impairments. Many children with physical disabilities, especially those with cerebral palsy, have atypical motor patterns and consequently have particular problems in executing movements and in gaining specific motor skills. Some motor *skills* require a high degree of precision: for example, picking up a paper clip from the table, or cutting with a knife.

Motor *patterns* are less precise and Lerner (1997) gives the example of throwing a ball at a target which may be a motor *skill*, but the ability of utilising this skill as part of a baseball game involves a motoric pattern which brings into play hand–eye co-ordination and many sets of complicated movements.

Movements take place in response to signals from the brain that alter the tension of specific groups of muscles. Such tensions are co-ordinated in set patterns or sequences, often involving different parts of the body. Sitting up, for example, requires a sequence of movement that involves the head, shoulders, hips and back (Glenn and Robertson, 2001). Brain damage can inhibit muscle co-ordination and consequently synchronised movements, such as sitting up, may be difficult. Children and adults with cerebral palsy are likely to find co-ordinated movements problematic and, as eye defects are common in people with this condition, orientation is also affected. Cerebral palsy can be classified in one or more of three general types (spasticity, athetosis and ataxia), each of which is characterised by a particular state of muscle tone and associated patterns of movement (for a detailed description, see Bleck and Nagel, 1982). Reasons for cerebral palsy are many and some of the causes include a lack of oxygen at birth, prematurity, infection, trauma and hereditary malformation (Miller, 1992). Those with cerebral palsy who are hypertonic (have increased muscle tension and tone) will have difficulty in carrying out smooth movements, and those who have a lack of muscle tone and are 'floppy' (hypotonic) will have difficulty in initiating or directing movement. In the case of Jaz, it is easy to see the implications of the lack of co-ordinated movements for the majority of classroom activities.

Jaz

Jaz is a Year 3 pupil who has cerebral palsy. Damage to the motor cortex at birth has resulted in spastic hemiplegia of the right side. Consequently his right leg is slightly shorter than the other, and he wears a built-up boot. He also wears leg callipers to provide extra support, but apart from a 'rolling gait' he walks around the environment without much difficulty (as long as there is enough space between pieces of furniture). The non-slip floor of his classroom provides a stable base for both him and another pupil in the class whose balance is also poor.

His severe squint and other eye problems are rectified by heavy lenses, but he dislikes wearing his glasses, and often attempts to remove them, a hazardous operation, as the groups of muscles in his arm make his movements very jerky. He often sweeps his glasses to the floor with disastrous results.

In an effort to help him to control his jerking arm and hand movements his teachers work closely with the physiotherapist (a member of the school staff) responsible for Jaz. The physiotherapist carries out specific movement programmes that are then taught to the teaching staff and these have become part of his teaching in all areas of the curriculum. Chairs and working positions are also considered in order to provide him with the best posture for learning. When engaged in individual tasks that involve fine motor movements, equipment (such as paper for writing or drawing) is 'fixed' to the work surface in order to provide a stable base from which to work.

Working with peers inevitably presents particular difficulties. Jaz is a sociable individual and enthusiastically takes part in group activities. The adaptations to the physical environment and the selected aids not only give Jaz better control over what he's doing (that is, compensating for physical difficulties) but they help him to be successful and more confident. Consequently his perception of his contribution to the work of the group is increased and by collaborating with his peers he is able to become more emotionally engaged and socially mature.

A lack of control over his movements, however, means that he is likely to sweep items off the table on which he and his peers are working, which is not only frustrating for Jaz but irritating for his friends. Recently, for example, in a design and technology session that focused on winding mechanisms, Jaz and his peers had planned and designed a simple winding apparatus which involved wheels, axles, pulleys and gears. Jaz had made many useful suggestions for the design, which the group had incorporated into the project. As his motor skills could inhibit the construction of the model, Jaz was given the task of passing large pieces of a construction kit to other children for them to incorporate into the composition. Unfortunately, when it was almost finished, his jerky movements sent the mechanism flying to the floor, which did not endear him to his peers. In consultation with the physiotherapist, 'Dycem' non-slip mats have now been introduced for such activities, and although Jaz still knocks things over on the table, the results are not so disastrous.

Jaz, in comparison with a child without such disabilities, is more dependent on the help of staff to enable him to develop, learn and progress. The aids to movement (fixtures to ensure that work does not move) and mobility (callipers, adapted footwear and non-slip flooring) are enhancing Jaz's competence. Such support systems, as we have pointed out earlier, are, in Bruner's terms, 'amplifiers' or tools for learning, which in Jaz's case are constructed by other people. Piaget emphasises the importance of action for perceptual development, and although not specifically emphasised in the example, it is likely that Jaz's orientation and spatial problems have added to his inability to control his movements. In their research, Foreman *et al.* (1989) found that children with cerebral palsy had difficulties in reconstructing accurate 'maps' of familiar places, and adding landmarks to them. Thus, when Jaz is working in collaboration with his peers, they are able to 'model' the correct responses for the correct placing of the parts (a technique discussed in relation to the learning theorists in Chapter 7).

In his interactions with his peers it is important that Jaz feels positive about his contribution to the work of others and that his self-esteem is preserved. Despite his motor difficulties, he has made a valuable contribution to the planning and design of the activity and his work is valued by his peers. They are allowing him (possibly without realising it) to control parts of the interaction. Research by Dallas *et al.* (1993) shows that children with cerebral palsy are often passive in their interactions, and other children (in their research, the siblings of the children under scrutiny) tended to control the situation. In terms of Erikson's first psychosocial stage, his peers' trust in Jaz's planning ability outweighs their healthy mistrust of his motor ability and, in turn, their trust in his capabilities encourages his own capacity to cope with the negative experiences of his body, and therefore helps him to 'trust' himself. His peers' positive but critical attitude towards the contribution Jaz can make to the work of the group 'challenges' him to take on board their views and encourages him to reorganise his thoughts. As Flanagan (1996, p.73) points out: 'children working together may promote learning not just because others may have greater knowledge but also because conflicting views necessitate negotiation which forces the individuals to reconstruct their ideas'.

Such socially supportive climates for learning have direct links to the Vygotskyan social-constructivist theory of learning (Watson, 1999). In addition, the collaborative approach taken by Jaz's teachers and physiotherapists in drawing up his specific physiotherapy programme helps to ensure that it becomes a basic part of teaching and learning which transcends all areas of the curriculum. The programme is designed to help Jaz to control his voluntary movements and to establish specific motor behaviours. In Piaget's view, motor behaviour linked to sensory stimulation is the basis of the development of cognition, and by careful consideration of his environment by the staff of the school and the provision of correct 'aids' to support his learning as he matures, Jaz *is* developing physically despite his physical impairments. It is important to emphasise that disorders of the nervous system, such as cerebral palsy, have encouraged many approaches to therapy and some, such as the particular patterning techniques of Doman–Delacato (Ziegler and Victoria, 1975) are not only highly invasive to the child and the family, but are considered by many researchers to be theoretically unsound (Cogher *et al.*, 1992).

Many therapists and teachers, however, have adapted some of the methods of the rehabilitation system *conductive education* (an approach developed in Budapest by Dr Andras Peto 1903–67). Conductive education is based on the notion of 'orthofunction' which aims to develop physical and emotional independence. As Coles and Zsargo (1998) emphasise, *orthofunction* is not a cure for disordered motor function but, they believe, helps the child to find some solutions to the problems of everyday life. Attitude is seen as vital: the ability to solve problems and to apply solutions based on one situation to another is very much part of the philosophy of the approach. Coles and Zsargo (1998) explain that children are 'taught to roll, crawl, and hold onto furniture and generally move as actively as possible' (p.71). The approach sets out to develop motor function and cognition holistically (for a full account of the theoretical framework on which the approach is based see Hari and Akos, 1988). However, research on an evaluation of the achievements of UK children using the original Hungarian approach showed that progress was modest and the claims made by the major educational establishment to use the approach in England were not realised (Bairstow *et al.*, 1993). Nevertheless, many schools have incorporated parts of the Peto methods (often called motor-based learning or motor education) into their curriculum. We mention it here because some of the strategies used by adults and caregivers to promote the development of the whole child resonate with the work of the theorists explored in this book, two of which are:

- the role of the conductor (the person in charge of the delivery of the programme);
- rhythmical intention.

The work of the conductor is to ensure that the individual capabilities and difficulties of each child are considered holistically. Coles and Zsargo (1998) explain that the children are given tasks that are just achievable and are therefore, in Vygotskian terms, within the child's ZPD. In addition, rhythmical intention involves all the children verbalising a goal set by the conductor. For example, the children may verbalise the goal 'I raise my right arm' and carry out the action to rhythmic counting. It is thought that verbalisation prepares the central nervous system for action and helps the pupil to create an internal picture: a 'motor memory' (Wilson, 2001). Such a process is in line with the Vygotskian *mediation* where the use of language is used to clarify, extend and make thoughts explicit (Hodapp, 1998).

In this approach, there is an emphasis on a teaching environment that promotes the application of the learned skills across all areas of the curriculum and Wilson suggests, for example, that a child in a design and technology lesson may require a specific grab rail in order to access tools. Group work is encouraged and, in line with the principles of the learning theorists, children are encouraged to model ways in which they have developed (or are going about the development of) motor skills in specific tasks. As in all group activities, there is the potential for developing interpersonal relationships and the facilitation of group practices. The emphasis on orthofunction means that children are taught to adapt, to cope and to be creative in order to 'find a way around a problem' (Coles and Zsargo, 1998, p.71). In other words, they are striving for independence, self-advocacy and autonomy.

Matthew

Matthew is six years old and attends a local education authority (LEA) maintained school for children with a physical disability. He has cerebral palsy of the athetoid quadriplegic type that affects all four limbs. He is described as a 'floppy' child whose movements are slow and writhing. He can weight-bear (take his body weight on his feet in a standing position) for limited periods only, and his 'aids' to movement include a wheelchair (with a special seating system to give extra support to his spine), a walker and an adapted bike (used with assistance from the staff).

Matthew also requires assistance to feed himself and use the bathroom but he can drink independently from a two-handled beaker. He has a limited range of vocal sounds and is very selective with whom he will communicate. However, when he chooses, Matthew can clearly communicate his immediate needs and preferences in a number of ways that require different aids and approaches. He can:

✓   eye point;
✓   reach or discard objects;
✓   use picture communication symbols (PCS);
✓   use a voice output communication aid.

Each week Matthew participates in three motor-based learning programmes, derived from the principles of conductive education. These programmes are designed to assist Matthew in all areas of his development. The following literacy lesson illustrates the holistic nature of the programmes

A literacy lesson

Linked to the National Literacy Strategy requirements for Year 1, Matthew and his peers are exploring traditional tales. This lesson is based around the story of *The Gingerbread Man* and is designed and delivered by a leader (the conductor) who incorporates the principles of motor-based learning into the content of the lesson. Matthew is supported throughout the lesson by a facilitator (another member of staff) with whom he works on a regular basis.

The development of gross and fine motor skills

Using a ladder-backed chair (as a Zimmer frame) Matthew is encouraged to get out of, and into, his wheelchair at the beginning and end of the lesson. (It is important to note that Matthew's motor-based learning programme is *adapted* from the Peto approach, and that in a 'pure' conductive education environment the use of a wheel chair would not be encouraged.) He sits on a slatted stool at a slatted table and both pieces of equipment are carefully measured to ensure that he maintains a correct body position. All physical positions can be achieved by using the equipment and some examples are:

✓   safe sitting (when listening to the story);
✓   steadying himself by holding onto a table slat with one hand in order to grasp and release objects, such as a gingerbread-man puppet or a wooden spoon, in the other;
✓   standing (by using the slats to pull himself up);
✓   kneeling (as if an animal in the story) by using the rungs of the ladder-back chair to support the descent.

Such physical tasks help to develop functional skills, all of which are used and practised at other times during the day. Tasks are set at a level that is achievable for Matthew, albeit with some assistance from either his equipment or his facilitator (as his physical skills develop, the amount of support required will decrease).

Fine motor skills are practised during several tasks linked to the story (for example: using a spoon to mix the gingerbread; rolling out the mixture; or using a 'gingerbread-man' cutter).

Intellectual and cognitive development and the development of communication

Matthew is currently being encouraged to increase the consistency with which he responds to people and events. He is particularly responsive to audio and visual stimuli, and a multi-sensory approach is adopted in all lessons. In this lesson he is, therefore, given opportunities to:

- ✓ smell and taste the gingerbread;
- ✓ handle dough;
- ✓ trace letters in a tray of sand to spell out important words in the story ('r' as in run, for example);
- ✓ use a voice activator in order to produce the key repetitive phrases that occur in the story;
- ✓ recreate the story using symbols of the characters.

Social and emotional development

Matthew works with five other pupils and is encouraged to collaborate with his peers. A 'registration time' takes place at the beginning of the session and the children identify each other by name cards or photographs. Throughout the lesson, Matthew has a set of *basic needs* symbols readily available in order that he can communicate his specific needs as the programme progresses (for example, 'my turn', 'more'). Matthew and his peers are involved in a process of self-evaluation at the end of each lesson and are encouraged to celebrate their own, and each other's, achievements. A 'well done' song provides a simple way for the children to give praise.

Throughout the lesson, the 'conductor' and 'facilitator' are consistent in their expectations of Matthew and adopt a compatible approach to the rewarding of appropriate behaviour.

As we have stated, we are not necessarily recommending such approaches to motor education: indeed we have emphasised that many researchers have serious reservations about its overall effectiveness (Bairstow *et al.*, 1993), as have people with a disability themselves (Oliver, 1989). We do, however, encourage an investigation of *all* classroom practices, particularly in terms of their potential for promoting self-advocacy and autonomy within the theoretical frameworks that we have explored.

In a consideration of physical development so far, we have only discussed the motor impairments of cerebral palsy and we wish to stress that this is only one of the many physical disabilities that result in barriers to learning and has the potential to affect normal development. It is important to bear in mind that the implications of one disability cannot unquestionably be generalised to others, but as a guiding principle, development which naturally enhances self-advocacy is the result of a complex interaction between the environment and the child and his or her own physical challenges.

The 'challenges' for Sue during her time in school were demanding for her and the staff. Now in her forties, Sue's physical disabilities were an outcome of the drug thalidomide (given to her mother during pregnancy) and resulted in Sue's arms (flippers) being attached directly to her torso. She also had some difficulties in learning, but these were unlikely to be related to the drug, although research by Decarie (1969) found that a high proportion of the thalidomide children she studied did have some difficulties in language and cognitive development. The example below, taken from a long list, shows some of the 'challenges' revealed by a functional assessment of Sue's daily living activities at the start of secondary education, undertaken by Sue herself, with the help of her teacher (one of the authors of this book).

Sue's challenges

EATING   Particularly cutting up food and using a knife and fork together; using some kitchen equipment; carrying out kitchen tasks such as lifting a kettle of water;

DRESSING   Including dealing with fastenings and putting on clothes, in particular bra, socks/tights, pants and trousers;

PERSONAL CARE   Washing trunk and below the waist; blowing nose acceptably; managing basic toilet hygiene and menstruation; brushing hair; cleaning teeth;

GENERAL CLASSROOM ACTIVITIES   Turning pages of a book; writing; manipulating objects and equipment and anchoring them down;

CURRICULUM   Some aspects of all subjects but particularly art and craft; music; science; geography.

Many of Sue's challenges were, however, 'inconveniences' and were overcome with the help of an occupational therapist and the provision of appropriate aids, adapted clothing (particularly important in enabling full use of her 'flippers'), tall working surfaces, and an adapted environment. Although some of the 'challenges' on Sue's list may look trivial in today's climate, at the time (without appropriate management) they could have quickly accumulated into an unnecessary pattern of dependency and greater disability. Sue would not, for example, be able to zip up her jeans without the long hook which was made especially for her and which she controlled by her teeth. Despite being labelled in the 1970s as having learning difficulties, Sue proved to be a self-directed learner, who was keen to take care of her physical management and therefore become more autonomous. Although her physical disabilities had the potential to inhibit other areas of development, her keenness to be autonomous meant, albeit unintentionally, that she made every effort to engage in activities that fostered physical development. For example, in learning to put her socks on by substituting her mouth for her hands, she was able to demonstrate greatly advanced motor skills (she could position her feet under her chin).

Steel (1996) gives an example of another teenager, Robert, whose physical challenges were different to Sue's but who took control of his own physical management in other ways, and whose physical development was of a very different order. Robert had brittle bones, and extreme care had to be undertaken in any physical manoeuvres, such as transferring Robert from his wheelchair onto a padded seat, as any pressure could result in painful fractures. Throughout his schooling, Robert had been encouraged to take charge of the situation, and as a teenager he was able to:

> … advise and direct his helpers, instruct them as to when he was ready for a particular manoeuvre, and thus ensure that transfers were effected smoothly and with appropriate care. Such tasks were never rushed and never undertaken until Robert was fully prepared.
>
> (Steel, 1996, p.62)

As a teenager with a physical disability Robert had learned to express his needs and then to anticipate the required manoeuvre, which resulted in minimal physical damage. He was his own advocate and earned the respect of the adults he was in contact with for his opinions, his efforts and hard work. He, like any teenager, resented being on the receiving end of discourtesies or disrespectful actions.

Our final example of a pupil with motor difficulties is that of James who was diagnosed as having dyspraxia. In the past he may have been considered to be a 'clumsy child', but it has been found that a number of children have difficulties carrying out a consistent range of motor behaviours (usually throughout their lives) for unexplained reasons. Consequently, terms such as dyspraxia, developmental co-ordination disorder (DCD) or specific developmental disorder (SDD) have replaced the notion of 'clumsiness'. It is worth noting here that dyspraxia comes within the category of specific learning difficulties: that is, it is not expected that dyspraxia will have any significant effect on *general* learning ability.

Some examples of the motor difficulties these children may have are in the following areas:

- self-help (for example, dressing, co-ordinating cutlery, cleaning teeth);
- dexterity (such as cutting with scissors, writing, using a ruler);
- carrying out spatial tasks (following maps or diagrams);
- organising themselves or being tidy;
- planning motor movements;
- balancing (riding a bicycle, roller skating), playing ball games;
- understanding or following rules (particularly games which require motor co-ordination).

(adapted from the information from the Dyspraxia Foundation website
http://www.dyspraxiafoundation.org.uk/)

James

James is a Year 9 pupil in a mainstream secondary school. He is diagnosed as having dyspraxia although cognitively he copes well with school (reading age 11+ in Year 7). The policy of the LEA does not allow additional support through a Statement of Need for pupils with dyspraxia, but the school has organized additional support of an occupational therapist (OT). The main tasks of the OT are to provide advice to staff and to attend reviews of James's educational progress.

James also receives regular weekly support from a learning support assistant because he struggles to organize himself (for example, he requires help to keep his bag and books in order). He also has difficulty in interacting with his peers as he is considered to be a bit 'different', particularly as he is not able to do the physical things that they can. His teachers note that he is the last one to be picked for sports teams.

The OT reports that James has difficulties with fine motor co-ordination which impacts on his handwriting and his ability to plan and organize himself and his work. He has these difficulties because he:

- lacks strength in his shoulders and trunk which means that he does not have a good support base from which to control his arm and hand movements;
- finds it difficult to use both hands together (for example, supporting paper when writing);
- has limited wrist and finger movements, is not able to isolate arm movements and, consequently, cannot produce smooth, controlled, writing.

In addition, James has poor concentration skills and is easily distracted. Members of staff think this is probably due to the fact that he is unable to filter out unwanted information and is therefore unable to focus on what is important. One teacher commented that 'he is unable to *tune out* classroom chatter and concentrate on what I am saying'.

In agreement with the OT, all staff are using the following three simple strategies to help James to compensate for his difficulties and to take control of his own development and learning:

✓ encouraging him to maintain a correct seating position with his feet flat on the floor, knees at a right angle, table at elbow height (to help improve his support base);
✓ ensuring that he faces the front of the classroom and does not have to turn to face the board or the teacher;
✓ making certain that the board is free of unwanted information.

Throughout this chapter we have emphasised that physically able people must not deny children and young people with physical disabilities opportunities to negotiate a position from which they can take control. Writers who are physically disabled themselves are quick to point out the social restrictions and the oppression they face from well-meaning but ill-informed individuals who fail to take account of their needs within the structures and organisation of society and, consequently, inhibit their participation within it (Oliver, 1996; Morris, 1991; Shakespeare, 1996). They, and others like them, constantly remind us that it is the collective responsibility of *all* to create an environment where physical disabilities are not an important issue and that enables those with such disabilities to contribute to society.

Sensory development

Although the majority of this section will focus on vision and hearing, it should be stressed that in order to make sense of the world a normally developing baby utilises the whole range of sensory input including touch, taste and smell, and it is important that these components are not overlooked. Piaget stressed that throughout infancy the child will be instrumental in procuring and organising all the experiences he or she encounters and Isaacs (1966, p.9) points out that the child:

> follows with his eyes, explores with them, turns his head; explores with his hands, grips, lets go, pulls, pushes; explores with his mouth; moves his body and limbs; explores jointly and alternately with eye and hand etc.

For many children with special educational needs, particularly those with profound and multiple learning disabilities, caregivers will need to help them to *assimilate* and *accommodate* their experiences through the exploitation of touch, taste and smell. The following example of the experiences offered to Mercy in an effort to help her to recognise her environment as she enters her school gives some indication of the importance of the involvement of all senses, and of the role the adult plays in helping her to structure her thinking.

Mercy's journey to her classroom

Mercy, aged 10, has complex learning difficulties which include visual and hearing impairments and physical disabilities (she is, however, able to reach out independently). She has been at her present school for one year and she is learning to adapt cognitively to a changed set of environmental circumstances. On arrival at school, she is met by a member of staff wearing a distinctive perfume as a means of identification. Time is allowed for Mercy to discriminate through smell, and also to feel the change of air, as her wheelchair is lowered from the transport and wheeled towards the door of the school. The pair stop at the door, and Mercy is encouraged to reach out to touch the brass plate beneath the door knob, a clue that she is about to enter the building. On entering the school the member of staff takes time to allow her to listen to any loud sounds within the building that she is able to pick up (children's voices, for example) which will give her a clue to her whereabouts. Time spent in this way will also help her to make sense of these sounds. Her journey to the classroom includes feeling a small number of objects (a glass display unit, the lintel of the secretary's door) in order to help her to get her bearings. A large shiny disk on her classroom door (which reflects the light and provides an interesting tactile experience) contains both the printed name of her classroom and a symbol (a pupil using a computer).

Once inside her classroom the regular 'greeting' routine includes a structured drinks time when all senses are utilised and Mercy is encouraged to:

- find her large red cup among those of different sizes and colours (vision and touch);
- choose a drink from a choice of two different tastes;
- listen to the liquid being poured into her cup;
- smell the liquid before drinking it.

Set within the Framework for New Learning, Mercy's learning experience has been enriched by a multisensory approach. Observations made by the staff have been interpreted in the following ways:

- When she *encountered* the school environment three months ago, her response to the sensory experiences that were offered (a loud noise or the bright disk) was simple and reflex.
- As she began to show an *emerging awareness* of her surroundings, she held up her face in order to feel the change in temperature from the inside to the outside of the transport, and once inside the school she put her head on one side as if to catch as much sound as possible.
- She now responds *consistently* to the objects along the corridors and puts her hand out to feel them. At present we (the staff) use a variety of methods (hand-under-hand, hand-over-hand, tapping items) in order to encourage her to reach out to objects and 'explore' them, rather than just touching them.
- During the routine greetings time, she is now *pro-active* in her interactions, showing a consistent dislike for certain drinks by turning her head away.
- In showing a preference Mercy is beginning to *communicate intentionally*, and it is this attainment that we are now working on. Hopefully, before she leaves school Mercy will be able to build on her *emerging communication* system and initiate interactions in a systematic way.

For Mercy to access the curriculum, sensory experiences are used throughout the day, but are structured with great care. The possibilities are endless: for example, the sense of touch is not just confined to sensations presented to her through her hands, but other areas of her skin (the sense organ that allows the discrimination of touch) such as feet and lips are brought into play. Smells are also used to alert her to the commencement of activities: a waft of her talcum powder indicates that it is time for her toilet routine; pine air freshener signifies 'home time'. It is possible to bombard Mercy with too many experiences which could result in confusion (Brown *et al.*, 1998; Davis, 2001). In another child, too many stimuli may result in hyperactivity or complete withdrawal. Initially, Mercy's efforts to communicate intentionally have been limited to the few staff who ensure that she receives consistent signals and that her emotional development is not impaired.

Sensory environments

In a number of schools, particularly special schools, specific sensory environments are constructed which have a range of functions. Some (white rooms, for example) are often made available for leisure, relaxation, aromatherapy and massage (Pagliano, 1999). Dark rooms, which cut down glare and reflection, are sometimes used with children with severe visual impairments, and enable them to focus on areas of bright light created by the use of such equipment as fibre optics or ultraviolet light (Best, 1992). Other specially constructed rooms are used for exploration, investigation and problem-solving, all of which lead to a sense of control and empowerment. If constructed and managed with skill and care, the sensory experiences which they provide can encourage the child to, in Piagetian terms, 'act upon the world', albeit a 'world' that has been carefully engineered by adults to meet particular needs. But caution is needed, as children may be faced with an overwhelming array of stimuli that are difficult to interpret (Porter and Ashdown, 2002).

It is also important to remember that when children need a great deal of support to explore the environment, as in Mercy's case, it is vital that changes are made in subtle ways in order to encourage them to adapt and build on their responses to gain the optimum measure of control. Adults will need to ensure that at all times Mercy's environment provides opportunities for stimulation and reinforcement coupled with both the right amount of challenge and the right level of expectation. In Vygotskian terms, the adults around her must be especially attentive and well-attuned to Mercy's zone of proximal development.

The development of vision

The visual skills of newborn infants are relatively underdeveloped, in contrast to hearing, although babies seem to be innately prepared to see what is crucial for their survival in the earliest weeks and months. Thus, their near vision functions effectively, but their visual acuity for stimuli at a distance is poor and the capacity of their eyes to accommodate to different focal lengths is restricted. Increased efficiency of the muscles that control focusing and the postnatal development of the retina, together with developments in the optic nerve and other neural pathways, bring about a gradual refinement of vision, but mature levels of functioning are not attained until about the age of five years. The relatively immature state of the visual system at birth means that it is vulnerable and can easily be damaged when infants are born prematurely, the most severe effects of which may result in blindness.

Degrees of loss of sight can be considered as points on a continuum and *visual impairment* is used as a generic term to cover all sight loss. Mason and McCall (1997) use the term 'blind' to describe children whose main access to learning is predominately tactile, and 'low vision' for children who are taught through methods that rely on sight (Mason and McCall, 1997, pp.xv–xvi). For children who have multiple disabilities and visual impairment the initials MDVI are often adopted (McLinden, 1999). The term does not, however, indicate an homogenous group as the combination and severity of each aspect of the disability and the totality of difficulties is unique to each person. The Royal National Institute for the Blind (1990, p.14) defines a child with MDVI as:

> ... one whose additional disabilities, physical, sensory, mental or behavioural are severe enough in themselves or in combination with their diminished vision to interfere with normal development or education ... The common factor in the diverse group is a visual impairment.

Such a definition would certainly apply to Mercy as her situation highlights her need for support from the staff of her school, the parents and caregivers, not only to gather sufficient information from the environment to *learn* independently, but also to make use of the environment to *function* independently (McLinden, 1999). The adults in Mercy's life are responsible for producing the 'culture' which Bruner sees as vital to foster maturity and growth.

As far back as 1948, Lowenfeld identified three limitations that were likely to affect the development of children and young people with visual impairment:

* the variety and range of the child's experience;
* the ability to move around (which includes orientation and mobility);
* his or her interaction with the environment.

However, as Kingsley (1997) points out, there is no firm evidence that these limitations restrict potential, and since Lowenfeld's work other researchers have attempted to analyse how visual impairment affects development. Opinions are divided and Stone (1997) identifies three main views:

* overall developmental delay, sometimes overcome by the time pupils reach adolescence (Tobin, 1979);
* detours taken to the developmental paths followed by most children with sight (Frailberg, 1977);
* no deviance from normal pathways as long as appropriate intervention is provided (Norris, Spaulding and Brodie,1957).

The research is inconclusive and in our view it is more important for practitioners to analyse *how* the child responds to external stimuli, and *what support* is necessary to encourage overall development, than to engage in comparisons between the three positions.

How children with visual impairments respond to stimuli will depend on the onset of the disability and the opportunities presented to them by other people. A child who is born blind will have a different perception of the world to one who loses his or her vision during infancy or in the teenage years. Such perceptions will be different from those of children whose visual impairment results in tunnel vision, lack of colour perception or acute problems with distance vision (for a comprehensive account of common eye defects and their educational implications readers are referred to Mason, 1997).

What is important to acknowledge is that experience will be unique to the individual and cannot be generalised. Take for example the visual differences experienced by two friends of one of the authors of this book. Both men had the same eye condition and the retinas in both eyes detached in the same way and at the same time in their careers (when they had just taken up their first jobs). In the case of the first, the onset of blindness was rapid and although he has visual knowledge acquired before his loss of sight, he has no idea of what his children, his wife and many of his friends look like. In contrast, although the second friend has a prosthesis in one eye socket, he retained some sight in the other eye up until his retirement. Consequently he has a visual image of all his family and friends. Both, however, rely heavily on sophisticated technology, mobility aids, a familiar environment and *other people* to create what Bozic and Murdoch (1996) term a 'functional system' for living, thinking and controlling events.

Vision helps us make sense of information received through the other senses and consequently to gather information on such attributes as size, colour, shape, use or location. As children who are blind cannot look around and experience objects visually, their experience of objects will be sequential, and will occur, in the main, through touching parts of an object. Not only is it more difficult to relate one part to another, but without vision it is also more difficult to become motivated to move or to extract the rules by which things happen. Lewis (2003, pp.55–6) gives an example of the latter in her comment on a sighted child watching an adult put up a picture:

> The sighted child can see all the preparations and can watch her parent line up the nail and raise the hammer to hit it. The sound of the hammer hitting the nail may be the first thing the blind child experiences. In this sort of way vision can often provide the context for events which helps the child make sense of them. In such a situation the child who is visually impaired will have to rely on verbal commentary in order to make sense of what is occurring. Such a commentary, in addition to contributing to Bruner's culture for learning, can also involve a task analysis approach to learning as advocated by the learning theorists.

The opportunities a child has for actively experimenting in the environment and the encouragement he or she receives are major determinants for development. In line with Lowenfeld's (1948) views it has been found that, in general, children with a visual impairment of greater or lesser severity are slower to crawl and walk, and they play less with other children. Turn-taking and games where social interaction depends on the sharing of toys and objects are activities that will be particularly difficult and may need to be 'stage managed' by an adult. Frailberg (1968, cited in Lewis 2003) found that object permanence occurred considerably later in children with a visual impairment; not surprising when, without the aid of vision, objects will cease to exist once they have left the grasp. In Piaget's view object permanence is crucial to the development of concept formation, but as we have pointed out in Chapter 9, when there are changed circumstances (that is, a lack of vision) it may be possible, as long as no other disabilities interfere with the visual impairment, to engage the other senses to allow conceptual structures to emerge intact (Warren, 1994). This is not to imply that children with a visual impairment have highly developed sensory skills (such as listening and exploring by touch) but, as we have implied throughout this section, greater emphasis needs to be given to enable these skills to be developed to the full. Once again, we emphasise the important role that the staff of schools have in becoming the facilitators for the pupil's own developmental processes.

As we have highlighted at the beginning of this chapter, vision and movement are major factors in learning, and visual impairment may restrict the quality and variety of experiences in exploring the environment. In some situations, as in the example of the child experiencing an adult putting up a picture, knowledge of the environment may only be gained second hand through verbal commentaries. Orientation, which involves the ability to understand where the body is in space, and mobility are important factors in acquiring such knowledge. As orientation and mobility are integral to overall development and learning, many children with visual impairment will require help to move in and around the environment. For many children, caregivers and staff can help to encourage these essential skills, but in some situations, where, for example, mastery of a long cane is required, expert help will be needed.

It is also important to bear in mind that the faces of some children with visual impairments, particularly those who are blind, may lack expression, which will impact on the way in which they are perceived by caregivers, staff and their peers who will need to be aware that lack of animation in the face does not mean lack of interest. Consequently they should not attach particular significance to the facial expressions of children who are blind but look for other indicators of interest and understanding. Children with visual impairments may also have difficulty in recognizing emotions and will lack information on the context in which particular emotions occur (Minter *et al.*, 1991).

At some stage in their development children who are blind are likely to be confused about their identity. A clear idea of the physical features of male and female, for example, is not helped by our culture taboos on touching the bodies of others, and the onset of adolescence is, in particular, likely to be a time of anxiety and bewilderment. Freud regarded the sight of body parts as an important element in a healthy attitude towards the body and sexuality, and Stafford-Clark (1965), writing on Freud's work, points out that 'to see and be seen are important parts of the emotional fulfilment and sexual excitation of children' (p.102). But as Warren (1994) points out, for children and young people who are visually impaired it is not the lack of vision that determines capacities and capabilities but the lack of *opportunities*. And as we have already highlighted in the discussion on physical development above, restriction of opportunity can be a major block to full and meaningful development.

The development of hearing

Recent evidence suggests that the hearing of newborn babies is very well developed (Aslin *et al.*, 1998, cited by Keenan, 2002), and it has been found that neonates can hear almost as well as adults. There are, however, differences, one of which relates to the infant's greater sensitivity to higher-pitched voices in comparison to low-pitched sounds. Such sensitivity may explain a feature of 'motherese' (see Chapter 8) in which mothers modify their normal speech in order to make it accessible to very young babies, and mature speakers (including young children) spontaneously raise the pitch of their voices. From an evolutionary perspective, it is likely that the predisposition towards female voices in preference to those of males arose in connection with the nurturing role of mothers.

Many children with hearing impairments have difficulty in hearing higher-pitch sounds, but in addition the *quality* and *amount* of language offered by mothers or caregivers to children with hearing impairments may be different to the language presented by mothers of children without such impairments. Cheskin (1982), for example, found that mothers of children with a hearing loss are less likely to speak to their children if they feel that little of what they say is being heard or to return verbal exchanges if they cannot make sense of their children's imprecise sounds. In such situations, common elements of experience may not be built upon and, as we have seen in our discussions on the development of language and communication, a lack of shared experiences is likely to lead to a lack of shared understandings which can seriously affect the nature of bonding between mother and child in the early years.

The state of an infant's hearing at birth is, therefore, crucial for many reasons, because of its impact not only on mother–child interaction, but on the acquisition of language and communication and on the development of cognition and social behaviour. In the first year, normally developing babies are able to pick up frequently occurring sounds and relationships between sounds, and they are able to 'screen out' sounds that are not in regular use by their caregivers. At the end of the first year, most are able to detect meaningful speech units, such as clause and word boundaries (Berk, 2003), and such sensitivity indicates how well prepared they are to acquire spoken language. At this stage, they understand and obey simple instructions, respond to their own name, listen with pleasure to sound-making toys, play pat-a-cake or wave goodbye on request.

Mercer (2000) makes the point that developmental psychologists (Bruner, in particular) have revealed how the individual development of children is shaped by dialogues with people around them. Children learn language through engaging in conversation with others and Mercer quotes the linguist Halliday who suggests that 'when children learn language they are learning the foundation of learning itself' (Mercer, 2000, p.11). There are, of course, important implications if the child has a hearing loss.

As in the case of visual impairment, children will vary in the degree of the loss they experience. Some may hear only loud sounds and not spoken language; others will hear some speech sounds when amplification is used; and background noise, or crowded rooms (where many conversations take place) may make it difficult for some children to decipher sounds. In the UK four categories of hearing loss are used to indicate the severity in terms of decibel (dB) loss:

- mild: 20dB to 40dB
- moderate: 41dB to 70dB
- severe: 71dB to 95dB
- profound: in excess of 95dB

(BATOD, 1997)

As with visual impairments many reasons and conditions can cause hearing impairments. Sensori-neural losses (including nerve damage and cochlea mechanism loss) can be caused by hereditary factors, or conditions that affect the foetus, or as a result of diseases contracted after birth (such as meningitis). Sensori-neural difficulties tend to result in the most severe or profound hearing loss and for some children cochlear implants can give some sensation of sound. The implants, however, do not restore hearing, and cannot be used at all times: they have to be removed at night or when the child swims or is out in the rain. The procedure is a relatively new intervention, but the results of some recent studies indicate that if the child receives the implant as early as possible the outcomes are generally favourable (Archibold, 1997; Robinson, 1998).

In contrast to sensori-neural losses, conductive deafness is often caused by problems in the outer or middle ear systems (such as blockages or damage to the ear drum) when the energy from the sound waves cannot activate the sensori-neural mechanisms. The results of conductive deafness are generally less severe than those of sensori-neural loss, and are often not permanent, but the amount of loss can vary from day to day and week to week and will influence the amount of support necessary (Fraser,1992).

Whatever the type of hearing loss, Meadow (1980) and Lewis (2003) emphasise that 'support' is needed in terms of skilled auditory assessment as soon as there is any indication of a hearing problem. Subsequently, it is likely that additional 'support' such as the use of hearing aids for some children and/or training in residual hearing will be necessary to encourage a child's response to sound and to help to promote the development of language and communication. Not all 'support' mechanisms need to be 'high tech': simple procedures, such as ensuring that the child can see the communicator's face and eliminating background noise, can greatly assist the developing child.

Greg, however, does have a severe hearing loss and a mixture of 'high-tech' and 'low-tech' support is necessary to allow him to be empowered.

Greg

Greg is a pupil in a mainstream school who has a moderate bilateral sensori-neural hearing loss and uses hearing aids in both ears. Although the aids can improve his sensitivity to sounds, other aspects of listening to speech are not improved by their amplification alone. His Statement of Special Educational Needs (SEN) entitles him to support in all classes and tutorials, and on the advice of skilled professionals Greg's teachers wear radio microlink transmitters around their necks, which transmit sound to receivers attached to his hearing aids.

The combination of his hearing aids and the FM radio aid system enables Greg to discriminate the majority of speech sounds in the normal delivery of lessons, but his teachers are mindful that listening fatigue and inconsistent concentration can hinder the level of success. In addition, it is necessary for Greg, his parents, the school staff and his peers to ensure that strategies are adopted to allow him every opportunity to develop and learn. These might include:

- keywords used in lessons and specific vocabulary lists that are created, and made available to him in both lessons and tutorials, to allow greater access to the curriculum;
- recognisable 'problem-solving' strategies that he uses to deal with the minor day-to-day challenges encountered at home and at school;
- structured opportunities that are created to encourage interaction with his peers.

With these support mechanisms in place Greg has successfully completed the first two years at secondary school and is moving into Year 9.

In the early years there is evidence to suggest that the 'supporter', the person who spends most time with the young child with a hearing loss (usually the mother), takes on the unnatural and unfamiliar roles of 'interpreter and intermediary' for her son or daughter, first within the immediate family and later with the outside world (Gregory, 1998). It is likely that the parenting of children with a severe and profound hearing loss, as with children with other disabilities, will take on a sharper dimension of 'teaching' not usually required in caregivers of normally developing children. As Gregory (1998) suggests, such a change in the parenting role has implications for changes in child–parent relationships and the dynamics of family life, and a fine balance needs to be struck between providing 'support' and inhibiting the child's opportunities to progress towards personal autonomy. As we have pointed out in our discussion on the educational implications of the learning theorists, the child may be denied the opportunity to take an active part in learning.

The majority of children who have severe hearing impairments (almost 90 per cent) are born to hearing parents and consequently grow up in a world dominated by spoken language, but it is likely that deaf children (usually those with a profound hearing loss) born to deaf parents will use sign language as their main means of communication. The efficacy of various methods of teaching language and communication to children with the full range of hearing loss has been hotly debated for many years (Meadow, 1980; Fraser, 1992; Gregory *et al.*, 1998) but the three main modes are:

* oral methods;
* sign language;
* total communication.

The latter is a combined method of speaking and signing, and a full account is given by Baker and Knight (1998). The other approaches are also discussed in depth in the same edited volume (Gregory *et al.*, 1998; for oral methods see Watson, 1998; for the development of signed languages see Woll, 1998).

Deaf children have the option of becoming part of a deaf community in which deafness is not regarded as an impairment, but as a culture. Deaf culture has its own language (sign language) and its users have come to be considered as an important linguistic minority group. Ridgeway (1998), using a capital D to provide emphasis, points out that members of the Deaf community have developed their own Deaf identity based on:

* interaction with others who are deaf and share similar beliefs and values;
* the identification of issues peculiar to the specific culture (such as feeling detached from those who do not have a hearing impairment);
* the use of sign language;
* pride in their separate identity.

In Ridgeway's view, Deaf culture contributes to a positive self-identity which is sought after by many other minority groups. Cass (1979) sees the development of the identity of *any* minority group as going through a number of stages: confusion, comparison, tolerance, acceptance, pride and finally synthesis. Cass's model appears to resonate with Erikson's stages of the development of identity outlined in Chapter 3. For example, it is possible to see the link between:

* confusion and Erikson's first stage of Trust versus Mistrust;
* comparison and Autonomy versus Shame and Doubt;
* tolerance and Initiative versus Guilt;
* acceptance and Industry versus Inferiority;
* pride and eventual synthesis and Identity versus Role diffusion.

From the research evidence, the accepted use of sign language, as a first language and as a means of natural communication, appears to contribute to the positive views many children and young people have about themselves in the deaf community, and how they adjust to their hearing loss. It is not only the deaf children of deaf parents who regard signing as important. Birkett (2003), in an article on the educational needs of deaf children, notes how the hearing parents of a seven-year-old boy with a profound hearing loss chose to send their son to a school for the deaf where signing was taught as a first language. Tyler's father argues: 'At his current school, the kids chat away in the playground in sign language. There are no communication problems. He needed a full language, with all its arts and poetry, and he has that now' (Birkett, 2003, p.2).

Other parents take a different stance: about 95 per cent of children are born into families where sign language is not an option and Birkett (2003) also documents Ellen, with a severe loss, now in a mainstream school where signing is not used. Ellen can hear certain frequencies through a digital hearing aid and lip-reads well. Her additional 'support' in helping her to develop language is through weekly sessions from:

- a speech and language therapist;
- a specialist teacher of the hearing impaired;
- a SENCo (special educational needs co-ordinator).

The arguments surrounding which of the three modes of communication is the most effective are inconclusive and will depend on particular circumstances. There is evidence to suggest that some children become proficient oral language users (Watson, 1998), but it has also been suggested that sign language is easier for some deaf children to acquire than spoken language. Indeed there is a strong argument that its use may actually facilitate spoken language.

However, the factors that influence the *whole* development of children with a hearing loss are, with the exception of the first two points, the same for all children:

- the hearing status of the parents, and the guidance provided to them to help them choose the most effective communication system for them and their child;
- the attitude communicators have towards the notion of deafness (in the past, to be deaf was linked to the concept of dumbness);
- the emotional support available;
- information on appropriate childrearing strategies;
- the provision of an environment that optimises development and gives high priority to opportunities for shared experiences and shared understandings.

As we have already stressed in this chapter, it is not the disability, in this case the hearing loss, itself that inhibits development, but the restriction of opportunities.

Multi-sensory impairment

A small number of children have a loss of both vision and hearing and are considered to be multi-sensorily impaired (deafblind). Best (1994) suggests that the percentage is around 0.018, but as there is no agreed definition of either multi-sensory impairments or deafblindness, the figures are approximate. Such terms are generally used to describe the continuum of individuals with congenital vision *and* hearing loss (Murdoch, 1997) and are in contrast to those with MDVI, previously discussed, where the loss of vision is the *principal* impairment amongst other disabilities. At one time the most prevalent cause of multi-sensory impairment was the viral infection rubella, contracted during pregnancy, but, as Murdoch (1997) points out, owing to medical advances and the increased survival rate of premature and vulnerable babies, the causes are now wide ranging. She emphasises that aetiological damage to both hearing and vision in these frail babies, or to the neurological systems that support the distance senses, tend to be very severe and can also damage other systems. Consequently some of the 'non-rubella' population may have other disabilities, but all children who are deafblind will have impairments of *both* distance senses which will drastically influence the quality of information they receive from the environment. McInnes and Treffrey (1982) emphasise that multi-sensory impairment cannot be considered as a combination of visual and hearing impairment: 'the deafblind child is not a deaf child who cannot see or a blind child who cannot hear' (p.2), but one who will receive distorted, unpredictable and very confused information through their damaged distance senses. For some children, the losses are so great that they receive no information at all, or they may develop unique learning styles in order to compensate for their difficulties. These authors suggest that children with multi-sensory impairments may experience acute problems in the following ways:

- establishing and maintaining interpersonal relationships;
- interacting with their environment in a meaningful way;
- gaining a perception of their world that is not distorted;
- anticipating future events or the results of their actions;
- becoming extrinsically motivated.

As we have shown above, this list could equally apply to children with visual or hearing problems only, but the developmental needs of the child who experiences losses in both distance senses are different and sharply focused. Without vision and hearing he or she will be limited to reacting to each passing event only, and will not have the sensory information to even begin to relate one event to another without the help of a partner with sight and hearing (Murdoch, 2001; Nafstad and Rødbroe, 1999). Vygotsky (1978) emphasised the role of other people, particularly adults, in the development of *all* children but their involvement is so critical to children with multi-sensory impairments that researchers use terms such as 'intervener' or 'co-creator' (Nafstad and Rødbroe, 1999) to describe the person who will help to interpret the physical and social world. For the majority of children with multi-sensory impairments, initial help to make sense of their environment and to progress towards autonomy will be through encouraging them to move around their surroundings and to react to the effects of their movements. Murdoch (2001) cites the five-stage movement approach developed by Writer (1987) as a useful model for the staff of schools to consider, and the approach has obvious links to the work of the theorists described in this book. It involves:

NURTURANCE (STAGE ONE)   The development of attachment between the child and a *restricted* number of adults who work in close proximity with him or her. Close proximity will help to signal the presence of another person, and allow the adult to help the child to repeat movements, particularly ones that he or she finds pleasurable. In addition, the adult and child will share the experience and there will be a greater chance of the development of shared understandings.

Opel

Opel (aged 5) had been at her new school for a few weeks when she suddenly developed a 'habit' of going towards the door and constantly crossing the threshold when working with her teacher. Initially he thought that he ought to try to divert Opel's attention away from the door as he considered her rather 'odd' behaviour to be meaningless and possibly ritualistic.

By observing her responses to her own actions over a few days, however, he noted that she showed some pleasure when crossing the threshold and held her head slightly on one side, possibly experiencing a slight change in light between the classroom and the corridor. He concluded that she had gained enough confidence in their relationship for her to explore a small part of her environment, and by moving through the same space over and over again she was beginning to make sense of one aspect of it. Rather than discouraging the behaviour he began to reward it.

In his work with Opel the teacher is drawing on many of the ideas offered by the theorists we have discussed. Teacher and pupil are, of course, working in partnership in relatively unknown territory for both of them and it is important that Opel's teacher does not dismiss her rather bizarre actions as being irrelevant, but regards them as clues to learning. At a basic level he has established a relationship built on trust and is reinforcing her confidence in him by using behaviourist techniques to develop her skills whilst working within her zone of proximal development, but readers will be able to use the work of the theorists to provide a deeper analysis.

ANTICIPATION (STAGE TWO)   Using the same stimulation to enable the child to anticipate events. In the example of Mercy (in this chapter), particular smells were used to alert her to the commencement of activities: talcum powder indicated her toilet routine; pine air freshener suggested home time. Routines which help to create 'memory scripts' are important and allow the child opportunities to anticipate events.

CO-ACTIVE MOVEMENT (STAGE THREE)   Total body movements or limb and hand movements are introduced. Murdoch (2001) suggests that co-active hand movements might involve the adult and child washing their hands at the same time, but hand over hand, or hand under hand, movements can provide the stimulus for children to explore.

DEFERRED IMITATION (STAGE FOUR)   The child imitates the adults' movements and activities after a period of time. At first the imitation happens almost spontaneously, but gradually lengthens.

NATURAL GESTURES (STAGE FIVE)   The child communicates spontaneously to indicate wants or needs (pulling an adult towards an object, for example, or pointing to a toy). Such natural gestures can lead to more formal systems of communication.

The five-stage model presented above reinforces the need for children with multi-sensory impairments to receive appropriate mediation in order to access and control their environment.

Conclusion

The examples of the children's 'challenges' in this chapter (linked to their difficulties) highlight the need for the children and their peers to have:

*   a basic understanding of the nature of the difficulties;
*   chances to express their feelings and to consider sameness and difference;
*   appropriate educational opportunities;
*   opportunities to make friendships;
*   every possibility to be independent;
*   practical and emotional coping strategies;
*   plans for the future with positive outcomes.

(adapted from Closs, 1998; p.114)

Equally importantly, children with sensory and physical disabilities will, at some stages of their lives, need the assistance of others to access the opportunities that they need to assume control and to become autonomous. But, as we have stressed, the assistance should be offered with caution and within a culture of 'valuing'. As Elizabeth Broberg (1996), a Swedish woman who was the first person with a range of disabilities (including intellectual disabilities) to become 'Woman of the Year', reminds us: 'One doesn't feel very valued when one constantly is anchored in situations where one cannot do for oneself' (p.56).

In this chapter we are aware that we have revisited many of the ideas raised in earlier chapters: for example, we have considered the cognitive development of pupils with sensory difficulties although it is discussed in Chapter 9. By re-examining these issues, together with the provision of more case study examples detailing the 'what to do', we hope that we have given readers an additional impetus to reflect upon the links between theory and everyday practice.

References

Archibold, S. (1997) 'Cochlea implants', in W. McCracken and S. Laoide-Kemp (eds) *Audiology in Education*. London: Whurr Publishers.

Bairstow, P., Cochrane, R. and Hur, J. (1993) *Evaluation of Conductive Education for Children with Cerebral Palsy. Final Report (Part 1)*. London: HMSO.

Baker, R. and Knight, P. (1998) '"Total communication": current policy and practice', in S. Gregory, P. Knight, W. McCracken, S. Powers and L. Watson (eds) *Issues in Deaf Education*. London: David Fulton Publishers.

BATOD (British Association of Teachers of the Deaf) (1997) 'Audiometric descriptors for pure tone audiograms', *BATOD Magazine*. September.

Berk, L.E. (2003) *Child Development* (6th edition). Boston, MA: Allyn and Bacon.

Best, A.B. (1992) *Teaching Children with Visual Impairments*. Milton Keynes: Open University Press.

Best, A.B. (1994) 'Developing and sustaining appropriate provision', in J. Summerscale and E. Boothroyd (eds) *Deafblind Education: Developing and Sustaining Appropriate Provision. Proceedings of the UK Conference held in Birmingham*. London: SENSE.

Birkett, D. (2003) 'A world of their own', *Guardian Education*. 29 July 2003, 2–3.

Bleck, E.E. and Nagel, D.A. (1982) *Physically Handicapped Children: A Medical Atlas for Teachers* (2nd edition). New York: Grune and Stratton.

Bozic, N. and Murdoch, H. (eds) (1996) *Learning Through Interaction*. London: David Fulton Publishers.

Broberg, E. (1996) 'Thoughts in me', in G. Dybwad and H. Bersani, Jr. (eds) *New Voices: Self-Advocacy by People with Disabilities*. Cambridge, MA Brookline Books.

Brown, N., McLinden, M. and Porter, J. (1998) 'Sensory needs', in P. Lacey and C. Ouvry (eds) *People with Profound and Multiple Learning Difficulties: A Collaborative Approach*. London: David Fulton Publishers.

Cass, V.C. (1979) 'Homosexual identity formation: a theoretical model', *Journal of Homosexuality*. 4, 219–35.

Cheskin, A. (1982) 'The use of language of deaf mothers of hearing children', *Journal of Communication Disorders*. 15, 145–53.

Closs, A. (1998) 'Quality of life and young people with serious medical conditions', in C. Robinson and K. Stalker (eds) *Growing Up with Disability*. London: Jessica Kingsley Publishers.

Cogher, L., Savage, E. and Smith, M.F. (eds) (1992) *Cerebral Palsy: The Child and the Young Person*. London: Chapman and Hall.

Coles, C. and Zsargo, L. (1998) 'Conductive education: towards an educational model', *British Journal of Special Education*. 25 (2), 70–4.

Dallas, E., Stevenson, J. and McGurk, H. (1993) 'Cerebral-palsied children's interactions with siblings: interactional structure', *Journal of Child Psychology and Psychiatry*. 34, 649–71.

Davis, J. (2001) *A Sensory Approach to the Curriculum for Pupils with Profound and Multiple Learning Difficulties*. London: David Fulton Publishers.

Decarie, T.G. (1969) 'A study of mental and emotional development of the thalidomide child', in B.M. Foss (ed.) *Determinant of Infants' Behaviour, Volume 4*. London: Methuen.

Dyspraxia Foundation *Dyspraxia Explained*. Available online at http://www.dyspraxiafoundation.org.uk.

Flanagan, C. (1996) *Applying Psychology to Early Child Development*. London: Hodder and Stoughton.

Foreman, N., Orencas, C., Nicholas, E., Morton, P. and Gell, M. (1989) 'Spatial awareness in seven- to 11-year-old physically handicapped children in mainstream schools', *European Journal of Special Needs Education*. 4, 171–9.

Frailberg, S. (1977) *Insights from the Blind: Comparative Studies of Blind and Sighted Infants*. London: Souvenir Press.

Fraser, B. (1992) 'Hearing impairments', in R. Gulliford and G. Upton (eds) *Special Educational Needs*. London: Routledge.

Glenn, I. and Robertson, C. (2001) 'Physical impairment', in C. Tilstone (ed.) *Reader for Learning Difficulties: Assessment and Curriculum*. (Distance Education Material for Teachers of Children with Learning Difficulties.) Birmingham: University of Birmingham, School of Education.

Gregory, S. (1998) 'Social development and family life', in S. Gregory, P. Knight, W. McCracken, S. Powers and L. Watson (eds) *Issues in Deaf Education*. London: David Fulton Publishers.

Gregory, S., Knight, P., McCracken, W., Powers, S. and Watson, L. (eds) (1998) *Issues in Deaf Education*. London: David Fulton Publishers.

Griffiths, R. (1967) *The Abilities of Babies*. London: University of London Press.

Hari, M. and Akos, K. (1988) *Conductive Education*. London: Routledge.

Hodapp, R. (1998) *Development and Disabilities: Intellectual, Sensory and Motor Impairments*. Cambridge: Cambridge University Press.

Isaacs, N. (1966) *The Growth of Understanding in the Young Child*. London: Ward Lock Educational Company.

Jackson, P. (2000) 'Health services: supporting children, families and schools', in A. Closs (ed.) *The Education of Children with Medical Conditions*. London: David Fulton Publishers.

Keenan, T. (2002) *An Introduction to Child Development*. London: Sage Publications.

Kingsley, M. (1977) 'The effects of a visual loss', in H. Mason and S. McCall (eds, with C. Arter, M. McLinden and J. Stone) *Visual Impairment: Access to Education for Children and Young People*. London: David Fulton Publishers.

Lerner, J. (1997) *Learning Disabilities: Theories, Diagnosis and Teaching Strategies* (7th edition). Boston, MA: Houghton Mifflin Company.

Lewis, V. (2003) *Development and Disability* (2nd edition). Oxford: Blackwell Publishing.

Lowenfeld, B. (1948) 'Effects of blindness on the cognitive functions of children', *Nervous Child*. 7, 45–54.

McInnes, J.M. and Treffrey, J.A. (1982) *Deaf-Blind Infants and Children*. Milton Keynes: Open University Press.

McLinden, M. (1999) 'Children with multiple disabilities and a visual impairment', in H. Mason and S. McCall (eds, with C. Arter, M. McLinden and J. Stone) *Visual Impairment: Access to Education for Children and Young People*. London: David Fulton Publishers.

Mason, H. (1997) 'Common eye defects and their educational implications', in H. Mason and S. McCall (eds, with C. Arter, M. McLinden and J. Stone) *Visual Impairment. Access to Education for Children and Young People*. London: David Fulton Publishers.

Mason, H. and McCall, S. (1997) 'Introduction', in H. Mason and S. McCall (eds, with C. Arter, M. McLinden and J. Stone) *Visual Impairment: Access to Education for Children and Young People*. London: David Fulton Publishers.

Meadow, K. (1980) *Deafness and Child Development*. Los Angeles: University of California Press.

Mercer, N. (2000) *Words and Minds: How We Use Language to Think Together*. London: Routledge.

Miller, G. (1992) 'Cerebral palsies', in G. Miller and J.C. Ramer (eds) *Static Encephalopathies of Infancy and Childhood*. New York: Raven Press.

Minter, M., Hobson, R.P. and Pring, L. (1991) 'Congenital visual impairment and theory of mind', *British Journal of Developmental Psychology*. 16, 183–96.

Morris, J. (1991) *Pride against Prejudice*. London: Women's Press.

Murdoch, H. (1997) 'Multi-sensory impairment', in H. Mason and S. McCall (eds, with C. Arter, M. McLinden and J. Stone) *Visual Impairment: Access to Education for Children and Young People*. London: David Fulton Publishers.

Murdoch, H. (2001) 'Multi-sensory Impairment', in C. Tilstone (ed.) *Reader for Learning Difficulties: Assessment and Curriculum* (Distance Education Material for Teachers of Children with Learning Difficulties). Birmingham: University of Birmingham, School of Education.

Nafstad, A. and Rødbroc, I. (1999) *Co-Creating Communication*. Dronninglund, Denmark: Forlager Nord-Press.

Norris, M., Spaulding, P. and Brodie, F.H. (1957) *Blindness in Children*. Illinois: University of Chicago Press.

Oliver, M. (1989) 'Conductive education: if it wasn't so sad it would be funny', *Disability, Handicap and Society*. 4 (2), 197–200.

Oliver, M. (1996) *Understanding Disability from Theory to Practice*. London: Macmillan Press

Pagliano, P. (1999) *Multisensory Environments*. London: David Fulton Publishers.

Porter, J. and Ashdown, R. (2002) *Pupils with Complex Learning Difficulties: Promoting Learning Using Visual Materials and Methods*. Tamworth: NASEN.

Ridgeway, S. (1998) 'A deaf personality', in S. Gregory, P. Knight, W. McCracken, S. Powers and L. Watson (eds) *Issues in Deaf Education*. London: David Fulton Publishers.

Robinson, K. (1998) 'Cochlea implants: Some challenges', in S. Gregory, P. Knight, W. McCracken, S. Powers and L. Watson (eds) *Issues in Deaf Education*. London: David Fulton Publishers.

Royal National Institute for the Blind (1990) *New Directions: Towards a Better Future for Mulitihandicapped Visually Impaired Children and Young People*. London: RNIB.

Shakespeare, T. (1996) 'Disability, identity and difference', in C. Barnes and G. Mercer (eds) *Exploring the Divide*. Leeds: The Disability Press.

Sharman, C., Cross, W. and Vennis, D. (1995) *Observing Children: A Practical Guide*. London: Cassell.

Sheridan, M. (1997) *From Birth to Five Years: Children's Developmental Progress* (revised and updated by M. Frost and A. Sharma). London: Routledge.

Stafford-Clark, D. (1965) *What Freud Really Said*. Harmondsworth: Penguin Books.

Steel, F. (1996) 'Physical disabilities', in V. Varma (ed.) *Coping with Children in Stress*. Aldershot: Arena Publications.

Stone, J. (1997) 'The pre-school child', in H. Mason and S. McCall (eds, with C. Arter, M. McLinden and J. Stone) *Visual Impairment: Access to Education for Children and Young People*. London: David Fulton Publishers.

Tobin, M. (1979) *A Longitudinal Study of Blind and Partially Sighted Children in Special Schools in England and Wales*. Birmingham: Research Centre for the Visually Handicapped, University of Birmingham.

Vygotsky, L.S. (1962) *Thought and Language*. Cambridge, MA: MFT Press.

Vygotsky, L.S. (1978) *Mind in Society: The Development of Higher Psychological Processes*. Cambridge, MA: Harvard University Press.

Warren, D. (1994) *Blindness and Children: An Individual Differences Approach*. Cambridge: Cambridge University Press.

Watson, J. (1999) 'Working in groups: social and cognitive effects in a special class', *British Journal of Special Education*. 26 (2), 87–95.

Watson, L. (1998) 'Oralism: current policy and practice', in S. Gregory, P. Knight, W. McCracken, S. Powers and L. Watson (eds) *Issues in Deaf Education*. London: David Fulton Publishers.

Wilson, J. (2001) 'Conductive education and the National Curriculum: an integrated approach', *British Journal of Special Education*. 16 (4) 168–173.

Woll, B. (1998) 'Development of signed and spoken languages', in S. Gregory; P. Knight, W. McCracken, S. Powers and L. Watson (eds) *Issues in Deaf Education*. London: David Fulton Publishers.

Ziegler, E. and Victoria, S. (1975) 'An experimental evaluation of sensorimotor patterning: a critique'. *American Journal of Mental Deficiency*, 79, 483–92.

Chapter 12

Conclusion

Many of the writers whose theories about development have been interpreted in this book lived and worked in another age. In some cases, theorists did not see it as necessary or appropriate to extend their research frameworks to consider outcomes for children whose development does not follow typical patterns. Those who did include a focus on children with difficulties in learning, wrote without the insights that support the approaches and pedagogies of the twenty-first century. For example, we recognise that the current emphasis on the inclusion in mainstream schooling of children with a range of medical conditions that give rise to special educational needs stems, in part, from improvements in the medical management of the conditions. Similarly, greater optimism about the potential of people with a range of severe and complex learning needs arises as a result of a more differentiated understanding of those needs that, in turn, derives from the findings of extensive psychological and educational research. Furthermore, the progressive deployment of sophisticated and imaginative technology has supported and enhanced the value of skilled teaching. These advancements have gone hand-in-hand with expressions of political will to promote the capacity of all individuals to assume full citizenship.

The aim of this book, therefore, has been to examine, within the framework of current knowledge and attitudes, seminal theories on development for their application to learners whose potential as autonomous citizens could be restricted. In England and Wales, following the Crick Report (DfEE, 1998), general principles of teaching that promote the active involvement of all individuals in public life were recently given added impetus when citizenship, along with personal, social and health education (PSHE), was designated a curriculum subject in the revised National Curriculum (DfEE/QCA, 1999). The extension of the National Curriculum to include Citizenship/PSHE may owe more to concerns about social control and aspirations for economic prosperity than to humanitarian considerations. Nonetheless, in considering the relationship between the individual and her or his society, it raised the profile of personal development, particularly with regard to personal autonomy, decision-making and empowerment, and Lawson and Fergusson (2001; Fergusson and Lawson 2003) have discussed these aspects in relation to pupils with learning difficulties. Elsewhere, Potter (2002) notes the type of individualism that has emerged in modern democratic societies. He observes that individuals, less constrained now by family ties or traditional class values, for example, expect the freedom and flexibility to choose and change the direction of their lives, pursuing personal goals through the exercise of autonomy. It is this notion of autonomy that Robertson (2001) attacks when he questions its centrality as 'an underlying goal of education' (p.121) in social systems where the principal purpose of education is to support economic growth.

We have, throughout this book, returned time and again to the theme of autonomy, arguing that striving to gain mastery over one's environment is a defining human activity. Further, we have made it our task to interpret developmental theories in terms that show how the young child is steadily empowered by his or her increasing competence, to assume a variety of roles in society. We have not, however, proposed that any individual can, or should, aspire to assert individualism as Potter has described it. Instead we align our view with that of Robertson (2001), as he develops his argument to propose that an essential dimension to human existence is dependency. According to this view, each of us, at some time or in some situations, has need of other people and so total empowerment remains beyond our grasp. This apparent individual frailty serves to strengthen social bonds, and interdependence results. As Sachs (2002, p.101), quoting Althusius (1603), acknowledges: 'Everyone … needs the experience and contributions of others, and no one lives to be himself [sic] alone.'

Much of our discussion of developmental theories has focused on the extent to which they promote the individual, first and foremost, as a social being. Further, we have considered the view that individuals build up their identity through the processes involved in social interaction, adopting and acting out the 'self' that they see reflected in the way other people respond to them. Along with this self-concept, the developing child starts to value him- or herself to acquire a level of self-esteem according to how parents and other caregivers meet his or her basic needs. Pringle (1986) asserts that, in meeting physical needs, sensitive caregivers will also meet the child's needs for optimal learning, which she summarises as the following:

• love and security
• new experiences
• praise and recognition
• responsibility.

We have argued, throughout, for these needs to be recognised, and met, in all children, including those with learning difficulties. However, the needs remain throughout the entire lifespan of every individual, taking different forms and requiring different responses as she or he moves into fresh environments. The first major step away from the familiarity of the home environment comes when the child enters school where learning, as the principal objective, takes on a formal quality. Here teachers are simultaneously agents through which formal learning will take place, and mediators of the new environment. Among all caring and guiding adults they are uniquely placed to promote learning and development, but we argue that this privileged position makes special demands in relation to children whose potential for learning may be compromised.

Current directives in England assert that 'all teachers are teachers of children with special educational needs' (DfES, 2001). We would like to propose possible implications of the assertion in terms of the themes developed in this book. First, we have presented an interpretation of teaching as the process of enabling a social dialogue with the purpose of enhancing knowledge and understanding. This social constructivist view importantly breaks down the traditional barrier between 'learner' and 'teacher' and in our case studies there are examples of where the two roles are indistinguishable, one from the other. Second, if all teachers are to 'enable a social dialogue' involving pupils with a diversity of abilities and a range of needs beyond those highlighted by Pringle, their own knowledge and understanding must be assured. Again in England, the Teacher Training Agency (TTA) has provided a framework, the 'Specialist Standards' (TTA, 1999), through which teachers can assess their competence to teach pupils with a range of special educational needs, and to identify where they need further training. However, while acknowledging the contribution that initial and post-experience training can make, we maintain that it constitutes only a part of the route to teachers' enhanced knowledge. Teachers' learning is set out, as it is for all learners, in the Framework for New Learning and is largely achieved through the teacher's openness to new experiences. Accordingly, we recognise that in the current climate all teachers are likely to *encounter* pupils with significant learning needs and, with successive encounters, to develop an *awareness* of those needs. Through increasing *engagement* with the range of pupil-profiles and *participation* and *involvement* with other professionals and the parents of pupils, teachers will *gain skills and understanding*. It is on this experience that formal training builds, but training can only be effective when teachers reflect on their experience, and how to apply their knowledge and understanding. It is our fervent hope that this book allows the staff of schools greater insights into the development and learning of all their pupils and equips them to reflect on ways of improving their own practice.

References

DfEE (1998) *Education for Citizenship and the Teaching of Democracy in Schools* (The Crick Report). London: DfEE.

DfEE/QCA (1999) *Citizenship*. London: DfEE/QCA.

DfES (2001) *Special Educational Needs: Code of Practice*. Nottingham: DfES.

Fergusson, A. and Lawson, H. (2003) *Access to Citizenship*. London: David Fulton Publishers.

Lawson, H. and Fergusson, A. (2001) 'PSHE and citizenship', in B. Carpenter, R. Ashdown and K. Bovair (eds) *Enabling Access: Effective Learning for Pupils with Learning Difficulties* (2nd edition). London: David Fulton Publishers.

Potter, J. (2002) *Active Citizenship in Schools*. London: Kogan Page.

Pringle, M.K. (1986) *The Needs of Children* (3rd edition). London: Routledge.

Robertson, C. (2001) 'Autonomy and identity: the need for new dialogues in education and welfare', *Support for Learning*. 16 (3), 117–21.

Sachs, J. (2002) *The Dignity of Difference: How to Avoid the Clash of Civilisations*. London: Continuum Books.

TTA (1999) *National Special Educational Needs Specialist Standards*. London: TTA.

Index